ANTHROPOLOGICAL PAPERS OF
THE UNIVERSITY OF ARIZONA
NUMBER 69

Ancient Maya Life in the Far West Bajo

Social and Environmental Change in the Wetlands of Belize

Julie L. Kunen

THE UNIVERSITY OF ARIZONA PRESS
TUCSON
2004

About the Author

JULIE L. KUNEN began research in Mesoamerica in 1995 and has conducted fieldwork in Belize and Guatemala. Her research interests include the archaeology of Mesoamerica and Southeast Asia, environmental archaeology, land use and social organization, and historical ecology, and focus on the role of ritual in community systems of natural resource management in early tropical states. During 2001–2002 she was Instructor in the Department of Anthropology at Northern Arizona University, Flagstaff. She became a Research Associate in the Department of Anthropology, Smithsonian Institution in 2002 and served as Adjunct Assistant Professor in the Science, Technology, and International Affairs Program, School of Foreign Service, Georgetown University in 2003. In 2003 she was named an American Association for the Advancement of Science Diplomacy Fellow assigned to the Forestry Team of the USAID Natural Resource Management Office. Dr. Kunen received a B.A. degree *cum laude* in 1990 from Yale University and M.A. (1995) and Ph.D. (2001) degrees from the Department of Anthropology at the University of Arizona, Tucson.

Research reported in this volume has been partially supported by an *Emil W. Haury Graduate Fellowship* awarded to Julie L. Kunen 1995–1998, Department of Anthropology, University of Arizona, Tucson.

Cover: Schematic drawing of use zones in the Far West Bajo of northwestern Belize, showing residential areas on hilltops, agricultural terraces on the bajo margins, and rockpiles and vegetation in the resource-rich bajo interior. Adapted from drawings by Mary Jo Galindo and Ron Redsteer.

THE UNIVERSITY OF ARIZONA PRESS

Library of Congress Cataloging-in-Publication Data

Kunen, Julie L., 1968-
 Ancient Maya life in the Far West Bajo : social and environmental change in the wetlands of Belize / Julie L. Kunen.
   p. cm. -- (Anthropological papers of the University of Arizona; no. 69)
 Includes bibliographical references and index.
 ISBN 0-8165-2235-9 (pbk. : alk. paper)
 1. Bajo Hill Site (Belize). 2. Mayas--Agriculture. 3. Mayas--Antiquities.
4. Excavations (Archaeology)--Belize. 5. Wetland agriculture--Belize. 6. Terracing--Belize. 7. Irrigation farming--Belize. 8. Belize--Antiquities. I. Title. II. Series.
 F1435.3.A37K86 2003
 972.82'6--dc22
         2003014273

Contents

FIGURES

TABLES

Preface

Research on the Far West Bajo was part of a larger regional investigation of ancient Maya land and water management strategies in northwestern Belize. In 1997, I joined a project co-directed by Vernon Scarborough, Nicholas Dunning, and Fred Valdez, Jr. that was studying the ways in which the Maya manipulated their natural landscape, creating a host of earthworks, stone features, and more subtle alterations of the physical environment that were designed to concentrate and conserve critical resources such as water and agricultural soils. This research proceeded through survey, mapping, and testing of drainages, depressions, agricultural features and related habitation sites in the vicinity of La Milpa, an important archaeological site in Belize. By 1997, significant results had already been achieved in the settlement center and along two of the drainages descending from the high ridge on which the center is located. One of these channels, Drainage 3, debouches into a small bajo (seasonal wetland) west of La Milpa in which Vern Scarborough was particularly interested.

With my colleague, Paul Hughbanks, I completed a survey along the lower third of Drainage 3, then turned to the bajo itself. Preliminary results from the 1997 season, including extremely dense concentrations of rubble features along the lower drainage and the discovery of an intriguing settlement on a karst hill within the bajo, convinced me that the Far West Bajo, as we named it, was critical to any reconstruction of La Milpa's land and water management strategies. I therefore focused my research on the evolution of settlement and agricultural systems in the bajo through a study of the archaeological features located in and around the depression. My understanding of these systems was complemented by a suite of analyses by my colleagues on the larger regional project that elucidated the paleoecological history of the bajo.

In 1998 and again in 1999 I returned to the Far West Bajo to conduct the mapping, pedestrian survey, and excavations that provided the core of the data presented in this volume. As the study progressed, two patterns became clear. First, several settlements of surprising size and complexity were located in or around the outskirts of the bajo, suggesting substantial occupation of the landscape. Second, clusters of rubble features that seemed to be agricultural indicated a hitherto unrecognized form of intensive agriculture, one that relied on the construction of terraces and berms to trap soil and moisture around the margins of the bajo. Taken together, these patterns suggested a degree of resource specialization and concomitant prosperity remarkable in a landscape that is today hot, humid, and devoid of human habitation.

Not until I turned from fieldwork to interpretation, and received the results of ceramic and geoarchaeological analyses, did these findings come into focus. Surprisingly, Kerry Sagebiel's ceramic analysis demonstrated that much of the settlement in and around the Far West Bajo was earlier than expected, with significant residential occupation in the Early Classic and early Late Classic periods. Normally, agricultural features indicative of intensive farming practices are associated with Late Classic settlement and are understood to represent intensification of production efforts as population density peaked in this period. The agricultural features of the Far West Bajo, however, were similarly early. What processes could have spurred such an unexpected and dramatic modification of the landscape? The paleoecological analyses provided an answer. Studies of the geomorphological and hydrological history of the bajo indicated that it began as a perennial wetland but was transformed into a seasonally wet depression by erosion and associated hydrological changes caused by massive clearance of the surrounding uplands. The timing of this transformation corresponds with the dates proposed for the construction of agricultural features designed to preserve the remaining fertility of the agricultural lands at the margins of the bajo. Based on careful synthesis of both paleoecological and archaeological data, I argue that the construction of agricultural terraces around the bajo was part of an accretionary transformation of the landscape in response to anthropogenic changes in the environment and the increasing need of specialized farming communities to conserve, improve, protect, and lay claim to agricultural lands. That this strategy was successful for several centuries before the Maya collapse is demonstrated by the quality, complexity, and longevity of the residential architecture in the settlements I studied.

The next several chapters tell the story of the Far West Bajo and the agricultural and settlement systems that developed in and around it in prehistory. After introducing the reader to the ancient lowland Maya, their history, and their environment, I summarize several decades of investigation of agriculture in wet environments that has led to controversy concerning their importance in Maya subsistence. I introduce the concept of resource-specialized communities, describing bajo communities as settlements specializing in the extraction and use of resources concentrated in the bajo landscape, the most important of which were soils and water.

Before turning to a description of the research methods used in this study, I summarize the history of archaeological research in northwestern Belize and then narrow my focus to the environment of the Río Bravo region, where the Far West Bajo is located (Chapter 2). Chapter 3 describes the bajo as it appears today, its vegetation, topography, and cultural features. I review the excavations that were conducted in the bajo, and indicate what these excavations and subsequent analyses tell us about the dynamic paleo-ecology of this wetland during the history of its occupation by ancient Maya farmers.

Based on mapping and excavation in four discrete agricultural zones, a picture emerges of the system of intensive terrace-based agriculture that the Maya developed on the bajo margins (Chapter 4). I argue that the accompanying settlement system developed out of innovative responses by the Maya to dramatic changes in their natural environment caused in part by their own activities. I then explore a pair of models that best explains the organization of the agricultural landscape and its corresponding settlement pattern. The garden-infield-outfield model accounts for the spatial arrangement of residential and agricultural features, and a model of community founders explains the presence of distinctive residential groupings in each of the settlements studied (Chapter 6). To conclude, I take a broad view of the Far West Bajo and describe what life would have been like for its inhabitants throughout its dynamic history. The volume ends with brief comments on the contribution this research in the Far West Bajo makes to the integration of environmental and archaeological analyses in the study of landscape history, a discipline that is better known in anthropology as historical ecology.

Acknowledgments

Research in the Far West Bajo was funded primarily by a dissertation improvement grant (SBR #9810002) from the National Science Foundation. Major support came from the Programme for Belize Archaeological Project, directed by Fred Valdez, Jr., and the Ancient Maya Land and Water Management Project, co-directed by Vernon Scarborough, Fred Valdez, Jr., and Nicholas Dunning, through an NSF grant awarded to Scarborough and Dunning (SBR #963–1024). For a portion of the 1998 season, I was hosted and provided with support by the La Milpa Archaeological Project, directed by Norman Hammond and Gair Tourtellot III.

Fieldwork support came from the Graduate College and the Social and Behavioral Sciences Research Institute at the University of Arizona. Throughout my years as a graduate student, the Department of Anthropology provided financial support in myriad ways. Most significantly, my development as a scholar was aided by the Emil W. Haury Fellowship, which was awarded to me for the years 1995–1998. In addition, grants from the Haury Educational Fund for Archaeology, the Comins Fund, and the Riecker Grant Fund facilitated my research in Belize for several years.

I am indebted to the Belize Department of Archaeology, who granted permission to conduct research under the auspices of the Programme for Belize Archaeological Project. Special thanks go to Charles Colby and the Colby family of Houston, Texas, on whose land much of the research took place.

My research in Belize would not have been possible without the tremendous efforts of my field assistants, including David McDow, Marc Wolf, Erin Chase, and especially Mary Jo Galindo. I am grateful to the

Mennonite community of Blue Creek, especially the Rempel family, and the men and women of San Felipe, especially the Dominguez and Magaña families, who welcomed me into their homes and their lives. I am indebted to Bruce Bachand, Holly Bachand, Corey Broehm, Jorge Cante, Eli Chi, Mariano Diaz, Emelardo Dominguez, Pastor Magaña, Pedro Magaña, Polo Magaña, Ubi Magaña, Sergio Murillos, Judith Silverman, Sarah Stoutamire, Noel Velasquez, and Amanda Wager for their skilled work in the field. I also thank the many hardworking field school students and volunteers who participated in this research.

Investigations in the Far West Bajo were facilitated by the support of many colleagues in Belize, notably Tim Beach, Sheryl Beach, Liwy Grazioso, Laura Kosakowsky, John Jones, Estella Krecji, Laura Levi, Kathy Reese-Taylor, Frank Saul, Julie Mather Saul, and Lauren Sullivan. Tim and Sheryl Beach, Alan Covich, Nick Dunning, and John Jones did the paleoecological analyses that so greatly enriched my interpretations of the Far West Bajo. Julie and Frank Saul conducted osteological analysis and are the authors of the summary of skeletal materials in Appendix G. Gair Tourtellot, Norman Hammond, and Amanda Clarke of the La Milpa Archaeological Project gave me rigorous training in architectural excavations and survey procedures.

Fellow graduate students and colleagues in Belize and at the University of Arizona provided moral and intellectual support: Jeff Baker, John Chamblee, Patti Cook, Gloria Everson, Pamela Geller, Jon Hageman, Mark Ingraham, Jon Lohse, Paul Hughbanks, Brian McKee, Rene Muñoz, John Murphy, Rissa Trachman, and Skye Wagner. Kerry Sagebiel provided superb ceramic analysis and was a wonderful roommate in field camp.

Hugh Robichaux generously allowed me to include data from his earlier research project in my analyses and to reproduce modified versions of several of his maps. Francisco Estrada Belli graciously provided digital data files from the La Milpa project for use in my GIS analysis. Brett Houk granted permission to use Figure 2.1. Gary Christopherson, Patrick Barabe, and Peter Johnson of the Center for Applied Spatial Analysis (University of Arizona) demonstrated extraordinary patience in assisting me with GIS. Marcia Bakry and Nicole Kilburn were invaluable in preparing figures, and Ron Redsteer at Northern Arizona University provided important assistance with illustrations. Dirk Harris, Senior Support Systems Analyst (University of Arizona), deftly managed complex computer graphics. Heather Knustrom took the photographs of artifacts (Figs. 5.7, 5.15, 5.20).

Nick Dunning and one anonymous reviewer shared many insightful comments and suggestions that greatly improved this volume. Norman Hammond and T. Patrick Culbert also reviewed sections of the text and Pat and Vern Scarborough provided guidance throughout. Carol Gifford edited and polished the manuscript, and it is much better as a result.

I am tremendously grateful for the love and support provided by my partner, Harold Smith. My parents, James and Mona Kunen, and my siblings, Sara and Michael Ackerman and David and Mandi Kunen have never failed to express support for my academic pursuits and pride in my accomplishments. For that, I cannot thank them enough, and this volume is dedicated to them.

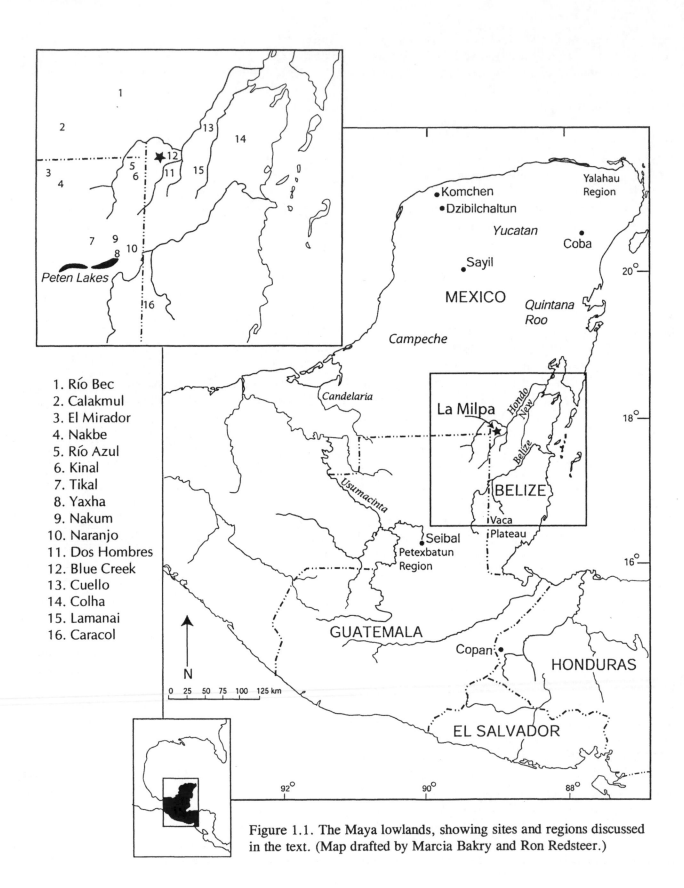

1. Río Bec
2. Calakmul
3. El Mirador
4. Nakbe
5. Río Azul
6. Kinal
7. Tikal
8. Yaxha
9. Nakum
10. Naranjo
11. Dos Hombres
12. Blue Creek
13. Cuello
14. Colha
15. Lamanai
16. Caracol

Figure 1.1. The Maya lowlands, showing sites and regions discussed in the text. (Map drafted by Marcia Bakry and Ron Redsteer.)

CHAPTER ONE

The Evolving Maya Landscape

Human activity during centuries of occupation significantly altered the landscape inhabited by the ancient Maya. In response, the Maya developed new techniques to harvest the natural resources of their surroundings, investing increased labor and raw materials into maintaining and even improving their ways of life. In some respects, the anthropogenic change to the landscape led to a serious degradation of the environment, spurring deforestation, erosion, and deterioration of water resources. But these human-induced changes also created new niches for exploitation and fostered innovative responses to altered conditions that allowed the Maya to survive for several centuries more, prior to their society's ultimate collapse. In presenting this agricultural landscape to the reader, I report on the history of settlement and farming in only a small corner of the Maya world. But the implication for any study of human-environment relationships is that these long term interactions are reflexive and that environmental history consists equally of ecological and cultural strands of influence.

This volume presents a study of an ancient Maya agricultural landscape in northwestern Belize. It documents a hitherto unrecognized form of intensive agriculture in the Maya lowlands, one that relied on the construction of terraces and berms to trap soil and moisture around the margins of low-lying depressions, called *bajos*. In the chapters that follow, I tell the story of a bajo on the outskirts of the major Belizean site of La Milpa. I trace the intertwined histories of residential settlements on nearby hills and ridges and agricultural terraces and other farming-related features around the margins of the bajo as these developed from the Late Preclassic period (400 B.C.–A.D. 250) until the area's abandonment in the Terminal Classic period (about A.D. 850). I then place this history within a reconstruction of the paleoenvironment of the bajo throughout this time. The reconstruction is based on

synthesis of numerous strands of ecological data provided by specialists in geomorphology, hydrology, soil science, and palynology. It is the thorough integration of all lines of evidence—the settlement system, the agricultural system, and the ancient environment—that breaks new ground in landscape research and, equally important, in the study of Maya non-elite domestic organization.

In examining the organization of three bajo communities with respect to the use and management of resources critical to agricultural production, I argue that differences in access to spatially variable natural resources resulted in highly patterned settlement remains. Ancient Maya farmers of the bajo distinguished and exploited three related environments: settling and gardening the uplands, terracing and farming intensively the low slopes surrounding the bajo, and extracting raw materials and obtaining water from the bajo itself. Access to the resources of each zone was not equal, however, as the first farmers to arrive settled in optimal locations and garnered for themselves the best quality and most diverse set of resources. For centuries, descendants of these community founders maintained their status as leaders in society. Even in the face of dramatic environmental change that demanded innovative human response to maintain a livable landscape, the socioeconomic differences established at the inception of bajo community life persevered until societal collapse.

MAYA PLACE AND TIME

The ancient Maya occupied an area that today stretches from the Yucatan peninsula in Mexico to the western frontiers of Honduras and El Salvador, and from the Pacific Coast of Guatemala to the Caribbean Sea off the coast of Belize (Fig. 1.1). The Maya lowlands encompass the Yucatan and adjacent areas of

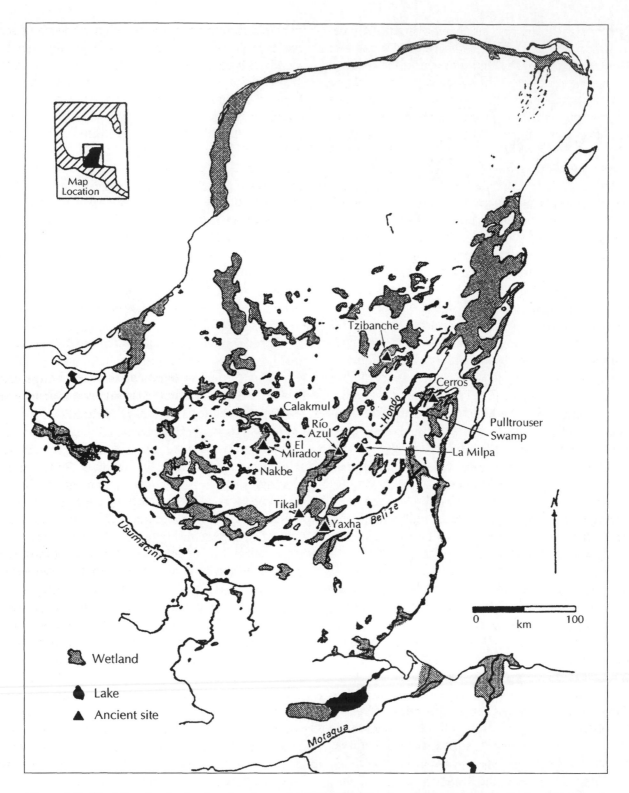

Figure 1.2. The Maya lowlands, showing the regional distribution of wetlands and pertinent sites. (Adapted by Nicholas Dunning from Pope and Dahlin 1989, Fig. 1, *Journal of Field Archaeology,* with the permission of the Trustees of Boston University, all rights reserved, and published in Dunning and others 2002, *Annals of the Association of American Geographers,* with permission from Blackwell Publishing Ltd.)

Mexico, all of Belize, and the Peten district of Guatemala. Traditionally, the lowlands are subdivided into drier northern and wetter southern zones; the focus of this study is a portion of the southern lowlands where upland bajos are especially common (Fig. 1.2). The first Maya settlements in the lowland area were established by approximately 1500 B.C. as small, scattered farming villages. Entry into the lowlands may originally have been through riverine channels such as the Usumacinta drainage and the rivers of the Belizean coastal plain. Cuello, in northern Belize, is a well-documented agricultural village dating from the Middle Preclassic (900–400 B.C.). Many characteristics later considered to be typical of the Maya like pole and thatch houses atop plastered platforms, human burials, ceramics, and tools for processing crops, were already present by this time. The earliest major centers, including El Mirador and Nakbe in northern Peten, flourished during the Middle and Late Preclassic (400 B.C.–A.D. 250) periods and contained some of the most impressive monumental architecture ever built by the Maya. Although these centers collapsed at the end of this period, most other Late Preclassic centers, such as Lamanai in Belize, continued to flourish in succeeding periods. By the end of the Preclassic, trappings of rulership such as hieroglyphic writing, stela portraiture, and recording of dynastic histories were established.

The subsequent Classic period is typically divided into Early (A.D. 250–600), Late (A.D. 600–830), and Terminal (A.D. 830–930) phases. For many, this period represents the apogee of Maya civilization, with settlement at its widest extent; the rise of most of the great centers of power, such as Tikal, Copan, and Calakmul; and extraordinary developments in art, architecture, cosmology, writing, and agriculture. By the Terminal Classic, most southern Maya states had collapsed and most settlements were occupied by only small remnant populations, but communities continued to thrive in the northern lowlands throughout this and the subsequent Postclassic period (A.D. 930–1500) until the Spanish Conquest.

Why focus so intently on a bajo landscape? Many of the best-known and largest Maya centers, including Tikal, Calakmul, Nakbe, El Mirador, and Río Azul, were built adjacent to the karstic depressions known as bajos. This is an intriguing spatial relationship, as today these seasonally wet, densely vegetated ecosystems are exceedingly inhospitable and seemingly devoid of valuable resources, not to mention evidence of settlement. More than 40 percent of the land of the southern lowlands is covered in wetlands of various types (Fig. 1.2). Considering the density of ancient Maya populations in antiquity and the importance of water and water imagery in Maya cosmology, it would be surprising if these lands were not utilized for settlement, agriculture, or the exploitation of a critical resource. Yet, despite their apparent importance in the development of Maya civilization and a growing number of research projects focusing on them, bajos remain poorly understood.

WETLANDS RESEARCH

Most studies involving bajos and other wetlands have focused on their modification and management for systems of intensive agriculture. Several different types of wetlands exist in the Maya lowlands and the differences among them are significant. Riverine floodplains and permanently inundated swamps are common in low-lying coastal zones such as northern Belize. Research on the modification of river floodplains for agricultural purposes has yielded evidence of wetland field systems along the Candelaria River in Campeche (Siemens and Puleston 1972) and in the floodplains of the New River and Hondo River in northern Belize (Bloom and others 1985; Lambert and Arnason 1983; Pohl 1990; Pohl and Bloom 1996; Puleston 1977; Siemens 1982). Channelized and possibly raised field systems were identified in a pioneering study of wetland agriculture in Pulltrouser Swamp, a largely permanent wetland in northern Belize (Turner 1993; Turner and Harrison 1983) as well as at Cobweb Swamp near the site of Colha (Jacob 1995). Canal irrigation and wetland agriculture is also well-documented for the Late Preclassic site of Cerros on the Belizean coast (Scarborough 1983, 1991).

Debate about the chronology, function, and extent of agricultural systems in riverine and permanent wetlands continues among researchers (see Turner 1993 for a thorough discussion), but there is now little controversy surrounding the idea that these areas were indeed utilized by the ancient Maya. The same cannot be said for the upland bajos of the interior southern lowlands, where questions persist about their suitability for cultivation. These karstic depressions, lying between higher ridges and hills, are today only seasonally flooded, remaining dry for several months of the year. Soils in many bajos are characterized as vertisols, whose mineral deficiency and susceptibility to seasonal shrinking and swelling leads some scholars to question their suitability for farming (Pope and Dahlin 1989, 1993). However, great variability exists among and even within bajos in terms of hydrological regimes, soil types, and vegetation association. This environmental heterogeneity may be indicative of differences that prevailed in ancient times and provides relevant clues to past land use patterns.

Peter Harrison first reported aerial observation of extensive field systems in the Bajo del Morocoy in southern Quintana Roo (Harrison 1977; Harrison and Turner 1978). Subsequent verification on the ground (called ground-truthing by archaeologists) revealed the presence of features interpreted as wetland fields in the bajo, near the site of Tzibanche (Gliessman and others 1983). However, later attempts to identify wetland fields by remotely sensed patterns recorded by radar that appeared to indicate widespread canals and field systems were flawed by "noise" in the system and other interpretive difficulties (Adams 1980, 1981; Pope and Dahlin 1989, 1993). Subsequently, ground reconnaissance has been the dominant mode of research.

Folan and his colleagues reported small raised rubble surfaces that potentially served as planting platforms in the Bajo el Laberinto in southeast Campeche (Folan and Gallegos 1998, 1999). Culbert and his colleagues identified features that appeared to be drainage ditches on the margins of the Bajo Pedernal near Río Azul in northern Peten (Culbert and others 1990). McAnany is continuing the research of Turner and Harrison in the seasonally inundated arms of Pulltrouser Swamp in northern Belize (Berry and McAnany 2000; McAnany 1998) and has mapped and tested a sample of wetland fields and canals associated with the adjacent site of K'axob. More recently, Gunn and others (2002) and Hansen and others (2002) presented evidence of terracing on the margins of the large bajos adjacent to Calakmul and Nakbe, respectively. Hansen also reports the presence of organic mucks imported from the bajo behind some of the terraces and across some agricultural fields.

Two recent studies of seasonal wetlands are particularly relevant to the research I present here. First, Fedick's investigations in wetlands in the Yalahau region of northern Quintana Roo extend the geographic range of seasonal wetland research and documents innovative use and manipulation of a wetland landscape (Fedick and Hovey 1995; Fedick and others 2000). Although most of the northern lowlands is significantly drier, flatter, and more sparsely vegetated than the southern lowlands on which this book focuses, the Holbox fracture zone Fedick studied contains wetlands similar in many respects to the upland bajos to the south. The fracture zone features a series of linear swales alternating with depressions that contain freshwater wetlands dependent both on water table fluctuations and on seasonal rainfall (Fedick and others 2000: 133). Research in one of these wetlands revealed numerous alignments of limestone boulders and slabs situated strategically with respect to small natural depressions within the larger wetland. Fedick interprets these features as the internal scaffolding for now-eroded earthen berms that controlled the movement of water in the wetland during the rainy season. He argues that such manipulation of water levels and sediment movement might have facilitated flood-recessional farming or a late dry-season crop. He also suggests that the wetland itself provided important natural resources, including wild foods and possibly fertilizer, that would have supplemented crops (Fedick and others 2000: 145). These interpretations are strikingly similar to ones I made after studying a southern lowland bajo. I, too, discovered that berms in a flat portion of the Far West bajo directed the flow of water and sediment and that these features facilitated flood-recessional farming near the edges of the bajo. The bajo itself was an extremely valuable landscape, containing not only water but also important raw materials such as chert and clay (Kunen 2001).

Finally, research in the Bajo la Justa, located between the sites of Yaxhá and Nakum in Peten, Guatemala, is of particular interest because it was the precursor to the research discussed here. The Bajo la Justa project was designed to resolve some of the wetlands controversy by testing the hypothesis that bajos were important loci of prehispanic Maya settlement and agriculture (Culbert and others 1995, 1996; Grazioso Sierra and others 2001; Kunen and others 2000). Project members, directed by T. Patrick Culbert and Vilma Fialko, mapped topography, vegetation zones, and settlement remains in the bajo, which measures approximately 10 km by 10 km (6 by 6 miles), and its immediate surroundings. Test pits in several sites located on ridges and hilltops within and on the edges of the bajo helped to establish a chronology of occupation. The crew also placed several small trenches in an area of the bajo near Yaxhá in order to identify possible modifications of the landscape associated with ancient agriculture and to study associated soils and pollen.

Settlement survey revealed that occupation on ridges of land around and within the bajo was ubiquitous and varied in size and complexity from small rural hamlets to minor centers like Poza Maya (Kunen and others 2000). Moreover, test excavations yielded evidence that these sites had long and varied histories of occupation, ranging in time from the Preclassic to the Terminal Classic, and did not represent merely ephemeral occupations. These settlements continued to be occupied and indeed flourished even as dramatic changes to the bajo environment surely affected the livelihood of residents.

Soil pits excavated in the Bajo la Justa produced evidence that portions of the bajo had once been perennially wet. A buried paleosol dating to A.D. 75 (calibrated) yielded an isotope signature indicative of its formation in a perennial wetland (Dunning and others 2002: 277). Moreover, some pollen recovered from this unit came from aquatic plants, including water lilies and cattails, whereas other pollen indicated that grassy areas once existed around the wetland's margins (Dunning and others 2002). After A.D. 75, colluviation led to infilling of the bajo, forming a gray, clayey surface that the Maya may have cultivated. Trenches excavated nearby revealed deep clay-filled cuts into underlying marl (Kunen and others 2000). These features appeared to be canals that might have provided the drainage necessary to bring the now-buried surface into production. Similar features were discovered by Fialko (2000; Fialko and Culbert 1997) in the Bajo de Santa Fe near Tikal and the Bajo la Pita near Naranjo. Despite the apparent transformation of at least parts of the Bajo la Justa from a perennial to a seasonal wetland, settlements around the bajo flourished, indicating that the bajo continued to play an important albeit changed role in the settlers' way of life.

Many scholars currently think that intensive agriculture involving the modification of wetlands was a central component of ancient Maya subsistence, supporting the maintenance of dense populations through centuries of complex social development (Culbert and others 1995, 1996; Harrison 1977; Harrison and Turner 1978; Turner and Harrison 1983). These scholars argue for a primarily Classic period reliance on wetland reclamation consonant with demographic and sociopolitical developments in the lowlands during this time. In contrast, other researchers (Fedick and Ford 1990; Pohl 1985, 1990; Pohl and Bloom 1996; Pope and Dahlin 1989; Pope and others 1996, 2000) have argued that wetland agriculture was neither as geographically nor as temporally widespread as its proponents believe, nor was it as significant a part of the subsistence base. These scholars advocate a primarily Preclassic period use, not of ridged or raised wetland fields, but of ditched or drained fields for floodwater recessional farming, a practice they argue was abandoned before the Classic period because of coastal flooding associated with a rise in sea levels. Many of these scholars question the evidence for cultivation of bajos, arguing that some of the features and buried soil layers cited by advocates of the first position are attributable to natural, not anthropogenic, environmental perturbations (Pohl and Bloom 1996; Pope and others 1996).

THE PATCHY LOWLAND ENVIRONMENT

With the controversy surrounding the use of seasonal wetlands for intensive wetland agriculture in full force, I approached this study of the bajo from a different perspective. My previous experience in the Bajo la Justa had indicated that the most definitive evidence for bajo use came from settlements on small ridges or "islands" of land within the depressions and from the ridges and hilltops around the margins of the bajo. It seemed imperative to sample the bajo interior thoroughly, both to map the environmental heterogeneity contained within the wetland and to record any settlement or agricultural features that might be present. Thus, I designed a project in which a long transect to obtain information from a cross-section of the bajo was complemented by a series of survey blocks that tested large areas of the bajo margins and surrounding ridges. These archaeological excavations were supplemented by a paleoecological study of the bajo directed by my colleagues Vernon Scarborough and Nicholas Dunning of the University of Cincinnati. The environmental reconstruction offered by their team was based in large part on a set of backhoe trenches dug into the bajo in various locations.

In combining studies of the bajo interior and margins, my explicit focus was *not* on searching for evidence of wetland reclamation in the form of ridged fields; rather, I sought to document two critical relationships. The first was the spatial relationship among cultural features in the uplands, bajo margins, and bajo interior. The second was the temporal relationship between the environmental history of the bajo and the agricultural and settlement history of its occupants. It quickly became apparent that the dominant agricultural practice in the bajo was not the use of fields in the bajo interior, but intensive farming of the bajo margins using terraces and berms to conserve soil and manage moisture.

Agricultural terracing has been extensively studied in four regions of the Maya lowlands: the karstic hills of the Río Bec region of Campeche, Mexico; the horst-graben topography of the Petexbatun region of the Peten, Guatemala; the rolling limestone plains of the Belize River Valley in western Belize; and the granite outcroppings of the Maya mountains and their limestone foothills on the Vaca Plateau of central Belize (Chase and Chase 1998; Dunning and Beach 1994; Dunning and others 1997; Fedick 1994, 1995; Healy and others 1983; Neff and others 1995; Turner 1983). None of these studies documents terracing around the margins of an upland bajo, however, and all of them postulate a Late Classic period date for peak use of the features. Ongoing research in the bajos near Nakbe and Calakmul also hints at the importance of terracing in our understanding of Maya use of bajos (Gunn and others 2002; Hansen and others 2002).

It is now evident that no single explanatory model of agriculture is valid for the entire Maya lowlands (see Dunning and Beach 2000). Rather, in response to the patchy nature of the lowland environment, the Maya developed suites of agricultural techniques tailored to the particularities of localized conditions. Recognition of this variability is beginning to coalesce in what Don Rice (1993) calls the multihabitat-multitechnology model or what Fedick (1996a) terms the managed mosaic. Current research on ancient Maya agricultural practices emphasizes the importance of fine-grained studies of environmental variation, resource diversity, and the arrangement of settlements in response to the distribution of critical resources (Dunning 1996;

Dunning and others 1998; Fedick 1995, 1996a; Kunen 2003; Turner 1993). Collection of vital empirical data, especially on the local level, is crucial to the development of this model. Based on careful synthesis of both paleoecological and archaeological data, I suggest that the Maya constructed agricultural terraces around the bajo as part of an accretionary transformation of the landscape in response to anthropogenic changes in the environment and the increasing need of specialized farming communities to conserve, improve, protect, and lay claim to agricultural lands.

RESOURCE SPECIALIZATION AND BAJO COMMUNITIES

Since the beginning of archaeological research in the Maya lowlands, models of subsistence production and models of settlement have developed hand in hand (Becker 1979). For example, the outmoded view of Maya sites as empty ceremonial centers surrounded by a thinly populated rural countryside was predicated on the notion that Maya farmers practiced simple swidden agriculture. As research beginning in the 1950s revealed evidence for much higher population densities than had previously been proposed, the dichotomous view of Maya society as consisting of priests and peasants, ceremonial centers and humble hinterland houses, was abandoned. A newer model was postulated, one of concentric zones of settlement in which both population density and social status dropped off as distance from the center increased. Implicit in this model was the association of high status with proximity to major architecture and low status with distance from monumental precincts. The classification of sites as either centers or hamlets now appeared untenable, considering the range of variation that existed between these two categories. Rather, the newer model described a central precinct of monumental architecture surrounded by concentric zones of increasingly less impressive buildings (Marcus 1983).

Recent studies of Maya economic organization (like McAnany 1989; Rice 1987), however, point to the existence of nodes of specialized production in non-site-center contexts. Such nodes indicate that a steady drop-off both of population density and of social status, as posited by the concentric zonation model, is an oversimplification of the lowland settlement pattern. There is no question that major cities were focal points for religious and political power and constituted the principal administrative centers for the polities to which non-urban settlements belonged. Nevertheless, the assumption that a single hierarchy existed, subsuming political, religious, administrative, and economic powers, is unproved. As Bray (1983: 174-175) wrote in his discussion of the organization of central places:

> We may imagine a political lattice organized on much the same principle as the market lattice, but it does not follow that the two lattices will be spatially congruent. The tendency has been to assume that all services will congregate, that political power and purchasing power (and also ritual and military power) will concentrate in the same towns and cities, and often in the same hands. This may be frequently true, but there are plenty of exceptions.

Recognition of the spatial noncongruence between various spheres of organization has led to a serious challenge of hierarchical core-periphery and zonation models of Maya social structure and settlement pattern. Couched in the language of heterarchy, which proposes a more flexible model for understanding the structure of complex societies, scholars have begun to document the importance of non-urban resource specialized communities (Scarborough 1999). Heterarchy recognizes that "political, economic and religious hierarchies . . . [in complex societies] were rarely isomorphic" (Marcus 1995: 19). The existence of multiple hierarchies (heterarchy) thus offers an explanation for the presence of these higher status, economically specialized communities in the hinterlands around large cities.

Many scholars now argue that economic specialization in the Maya lowlands was tied not to central places but to the spatial structure of resources (Fedick 1995; Harrison 1989; Potter and King 1995; D. Rice 1993; P. Rice 1987; Scarborough and others 2003). Because the lowland environment was patchy, certain biotic and abiotic resources were highly localized. Settlements that developed near concentrations or "patches" of critical resources may have become specialized producers by exploiting these resources (Scarborough and others 2003).

Potter and King (1995) used ceramic and lithic production as examples to illustrate their argument that economic organization in the Maya lowlands was heterarchical. Distinguishing between utilitarian and prestige good production, they argued that producers of utilitarian ceramics were located near clay sources in a system of dispersed localized community specialization, whereas luxury ceramics were produced in city centers where production was subject to elite oversight (Potter and King 1995: 25). This pattern is documented at places like Tikal and Palenque (Fry 1980; Rands and Bishop 1980; P. Rice 1987).

Similarly, lithic producers may have been located literally on top of the resource, as at Colha, Belize, where again, researchers identified autonomous or loosely organized household or community-level producers (King and Shaw 2003; Shafer 1983). Specialized lithics, such as chert eccentrics, which were also produced at Colha, entered into a separate, highly centralized distribution and exchange network. In discussing utilitarian ceramic production, Prudence Rice (1987) noted that there is little evidence for a strong directive role played by major centers in economic organization. Rather, the pattern seems to have been one of non-urban, spatially dispersed specialization. Mark Aldenderfer generalized this argument by noting that attached specialists producing low volumes of specialized goods were likely to be found in major centers, whereas high-volume production of "industrial" or subsistence goods were dispersed into areas where the resource under production was abundant (Aldenderfer and others 1989: 58).

Settlements that were directly involved in agricultural production were similarly oriented, not toward political or religious centers, but toward the spatial distribution of agricultural resources (Fedick 1995). It is not immediately evident that agricultural production was organized in the same manner as craft production. On the contrary, it might be argued that agricultural land was not a spatially discrete resource in the same way that clay, chert, or salt were. Rather, there is plentiful evidence that agriculture was almost universally practiced throughout the Maya lowlands in a variety of environmental settings (Dunning and others 1998; Flannery 1982; Harrison and Turner 1978; Pohl 1985). However, some "patches" of agricultural resources were improved by labor inputs, which had the effect of further localizing these resources (Potter and King 1995: 19).

Such improvement was especially visible in systems of intensive agriculture, where construction and maintenance of agricultural installations like terraces, check dams, wetland fields, and drainage canals were necessary to maintain high levels of production. These types of landscape modifications could not be made everywhere, but were found in specific environmental zones, be they wetlands, areas with particular slopes or vegetation signatures, or soil types well suited to manipulation (Harrison and Turner 1978). Thus, agricultural lands suitable for *intensive* production strategies may be viewed as localized resources made more localized through labor inputs. Some communities whose residents exploited these resources became loci of economic power spatially discrete from the centralized political forces of the major centers.

I propose that a special type of settlement, a "bajo community," existed in the Maya lowlands that was organized primarily around intensive terraced agricultural production and secondarily around the extraction of bajo resources such as chert, clay, and organic soils. Bajo communities are thus examples of what Potter and King (1995: 19) call specialized producer extractor sites and what Scarborough (1999) refers to as resource specialized communities. According to Scarborough, Maya settlements did not simply expand in regular, concentric circles around monumental centers. Rather,

the dispersed nature of resources in the lowlands prompted the "hiving off" of segments of the population who relocated to environmentally favorable locations. The result was the creation of numerous settlements founded on a strategy of exploitation of the local environment's set of productive resources. Although inhabitants of these settlements presumably participated in the political life of the polity whose center was the monumental precinct, they also developed a more autonomous economic specialization. This specialization in turn enhanced the social status of at least some community members.

In the following chapters I explore two questions that arise when documenting the particular pattern of intensive agricultural production that developed in one small area of the Maya lowlands, the Far West Bajo. First, how was the bajo landscape organized and utilized by its ancient Maya inhabitants? Second, how did environmental changes and human activities interact and influence each other through time? The answers to these questions contribute to our understanding of the important role of bajos in the development of Maya civilization and of the enduring ingenuity of human cultural groups in the face of dramatic anthropogenic environmental changes.

CHAPTER TWO

Investigating the Bajo

The Far West Bajo is located close to the Guatemalan and Mexican frontiers and slightly northwest of the monumental center of La Milpa (Fig. 2.1). I chose to study this particular seasonal wetland for two reasons. First, it had been investigated briefly as part of a comprehensive program of research on ancient land and water management techniques around the La Milpa polity initiated by Vernon Scarborough and Nicholas Dunning in 1992. This initial exploration had demonstrated that the bajo lay at the terminus of an important stream channel draining La Milpa center and was therefore in a prime location to play an important role in agricultural production for the polity (Scarborough and others 1992). Second, the Far West Bajo was a small-scale counterpart to the Bajo la Justa in neighboring Peten, where data concerning settlement patterns, occupational history, and agricultural practices were beginning to coalesce. The Bajo la Justa was large in area, and Pat Culbert's team had been conducting a necessarily limited sampling program. The Far West Bajo presented an opportunity for the first thorough exploration of a bajo interior and its margins through transects, survey blocks, and excavations that would test a large portion of the depression. My project was designed in part to determine whether the patterns of settlement and agricultural practice emerging from the Bajo la Justa also characterized the more circumscribed Far West Bajo.

PREVIOUS RESEARCH IN NORTHWESTERN BELIZE

Little exploration, archaeological or otherwise, took place in remote northwestern Belize prior to the 1980s. Exceptions included brief investigation of La Milpa by noted Mayanist J. Eric S. Thompson, reconnaissance by oil company workers, and visits by various personnel of the Belize Department of Archaeology who investigated reports of looting, particularly at La Milpa (Guderjan 1991). Since then, archaeological research in the region has been undertaken principally by three projects: the La Milpa Archaeological Project (LaMAP), the Programme for Belize Archaeological Project (PfBAP), and the Blue Creek Project. In addition, the Ancient Maya Land and Water Management Project, a collaborative undertaking with the PfBAP, focuses explicitly on the relationships between settlement and natural resource use in the vicinity of La Milpa.

La Milpa Archaeological Project (LaMAP)

La Milpa is a midsized Maya center in northwestern Belize, approximately 90 km (56 miles) northwest of Tikal in the central Peten, 20 km (12 miles) east of Río Azul in northeastern Guatemala, and 40 km (25 miles) west of Lamanai, on the New River Lagoon in Belize (Hammond and others 1998: 831). The site core sits atop a locally prominent limestone ridge about 180 m above sea level. La Milpa is the largest site in the Río Bravo Conservation Management Area (RBCMA), a 105,300–hectare (260,000–acre) preserve (Fig. 2.1) dedicated to maintaining Belize's natural and cultural heritage administered by the not-for-profit Programme for Belize (PfB). The site was first discovered by Eric Thompson in 1938 (Guderjan 1989; Hammond 1991), who mapped the main plaza and made notes on its stelae and monumental architecture. In 1992, Norman Hammond and Gair Tourtellot III initiated LaMAP to investigate social structure, political organization, and settlement history at La Milpa and its sustaining area (Hammond 1991; Hammond and others 1996; Hammond and others 1998; Hammond and Tourtellot 1993, 1999; Tourtellot and Hammond 2000; Tourtellot and others 1993; Tourtellot and others 1994; Tourtellot and

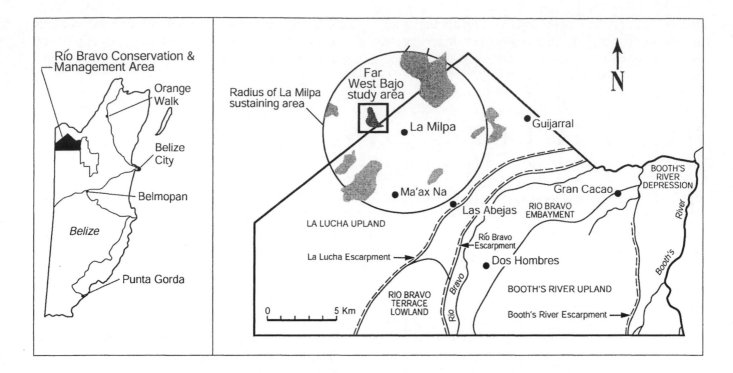

Figure 2.1. The Río Bravo Conservation Management Area, showing its location in Belize, major sites of the area, and physiography. (After Houk 1996: 84; reproduced courtesy of Brett A. Houk and the Programme for Belize Archaeological Project.)

others 1996; Tourtellot and others 1997; Tourtellot and others 1999; Tourtellot and others 2002). Excavations in the site center under Hammond's direction have established a preliminary chronology for the site, revealed much about the architectural style of some of the principal buildings, obtained substantial information about construction history through the recording of looters' trenches, and documented the placement and dates (when present) of 20 stelae (Grube 1994; Grube and Hammond 1998; Hammond 2001; Hammond and others 1998; Hammond and Tourtellot 1999; Kosakowsky and Sagebiel 1999). The site core follows the topography of the ridge and is laid out in a roughly linear arrangement. In the northern part, the center features an imposing main plaza (Plaza A) surrounded by large pyramidal buildings and long range structures. Within the plaza are a large pyramidal structure, two ball courts, and a line of stelae running north-south in front of the set of temples that define the eastern plaza edge. Many of the stelae are not in situ and appear to have been reset in the plaza during the Postclassic period or later. In 1996, a royal tomb dating to around

A.D. 450 was excavated near Stela 1 at the corner of Structure 1, the tallest structure at La Milpa. (Hammond and others 1998: 831). Evidence of a Late Classic ruler named *Ukay* is on Stela 7, located in front of the much smaller Structure 5, which depicts him along with a date of November 30, A.D. 780. A causeway links Plaza A to the smaller Plazas B and C to the south, passing by a large reservoir that likely served much of the center's water storage and drainage needs. Dominating the southern part of the site is the acropolis, a series of elevated structures and courtyards thought to have been the residence of the rulers of La Milpa (Hammond and others 1998). Excavations by LaMAP demonstrate that La Milpa was initially settled during the Late Preclassic period (about 300 B.C.) and had an established royal dynasty but only a small resident population during the Early Classic. It reached its zenith during the Late/Terminal Classic period, during which most of the visible monumental architecture was built, but after which it was subsequently abandoned save for a remnant population. Exploration of looters' trenches in several of the elaborate courtyards of the acropolis have resulted in an argument for north-to-south expansion; there is also evidence for the abrupt cessation of elite construction as La Milpa declined, leaving unfinished structures in several places, including a major expansion of the acropolis at the southern end of the site center (Hammond and others 1998; Hammond and Tourtellot 1999).

In addition to research on the monumental architecture of the site core, the central square kilometer of the site was mapped in detail under Gair Tourtellot's direction (Tourtellot and others 1993; Tourtellot and others 1994). Locational control was provided by an imaginary grid laid across the site, which I also used to link my maps to those of the La Milpa project. The origin of this grid, designated E6000/N6000, lies in the center of the 6–km (3.7–mile) radius circle that essentially delimits the boundaries of the La Milpa polity. In addition to the central square kilometer, Tourtellot and his team extended their surveys to a set of transects emanating in cardinal directions from the main plaza (Tourtellot and others 1996; Tourtellot and others 1997). Along each of the southern and eastern transects, surveyors discovered a smaller minor center 3.5 km (2.2 miles) from the site core on elevated ground high enough to be intervisible with Structure 1 at La Milpa center; purposive survey located complementary western and northern centers similarly placed (Tourtellot and others 2002). The minor center designated La Milpa West (Tourtellot and Hammond 2000) is just a few hundred meters from one of my survey blocks. Ongoing mapping and limited test excavations along these transects are providing data on settlement history, population dynamics, agricultural production, and household organization in the La Milpa sustaining area (for example, Tourtellot and others 1999). John Rose (2000) studied 15 randomly located survey blocks within the La Milpa sustaining area and found evidence of extremely high population densities, testifying to substantial growth of the polity during the Late Classic period. Gloria Everson is completing research on household archaeology, focusing on a random sample of test excavations in house groups and examining middens along the eastern transect (Everson 2003). Jason Gonzáles, along with Marc Wolf and Chantal Esquivias, tested some of the many linear features in the La Milpa area, including terraces and berms, that appear to be related to land management (Tourtellot and others 1999). Finally, Kerry Sagebiel (1999,

2003), who is responsible for the ceramic analysis reported here, is investigating issues of vessel function in her analysis of LaMAP ceramics.

Programme for Belize Archaeological Project (PfBAP)

Whereas LaMAP takes as its focus La Milpa and its sustaining area, investigation of all other archaeological remains within the RBCMA is the responsibility of the Programme for Belize Archaeological Project. PfBAP is a multiyear project that began in 1992 and is designed to locate, record, and test archaeological sites throughout the RBCMA in an effort to reconstruct regional settlement patterns. Originally under the direction of Richard E. W. Adams, the project has been directed since 1995 by Fred Valdez, Jr. Research under the auspices of the PfBAP includes site-based investigation of both large and small centers as well as systematic sampling along transects and nonsite-based research on agriculture.

South of La Milpa, Eleanor King and Leslie Shaw are conducting mapping and limited excavations to address questions of site planning and occupational history at the large site of Ma'ax Na and its smaller neighbor, Bolsa Verde, (King and Shaw 1998, 2003; King and others 1999; Shaw and King 1999; Shaw and others 1999). Their research has identified Ma'ax Na, whose site center includes a number of caves, as a ritual center with a power base rooted in ideology. In contrast, Bolsa Verde appears to be a resource-specialized community emphasizing intensive agriculture. The large site of Dos Hombres, below the Río Bravo escarpment and only slightly smaller than La Milpa, was the focus of dissertation research by Brett Houk (1996), who used research at the site to investigate the relationship between sociopolitical developments and principles of site planning. In a complementary project, Jon Lohse (2001) has recently reported on social status and community organization among households in the sustaining area around Dos Hombres, and Rissa Trachman (2001) is completing an analysis of domestic labor organization through a study of Dos Hombres households.

Laura Levi has been sampling survey blocks near the large sites of Wari Camp and 200 Meter Ridge close to the Río Bravo escarpment as part of a study refining her understanding of domestic group organization and its architectural expression. Kathryn Reese-Taylor worked for several seasons in the area closest to the Guatemalan border in an investigation of regional political relationships, especially between Río Azul and La Milpa. Brandon Lewis is continuing his work on the organization of lithic production, focusing in particular on identifying attached versus independent production. Examining data from several sites throughout the RBCMA, he argues for independent specialization in agricultural tool production (Lewis 1995). Lauren Sullivan conducted excavations at the minor center of Las Abejas, adjacent to the Gallon Jug road that bisects the RBCMA; she is the PfBAP ceramicist.

Research focused on rural settlement and agriculture includes that of Hugh Robichaux (1995), who conducted a study on settlement patterns in a set of eleven survey blocks located along two transects: the western PfB property line near La Milpa and a seismic transect near Dos Hombres. Three of his survey blocks near La Milpa are within the Far West Bajo study area. With Robichaux's gracious permission, data from these blocks (here designated survey blocks 6-8) are included in subsequent chapters. Paul Hughbanks (1998) directed a project investigating the relationship between settlement and the management of natural resources at the minor center of Guijarral, near Wari Camp. He documented an array of agricultural and land management strategies across the varied microenvironments of the site. Jon Hageman (1999a, 1999b) is completing a study of community-level social relationships among non-elite, non-urban Maya. Through survey and excavation, his work investigates the correlates and implications of lineage-based social organization in three locations within the RBCMA. Jeffrey Baker (2002) conducted research on intensive wetland agriculture near Sierra de Agua in the southern part of the RBCMA, near the Gallon Jug property. Estella Krejci is studying small depressions throughout the RBCMA, as well as at the minor centers of La Milpa East and La Milpa West under the auspices of LaMAP. She finds that many of these depressions (called *pozas*) served as cisterns for the ancient Maya inhabitants of the area. This finding brings hypotheses about centralized water management into question (Weiss-Krejci 2000; Weiss-Krejci and Sabbas 2002). Stan Walling (1995; Walling and others 1995) directed a study of the relationship between terracing and settlement along the Río Bravo escarpment near Dos Hombres. He and his colleagues

used survey and excavation to document substantial labor and material investment in terraces and ground penetrating radar to investigate buried terrace and residential construction (McIntyre and others 1996).

Finally, several scholars conduct specialized analyses for the PfBAP, and they have contributed much of the paleoecological analysis herein. Vernon Scarborough oversees research pertaining to water management throughout the RBCMA, including La Milpa. Similarly, Nicholas Dunning directs geoarchaeological research, conducting a program of coring and test excavation designed to investigate soils and geomorphology. Timothy Beach and Sheryl Luzzader-Beach research soils and hydrology of the region, and John Jones conducts palynological research throughout the RBCMA. Frank Saul and Julie Mather Saul are the PfBAP osteologists; Pamela Geller is conducting doctoral research on material from burials throughout the RBCMA. Alan Covich is responsible for analysis of shell, and David Lentz and his students have conducted limited macrobotanical analyses, particularly on samples collected by Hughbanks.

Ancient Maya Land and Water Management Project

A major collaborative research program co-directed by Vernon Scarborough, Fred Valdez, Jr., and Nicholas Dunning was undertaken jointly with the PfBAP; its members are investigating ancient water and land management practices in the RBCMA (Dunning and others 1999; Dunning and others 2002; Dunning and others 2003; Scarborough and Dunning 1995). This project seeks to document the systematic ways in which the Maya manipulated the natural landscape, transforming it into an engineered environment designed to provide basic resources such as water and agricultural lands. A major objective of this research is the examination of ancient Maya land-use adaptations through survey, mapping, and testing of significant drainages, depressions, *aguadas* (natural or modified sinks that hold water), agricultural features, and related habitation sites (Scarborough and others 1992; Scarborough and Dunning 1995).

The land and water management project initially conducted research at Kinal, a ridgetop site near Río Azul. The project investigated a reservoir system designed to divert runoff from the monumental architecture of the site center into downslope storage tanks (Scarborough and others 1994). More recently, the project has focused primarily on La Milpa and its environs. As part of this research, Scarborough and Dunning have documented the presence of a well-defined water control system at La Milpa featuring a system of reservoirs and drainages that regulated the storage and release of water to dependent zones below the monumental center (Scarborough and Dunning 1995; Scarborough and others 1992). Nicholas Dunning reported to me in 2001 that the system may also have been responsible for ridding the center of excess water during heavy rains and preventing uncontrolled floods from destroying fields and settlements downstream. As part of this research, the La Milpa aguada, a crucial source of water for the center, was systematically cored and tested in several locations (Hughbanks and Kunen 1997; Scarborough and others 1992). Dunning also excavated soil pits and test trenches in a small bajo at the terminus of Drainage 1, which descends from the northeast portion of the La Milpa center (Dunning and Beach 2000). Drainage 1 is marked by a number of check dams or cross-channel terraces that controlled the flow of water downslope.

Drainage 3, which drains the west side of La Milpa and empties into the Far West Bajo, was the focus of several seasons of research by this project. In 1992 Scarborough and his colleagues began a survey of the drainage channel and of a swath of land 200 m wide on either side of the drainage (Scarborough and others 1992); it was continued by Hughbanks and myself in 1997 (Hughbanks and Kunen 1997) and completed by Skye Wagner in 1998. These surveys revealed extensive zones of terraces, berms, and other land management features near the drainage, although no features such as check dams were found in the channel itself. Dunning excavated two test trenches at the mouth of Drainage 3 to investigate whether the channel had been artificially manipulated in ancient times. He also supervised excavation of 15 backhoe trenches in the Far West Bajo, some of which yielded crucial radiocarbon dates and preserved pollen (Dunning and Beach 2000; Dunning and others 1999; Dunning and others 2002; Dunning and others 2003). These investigations form the core of the paleoenvironmental reconstruction presented in the next chapter.

In addition to research at La Milpa, land and water management studies have taken place elsewhere in the

RBCMA. A small lake on the Río Bravo floodplain near Dos Hombres was cored, and the fossil pollen retrieved was analyzed (Dunning and others 1999; Jones 1999). Significant quantities of maize pollen attest to widespread cultivation and deforestation around the lake extending from 500 B.C. to A.D. 1000 (Dunning and others 1999: 654). A pollen core from the aguada near Sierra de Agua also contained both maize and manioc pollen, indicating cultivation in the associated wetland field systems (Baker 1997; Dunning and others 2003). Mapping and test excavation of various kinds of agricultural features, especially terraces, occurred along the Río Bravo escarpment (Beach and others 1999; Paxton O'Neal 1999) and the periphery of Dos Hombres (Beach and others 2002). Taken together, this research demonstrates that the environment inhabited by the ancient Maya of this region was the product of a long-term interactive sequence of environmental change and human response for more than a millennium of occupation.

Blue Creek Project

The Blue Creek project is an ongoing regional research effort that developed out of reconnaissance in northwestern Belize by Thomas Guderjan in 1988. His efforts were initially directed at exploration of sites in the RBCMA and adjacent Gallon Jug property (Guderjan 1991). As part of this reconnaissance, major sites, including La Milpa, Chan Chich, and Punta de Cacao, were mapped. Beginning in 1992, Guderjan began to focus on the center of Blue Creek, which is just east of the RBCMA at the edge of the Río Bravo escarpment, and on the nearby settlement area of Chan Cahal located just below the escarpment (Clagett 1997; Guderjan and Driver 1995; Guderjan and Lichtenstein 2001; Guderjan and others 1993; Guderjan and others 1994; Guderjan and others 1996; Hanratty 2000; Popson 2000; Popson and Clagett 1999). Crews conducted regional reconnaissance and limited test excavations in surrounding settlement areas (Baker 1996; Guderjan and Lichtenstein 2001; Lichtenstein 2000) and initiated research in the ditched-field agricultural systems below the escarpment, including backhoe excavations across several of the agricultural fields and testing water control features (Baker 2002; Guderjan and Lichtenstein 2001). Beginning in 2001, under the directorship of Jon Lohse, the project has turned to questions of political ecology, focusing on local and regional adaptations to the distribution of important resources and the ways in which local responses to environmental conditions shaped regional political and economic integration. Included are continued investigations in the expansive ditched-field system, under the direction of Tim Beach, Sheryl Luzzader-Beach, and Jon Lohse. Additional survey and excavations are now focusing on evaluating two "research corridors," one several kilometers west of the escarpment ranges atop the Peten Plateau where upland hills and bajos dominate, and one along the Río Bravo escarpment extending south to the La Lucha and Booth's River escarpments as they represent an ecotonal setting at the convergence of the Peten Plateau and Belize Coastal Plain.

THE BRAVO HILLS REGION

The Far West Bajo study area lies within the RBCMA and on private lands immediately to the west. This corner of the Maya world is part of the large karstic limestone platform of the Yucatan peninsula. The terrain is heavily faulted, forming areas of rolling and hilly uplands interspersed with low-lying bajos. Frequently, rivers and streams are bordered by steeply uplifted escarpments. Northwestern Belize above the Río Bravo escarpment is similar in physiography to the Peten region of Guatemala, which borders it on the west. General descriptions of vegetation, climate, and topography by Cyrus Lundell (1937) and Don Rice (1993) are applicable.

The RBCMA is within the Bravo Hills land region, which is bordered by the Belize River Valley on the south, Blue Creek on the north, and the Booth's River escarpment on the east (King and others 1992: 35). The area is drained by three rivers, earning it an alternative designation, "the Three Rivers Region." The Río Bravo, which begins in Guatemala, travels through the area from southwest to northeast. To the south of the RBCMA lands, this river is known as Chan Chich Creek (Houk 1996: 85). The river travels along the base of the Río Bravo escarpment and is eventually joined by Booth's River, which flows northward farther to the east. Together, these two rivers join the Río Azul to form the Río Hondo, which marks the border between Belize and Mexico to the north of the RBCMA. The Río Azul, which flows eastward from

Guatemala and is known as Blue Creek in Belize, drains along the northern border of the region before entering the Río Hondo.

Physiography

The Bravo Hills region is characterized by faulted limestone, broken into a series of undulating plains and karstic hills. Several steep escarpments mark the western sides of river floodplains. From east to west, the terrain rises in height from the Booth's River escarpment to the Río Bravo escarpment and finally to the La Lucha escarpment (which is not associated with a river drainage). Above the escarpments lie much higher lands known as the Booth's River upland, the Río Bravo Terrace upland, and the La Lucha upland (Dunning and others 1999; King and others 1992). La Milpa and the Far West Bajo study area are within the La Lucha upland, which extends westward into Guatemala. Elevations in some places near the Guatemalan border reach 300 m above sea level (King and others 1992: 35).

Locally abundant and variably sized enclosed bajos located between higher ridges and hills are important physiographic components of the Bravo Hills region. During the rainy season, portions of many of these bajos hold standing water. In the dry season, the clay soils of some bajos are "edaphically dry," meaning that although water is present in the soil it is not available to plants (Brokaw and Mallory 1993: 23; Dunning and others 2003). The Far West Bajo is one example of the many small bajos throughout the area.

Rainfall

The Bravo Hills region is within the neotropics and is therefore subject to highly seasonal rainfall. On average, the area receives about 1,500 mm of annual rainfall, but there is a great deal of variation from year to year (Brokaw and Mallory 1993: 12). Moreover, despite the large amount of rain, more than 90 percent of it arrives during the rainy season, meaning that the region experiences four especially dry months (Dunning and others 2003). The wet season extends from May to December, with an average of 200 mm per month of precipitation. The dry season, from January to April, receives less than 100 mm per month of rainfall (Brokaw and Mallory 1993: 13).

Figure 2.2. Howler monkey in an area of upland forest

Soils

Soils of the region, which derive from the underlying limestone of the Yucatan shelf, have been studied by King and others (1992) and Wright and others (1959), who are in general agreement regarding terminology. More detailed studies of the area have been conducted by Dunning and his colleagues as part of the land and water management project (Beach and others 2003; Dunning and others 2003). Upland soils are fertile but shallow, forming fairly well-draining clay mollisols or rendzinas. Bajo soils are dark and slow-draining clay vertisols, mollisols, and histosols that are frequently inundated during the wet season, then dry out and crack during the dry season (Beach and others 2003).

In the terminology of Wright and his colleagues (1959), soils are predominantly Yaxa and Jolja clays and gravelly clays. In the classification by King and his colleagues (1992), the soils of the region are part of the Yaxa suite, particularly the Jolja and Yalbac subsuites. Jolja soils in particular feature surface or subsurface layers of chert that were undoubtedly an important resource for the ancient Maya (Dunning and others 2003; King and others 1992).

Animal Life

Belize is justifiably famous for the richness of its animal life, which inhabits Caribbean cayes and coral reefs as well as inland forests. The RBCMA, protected from hunting and preserved in part for ecotourism, boasts a remarkable array of bird and mammalian life in addition to amphibians and reptiles, including noisy nocturnal frogs and poisonous snakes such as the fer de lance. Almost 400 species of bird are resident, including many types of hummingbirds and parrots, colorful toucans, and oscellated turkeys.

Howler and spider monkeys frequently travel through the treetops and often harass archaeologists working on the ground below with loud chatter and the occasional tossed branch (Fig. 2.2). Small ground-dwelling mammals such as agouti, opossum, and coatimundi are often spotted, along with large herds of peccary.

White-tailed and brocket deer are prevalent. Rare but not uncommon are magnificent jaguars, who cross the Gallon Jug road silently at dusk. Much more difficult to spot are the other cats, including mountain lion, ocelot and jaguarundi, who call this corner of forest home.

Vegetation

Vegetation in the region is a factor principally of soils and drainage. Lundell's (1937) study of vegetation in Peten is relevant for northwestern Belize, which, like Peten, is considered a zone of tropical wet-dry forest. Beginning with Lundell (1937), Wright and others (1959), King and others (1992), and Brokaw and Mallory (1993) are all in agreement as to the general categorization of forest types in the area, although their terminology varies somewhat.

In broad terms, vegetation can be divided into forest types along a gradient of elevation. Brokaw and Mallory (1993) have made a detailed study of modern vegetation within the RBCMA, most of which they classify as semideciduous broadleaf forest. This is upland forest with a canopy 15 m to 20 m high, located in well-drained areas atop ridges and hills (Fig. 2.2). Many economically valuable tree species such as sapodilla-chicle (*Manilkara zapota*), cherry (*Pseudolmedia* sp.), mamey (*Calocarpum mammosum*), copal (*Protium copal*), and various hardwoods, including mahogany (*Swietenia macrophylla*), exist today in these forests. Brokaw and Mallory conclude, however, and the paleoenvironmental data concur, that much of the original upland forest was cleared by the ancient Maya, and what is present now represents regrowth following the Maya collapse (Brokaw and Mallory 1993: 14).

Whereas upland areas are marked by high-canopied broadleaf forest, gentle slopes between the uplands and the low-lying bajos are generally covered in transitional forest. It has many of the same species as the upland forest, but the canopy tends to be lower. If large numbers of palms are present, the vegetation is called mixed palm-transitional forest (Fig. 2.3). The escoba palm (*Crysophila argentea*) in particular often grows in this forest, which is why some scholars (like Lundell 1937) identify it as escoba bajo. Because mixed palm-transitional forest usually does not occur in very low areas, I do not use this term here except when referring to low-lying areas of palm bajo in which the escoba palm dominates. As Houk (1996) notes, and as all scholars who work in the region can attest, no sharp division separates upland and transitional forests. Instead, a gradient between the two exists, so that it is not really possible to point to a line on the landscape at which upland forest ends and transitional forest begins.

Figure 2.3. Mixed palm-transitional forest.

In contrast to transitional forest zones, bajo zones are clearly demarcated. Low-lying bajos, because of their poorly draining clay soils and frequent inundation, cannot support tall forests and are instead marked by stunted trees and shrubs (Fig. 2.4). The canopy is low with a dense understory that can be almost impenetrable. Traditionally, these forests have been referred to as *tintal* bajo, after a particular woody shrub known as *palo de tinto* or logwood (*Haematoxylum campechianum*). In reality, however, several different kinds of bajo forests exist, including mixtures of different types of palms, low trees, epiphytes, and grasses or sedge. These distinctions are discussed in more detail in Chapter 3. In some areas, cohune palm forest (called *corozo bajo* in Spanish), a particular type of bajo forest in which the dominant species is the cohune palm (*Orbignya cohune*), grows in deep, well-drained soils at moderately low elevation (Fig. 2.5). Cohune forest

Figure 2.4. Scrub bajo forest.

Figure 2.5. Corozo bajo forest. (Photograph by T. Patrick Culbert.)

may be a successional forest representing secondary growth in areas benefiting from deposition of eroding soils from surrounding slopes (Dunning and others 2003). Corozo bajo (as it is called here) is recognized by scholars and local farmers alike as indicative of good land for milpas (Dunning and others 2002; Kunen and others 2000; Wright and others 1959).

Much of the land in the Far West Bajo study area is just outside the western boundary of the well-protected RBCMA and has therefore been disturbed by modern human activity. This area has been subject to extensive logging and clearing for cultivation and is today scarred by multiple logging roads and large patches of secondary growth in now abandoned milpas. Most of the areas that appear on the vegetation maps as "disturbance growth" are products of these modern activities.

RESEARCH METHODS

One day during my first field season in the RBCMA, when I was the most junior person on the project, I spent a few hours with two colleagues in the forest around La Milpa. My goal that summer was to decide

on a research project for my doctoral dissertation, and I was becoming convinced that a study of the Far West Bajo offered the most intriguing possibilities for examination of a dynamic agricultural landscape. That day I was walking with Paul Hughbanks, a fellow graduate student, and Nick Dunning in an area near the base of Drainage 3, which empties into the bajo. We were studying a feature that appeared to be a low causeway leading from the drainage to an unknown location. As we stood discussing ideas about its potential terminus (maybe it was a direct link between this important stream and the main plaza at La Milpa!), a sharp, strong, musty odor suddenly surrounded us. I, the most inexperienced of the three, stood surveying our immediate surroundings quizzically, while Nick, the senior researcher among us, did the most practical thing, which was to look quickly for a tall sturdy tree to climb, or at least hide behind. No sooner had I noticed his odd behavior when a pack of about 40 peccary appeared, snuffling at the ground and heading right toward us. As a graduate student in Arizona, I knew that peccaries can be aggressive and, what's worse, have terrible eyesight, so Paul and I quickly followed Nick's lead and hid behind the few tall trees we could find. Fortunately, no climbing was necessary, and we merely waited silently until the herd passed us by. This incident, although humorous in retrospect, nevertheless forced me to accept that if I decided to undertake research in the bajo, certain unorthodox ground rules were needed. Of these, the most basic were: don't survey close to the tree where the enormous poisonous snake lives (always be aware of your surroundings), when the forest goes utterly silent save for a gruff barking sound, a jaguar is close by (don't wander about alone in the bajo), and if it's raining too hard to survey, try digging instead (be prepared to problem-solve creatively).

This anecdote serves as a preface to my discussion of research methods. No scholarly discourse about sampling strategy and excavation methods can truly do justice to the decisions that must be made in the tropical forest on a daily basis in extremely difficult circumstances. Simple inconveniences like rain often cut short a day of mapping, since the electronic instruments should not get wet. Sometimes, the work day ended early when a student suffered the ill effects of heat and had still to contend with a 7–km (4–mile) walk back to the truck. When surveying, several structures could not be mapped in detail because they sat adjacent to hives of "killer" bees or, in one case, near an extremely large, coiled fer de lance hiding under a fallen tree trunk. At times, tape measures used to stake out lines had to be stretched creatively, to avoid the inevitable tree trunk blocking the path. Decisions about where to excavate, in principle made to test a representative sample of structures, were often in reality decided through selection of mounds that were not almost completely buried under the roots of a large tropical tree, as so many are. Occasionally, survey trails that we intended to cut straight veered around trees and never quite regained their proper orientation.

The specific focus of this study is the western portion of the La Milpa sustaining area centered on the Far West Bajo and its immediate environs (Fig. 2.6). The Far West Bajo is located approximately 3 km (1.8 miles) west-northwest of the center of La Milpa. Covering roughly 3 square kilometers (1.2 square miles), the bajo lies at the terminus of Drainage 3, a natural intermittent stream channel that emanates from the site core of La Milpa and courses in a generally western direction until debouching into the bajo (Scarborough

and others 1992). The bajo is teardrop shaped, with the bulbous end toward the south and a narrow neck extending to the north. The depression is almost completely enclosed by surrounding uplands, except for the neck, a strip of low-lying land through which runs an intermittent stream that eventually drains into Blue Creek to the north. This stream channel, for much of the year a dry arroyo, meanders through the bajo study area. At its lowest point, the bajo is 105 m above sea level. The edges of the bajo are slightly higher, about 111 m above sea level. On all sides, the terrain slopes up from the bajo, peaking at ridges 145 m above sea level. On the eastern and northern sides, the slope is gentle, but on the southern and western edges, steep ridges rise abruptly from the bajo edge. Near the eastern edge of the bajo, an isolated hill (hereafter referred to as the bajo hill) rises approximately 20 m from the surrounding low terrain. This hill is near a small aguada, into which run several small, intermittent streams.

Location of Survey Blocks and Transects

The small size of the Far West Bajo provided an opportunity for thorough sampling through a combination of transects and survey blocks, which were subject to topographic mapping, pedestrian survey, vegetation mapping, and test excavation. Eight survey blocks covering a total of 79 hectares were located in and around the bajo. Block 1 was centered on the bajo hill mentioned above. Blocks 2 through 5 were located on the margins of the bajo, covering parts of its interior, the slopes on the bajo margins, and the surrounding uplands. Blocks 6 through 8 were laid out by Robichaux along the PfB boundary line that crosses the southeast edge of the bajo. Blocks 6 and 7 were largely in the bajo, and Block 8 was situated on a high ridge overlooking the bajo on the southwest. The blocks were originally designed to be 300 m by 300 m. The crew made extensions in Blocks 1 and 3 to facilitate the inclusion of important natural and cultural features and, as a result, these blocks were irregularly shaped. I investigated Blocks 1 through 5 between 1997 and 1999 (Hughbanks and Kunen 1997; Kunen 2001). The remaining three blocks (Blocks 6-8) were mapped and tested by Hugh Robichaux (1995) in an earlier project with different goals; consequently, some data, such as

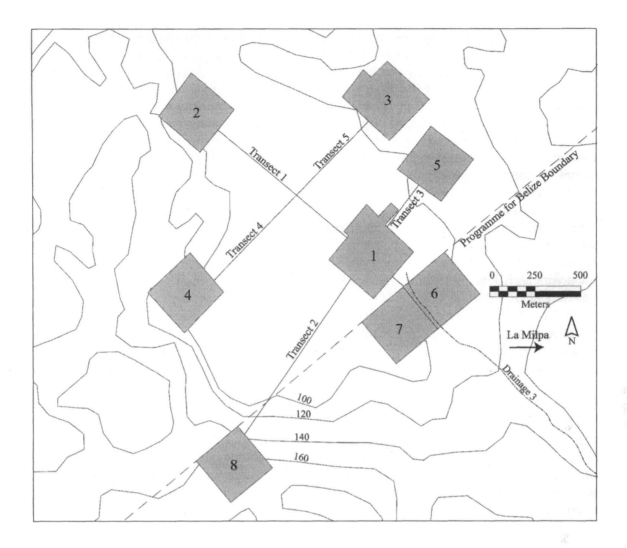

Figure 2.6. The Far West Bajo, showing the position
of survey blocks, transects, and Drainage 3.

detailed topographic information, are missing from
these blocks.

In addition to the survey blocks, Transect 1 (100 m
by 1,850 m) crossed the bajo from southeast to northwest and formed the baseline for a survey across the
bajo. This survey recorded detailed information on
vegetation zones and topography as well as cultural
features. Additional traverse lines (Transects 2 through
5), totaling more than 3 km (1.8 mile) in length,
crossed the bajo in various locations and connected the
survey blocks. The result was an interlocking system of
survey blocks and transects that sampled areas of the
bajo interior, the slopes surrounding the bajo, and the
higher ridges above it.

Topographic Mapping Methods

To facilitate mapping within the survey blocks, I
established a baseline along the midline of each block.
One exception was Block 4, in which the baseline was
offset by 50 m to the east to include more upland
terrain in the block. Each baseline was sighted in with
a Suunto sighting compass and cut by a group of
macheteros (local Belizean workmen who are expert in
cutting trails with machetes) backsighting on marked
stakes. Because of the densely forested terrain, the
alignment of the baselines and subsidiary *brechas*
(survey trails) was occasionally skewed. Because each
survey block was located along a transect or traverse

line, the midlines of each block generally followed the headings of the transects. Consequently, the blocks were not oriented to the cardinal directions. Each baseline was staked every 25 m, as measured with a meter tape, and the stakes labeled 0 m, 25 m, 50 m, and so on down the baseline to the far end of the block, which was ordinarily at 300 m. At each one of these stakes two brechas were cut at right angles to the baseline, staked, and labeled every 25 m as well. The result was that each survey block was overlain by a 25-m grid of labeled stakes.

The entire local grid system was tied into the La Milpa coordinate mapping system established by Gair Tourtellot for LaMAP. The connection was established by mapping with an EDMI (Electronic Distance Measuring Instrument; in different years either a Sokkia Set5 or a Sokkia Set3B) from a known stake in the LaMAP system (at the southwest corner of the central square kilometer of La Milpa (E5500/N5500), down Drainage 3, across the bajo, along each transect and into each survey block. Thus, every grid stake in this study was identified both by a set of local grid coordinates and by a set of LaMAP system coordinates, which was based on the E6000/ N6000 imaginary point located in the center of a 6-km (3.7-mile) radius circle around La Milpa center. In addition, the local coordinates have been transformed into UTM coordinates through correlation with numerous GPS readings provided by LaMAP for La Milpa's main plaza.

Topographic mapping of the survey blocks as well as along each of the five transects and traverse lines was done primarily with the EDMI. Due to difficulties with the instrument and time constraints at the end of the 1997 season, Transects 4 and 5 were mapped with a meter tape, sighting compass, and hand level. Blocks 1 through 5 were mapped in detail, but mapping was not done in the three survey blocks studied by Robichaux.

Each transect was mapped in a single line, taking the farthest shot visible in the dense forest, in order to move as rapidly as possible across the bajo into each survey block. Survey blocks were mapped by systematically recording coordinates and elevations for each of the labeled grid stakes, placed as described above. This procedure involved multiple set-up stations and traverse shots whenever poor visibility precluded a sightline from one gridstake to the next and was an extremely time-consuming process.

In Blocks 1, 2, and 3, point maps of the locations of each grid stake were printed out using the computer mapping program Surfer (version 7). These maps were then used in the next phase of the project, pedestrian survey. Because of the difficulty of mapping in densely forested, rolling terrain, the actual location of each grid stake varied slightly from the ideal, despite their labels. Maps such as these thus provided a more accurate picture of where each grid stake was located as opposed to an idealized schematic in which every grid stake was exactly 25 m from its neighbors. Lack of access to Surfer during the 1999 season precluded the use of this mapping aid in Blocks 4 and 5; pedestrian survey in these blocks was based on an idealized picture of the location of grid stakes and the accuracy of the resulting maps is slightly reduced.

During field mapping we entered the coordinate data and elevations generated by the EDMI for each grid-stake and traverse shot directly into a Sokkia SDR-33 data collector attached to the instrument. We then downloaded these data into a Microsoft Excel spreadsheet in the field lab. At the Center for Applied Spatial Analysis (CASA), a Geographic Information Systems (GIS) lab at the University of Arizona, I created digital elevation models (DEMs) from these data in ArcInfo, a GIS software package, using the Topogrid command sequence. I then prepared contour line and slope maps from the DEMs. Topographic mapping in each of the five survey blocks I mapped produced contour maps with 2 m contour intervals. Because I did not conduct any additional mapping in the three blocks studied by Robichaux, topographic information for these blocks derives from Robichaux's dissertation (1995). He used estimated elevations from Sheet 8 of the Ordnance Survey Maps compiled by the British Government Directorate of Overseas Surveys. These maps are at a scale of 1:50,000 and have a contour interval of 20 m (see Fig. 2.6). Consequently, the level of description of the terrain is less detailed for these three blocks.

Settlement Survey Methods

Pedestrian survey followed topographic mapping in Blocks 1 through 5 but not in Blocks 6 through 8, which had already been surveyed by Robichaux. The procedure I developed after some trial and error involved a team of three surveyors, always including myself and at times either student field assistants or well-trained local workmen. The one exception was the western half of Block 4, where Marc Wolf, who directed topographic mapping that season, was the survey supervisor. To begin, members of the team stood approximately 8 m apart on the midline of the block, facing perpendicular to it, with the middle surveyor standing at the designated grid stake. This distance ensured that our fields of vision overlapped slightly in the heavy vegetation. The middle team member, carrying the mapping board, walked down the brecha emanating from the grid stake, and the other two team members walked through the forest looking from side to side and using machetes when needed to clear a small path on either side of the brecha. All cultural features and significant natural features such as pozas or small stream channels were recorded as they were encountered. The surveyors positioned pin flags to mark the corners of features, and two team members measured distances and sighted angles between the feature to be mapped and the nearest marked grid stake using a sighting compass and meter tape. The third team member drew each feature to scale at 1:1000 on graph paper on the mapping board, using measurements from the grid stake to position it properly. This procedure was repeated until all team members reached the far edge of the block, then they returned to the midline and repeated the process on the other side of the block. To continue, they moved down to the next grid stake on the midline and began the procedure again. In this manner, surveyors covered the entire block systematically and produced scale maps in the field, which could be ground checked for accuracy. At the CASA lab, I digitized these paper maps on an electronic digitizing tablet; Blocks 1 and 2 were digitized in AutoCAD, and Blocks 3 through 5 were digitized in Arc/Info. Robichaux's three survey blocks were digitized in GRASS by Francisco Estrada Belli (then of Boston University), who generously provided me with the digital files. All the digitized maps were eventually combined in Arc/Info, along with topographic and vegetation maps.

Sample Transect Survey Methods

Transect 1 was the baseline for a feature and vegetation survey that crossed the length of the bajo. Transect 1 was originally mapped during the 1997 season with the EDMI, and therefore had stakes along its length at irregular intervals. To facilitate survey, the transect was restaked every 25 meters, as measured by a meter tape. At every other stake, a pair of brechas 50 m in length were cut at right angles to the transect. These were staked at 25 m intervals, thus forming a 100 m wide by 1,850 m long grid across the bajo. The areas between 300 m and 600 m, and between 1,550 m and 1,850 m were within Blocks 1 and 2, respectively, and thus were surveyed as parts of those blocks (see Fig. 2.6).

The extremely dense vegetation of the bajo precluded pedestrian survey between the brechas, even with heavy use of machetes. Instead, a three-person survey team walked together down each brecha, looking carefully from side to side. Despite the difficulty in walking, visibility was actually good and in most cases extended at least halfway to the next brecha. All cultural features observed were mapped in the manner described above. In addition, the team made detailed notes on vegetation at every grid stake, recording information on the general class of vegetation, canopy height, density of the understory, and surface topography. Changes in vegetation type were noted on the feature maps. The result was a vegetation and feature map of a sample transect through the bajo from edge to edge that I digitized at the CASA lab in Arc/Info and combined with the other topographic and survey maps from the study area.

Surveyors recorded cultural features along the four remaining traverse lines as they were encountered opportunistically while walking and noted changes in vegetation. No lateral survey along these lines, however, was undertaken.

Excavation Methods

Following completion of the pedestrian survey in each survey block and along Transect 1, I selected features for test excavation. Because the number of test excavations I was able to complete in either residential or agricultural features was small and not statistically significant, I emphasized criteria other than random sampling. After categorizing each feature as either residential (including houses, house platforms, patio walls, and pyramidal or range structures) or agricultural (including terraces, berms, and rockpiles), I chose a subsample of each type for excavation. For residential features, the selection included mounds of different sizes that were located in groups of varying configurations and in different vegetation zones and types of terrain. Often, the size and condition of the feature and presence or absence of large trees or tree roots were factors in the decision. I placed off-mound test pits in plazas, suspected garden areas, and other extramural areas. For agricultural features, I chose minimally one of each type of feature in any area in which such features were concentrated. In total, 75 excavations were completed throughout the study area in walled structures, platforms, patio walls, plazas, extramural spaces, terraces, berms, field walls, and rockpiles: 28 in Block 1, 8 in Block 2, 16 in Block 3, 10 in Block 4, and 9 in Block 5, and 2 test pits in features along Transect 1 and 2 along Transect 4. Two other excavations involved cleaning looters' trenches (in Block 1 and Block 5) and one involved a series of shovel tests (in Block 5).

Most excavations were test pits, ranging from 1.0 m by 0.5 m to 3 m by 3 m in size. As warranted by the architecture or other findings, the crew often expanded these test pits horizontally. In no case, however, was an entire mound stripped. The usual placement of excavation units on architecture was on the front of the mound, although occasionally the side or back was chosen if trees or other obstructions hindered excavation. These obstructions sometimes precluded deliberate selection of structure centerlines. The units were placed specifically to encounter architecture, particularly floors and walls, to provide some context for any artifacts found. Placement of excavation units on agricultural features depended on their size and shape. We trenched small terraces and berms from front to back, and tested larger terraces and berms as well as circular rockpiles by units beginning on top of the features at the highest part and extending down to, or beyond, their lateral edge.

For excavation provenience we adopted the operation-lot system used by the PfBAP. All operations in the bajo carried the prefix "V" for Vernon Scarborough, who initiated the project. Operations refer to groups of excavations conducted in the same general vicinity, numbered sequentially (V39, V40, V41). Within each operation, suboperations designated individual excavation units, which were in almost all cases rectangular pits or trenches. Suboperations were lettered (V39A, V39B). Lots within each suboperation represent strata or architectural features excavated as units. The lot was thus the minimal unit of provenience (V39A-1, V39A-2), and all artifacts of a particular class collected from a lot were bagged together. The only exceptions to this organizational system were the nine units excavated in 1997 (Ops. V27-V37). These units were each considered individual operations, so that even excavation units located in the same vicinity were given different numbers. For instance, Ops. V27 through V29 were all excavated in the same architectural group. As a result, no suboperation letters were used with these excavations, with the exception of Op. V35, which included two adjacent excavation units.

All excavations proceeded in natural stratigraphic levels; in a few special cases extremely fine control of context was necessary and arbitrary levels were used. In general, architectural fill was excavated with shovels, picks, hand-picks, and trowels; burials, caches, and other special contexts were excavated with trowels, dental picks, and paint brushes. All fill from residential features was screened through ¼-inch mesh. Burial and cache contexts were screened through window screen. Because of the difficulties of excavating through clay, fill from agricultural features was subsampled, with 25 percent screened through ¼-inch mesh (33% of fill from the agricultural features along Transect 1).

All artifacts from all contexts were collected by lot, bagged, catalogued, and analyzed in the PfBAP field lab (Appendixes A–F; in Appendixes A-C all lots are listed and their similar page positioning facilitates cross tabulation to ascertain total lot contents). All lots were documented carefully in the field on lot record forms. At least one plan map and one profile map were drawn of each excavation unit, and photographs were taken at pertinent points throughout the excavation.

Vegetation Mapping Methods

One obstacle to understanding landscape use in Maya bajos is the misperception that bajo environments are homogeneous, and a primary research goal of this project was the investigation and documentation of variability among bajo microenvironments. Although some may argue that the modern environment in and around bajos may not accurately reflect conditions existing in antiquity, it is clear that the substantial environmental heterogeneity that exists today is in-dicative of variability that likely prevailed in ancient times.

Each bajo microenvironment is distinguished not only by a characteristic vegetation association, but also by differences in canopy height, understory density, and ground topography. Surveyors recorded these categories of information on survey maps for each labeled stake throughout the detailed vegetation survey conducted along Transect 1. In the survey blocks, team members also observed the surrounding vegetation, denoting the boundaries of vegetation zones on the survey maps. As a result, a complete vegetation map exists for all parts of the Far West Bajo study area that were subject to systematic pedestrian survey (Chapter 3). The next several chapters tell the story of the Far West Bajo and the agricultural and settlement systems that developed in and around it in prehistory.

CHAPTER THREE

Environment of the Bajo Interior

Each day in the field in the months before the onset of rain in late May or early June, I would drive my field assistant, assorted field school students, a graduate student or two, and a team of Belizean workmen down a narrow, rocky, stump-filled logging road in our field vehicle, a pickup truck affectionately known as Hoss, to the edge of the bajo. Those in the bed of the pickup quickly learned to duck whenever a thorny *bayal* vine brushed by overhead. They also learned to brace themselves for my driving technique as I slewed the truck around tree stumps, protruding rocks, and potholes in an effort to preserve our tires. We knew we had arrived at work when the lush, high-canopied forest of the surrounding hills gave way to either leafy stands of tall, fanlike corozo palms or, less appealingly, dense thickets of stunted trees laden with epiphytes rising out of a bed of sawgrass. Once the rains began, access to the bajo was more difficult, and we could no longer drive down the logging trail for fear of bogging down in the mud. Instead, we parked at the head of the road and hiked in, carrying excavation equipment and at times the heavy total station, and hiked out carrying bags of artifacts. We came to dread the days when excavation produced large quantities of groundstone.

One advantage to walking in and out of field sites on the rainy days was the opportunity to enjoy the peace and beauty of the surrounding forest. We often spotted birds, agouti, and the occasional opossum or deer. The crew would usually spread out along the road, talking in small groups while keeping an eye on the ground for snakes. One day, we noticed with excitement the distinct paw prints of a large cat traversing our logging road. We looked at each other with anticipation (for some, it was fear) and I thought yes, *finally*, I will see a jaguar. The RBCMA has one of the densest concentrations of jaguars in Belize and most other long-time researchers had at least one, if not several, sightings of the cat from the Gallon Jug road or on the trails; I had not been so lucky. For several days after our first sighting of the cat tracks, we would find fresh evidence of the jaguar's proximity, and our workmen would nod and, observing my excitement, say to me, yes, it is probably close, these tracks are very fresh. Coincidentally, at this same time my university department head was visiting our field site and had volunteered to join our team for a few days. This was John's first visit to interior Belize, and he was particularly enthralled by the jaguar's presence. After an unpleasantly long, hot, difficult day of excavation in the bajo, I was among the stragglers hiking out to the truck. Most of the students and workmen had preceded me by about ten minutes, but on this day my mind was focused on juggling the logistical difficulties of dividing a crew of more than fifteen among test pits spread out between two survey blocks and one transect in the bajo and had spent the day violating my own rule, hiking back and forth between them through the bajo, alone. When I finally emerged from the brush onto the road next to our truck, I saw John standing amid a small knot of team members, grinning widely. He and Ubi, one of our workmen, had been chatting on the hike out, rounded a bend in the road, and come face to face with the big cat. According to them, and the others who saw it, it stood still in the road for a moment, took a single step toward them, then turned and walked silently away into the bush. It was, according to John, one of the most beautiful sights in nature he had ever witnessed. Glumly, I thought to myself, great, how come *you* get to see the jaguar when you've been here less than a week? *I've* been working here for three years and I've never seen a jaguar.

The kind of archaeological research we did in the Far West Bajo is one of the least glamorous pursuits I can think of. At the end of almost every day, we were exhausted, footsore, wet, muddy, and bug-bitten. We

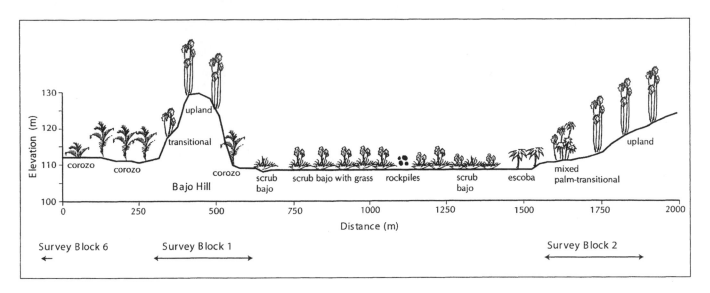

Figure 3.1. Cross-section of the Far West Bajo along Transect 1 from southeast to northwest, showing changes in elevation, topography, and vegetation. (Drafted by Ron Redsteer.)

spent endless hours digging through nearly sterile, sticky clayey soil to define ephemeral agricultural features defined at best by a single stone's width cobble wall. Yet it is the meticulous accumulation of data on vegetation changes, stratigraphy, artifacts, feature construction, and paleoecology, the slow addition to our knowledge of these difficult environments, that allows us to interpret their important role in the development of ancient Maya lifeways. A "temples and tombs" approach will not work in the bajo and jade and jaguars are not our rewards.

A CROSS-SECTION OF THE FAR WEST BAJO

Research along the transects that cross the bajo included not only recording of cultural features but also topographic survey, mapping of vegetation types, and excavation. In addition, my colleagues on the project conducted extensive soil pit operations as part of their paleoecological research. Pedestrian survey identified only a small number of features in the bajo interior, in contrast to the abundant features located on the bajo margins and surrounding hills and ridges. The survey results, the two concentrations of features discovered in the bajo interior, and the excavations in these areas demonstrate the role of the bajo interior as a resource extraction zone for residents of nearby settlements.

Transect 1 was a 100–m wide swath that extended for 1,850 m across the long axis of the Far West Bajo from southeast to northwest. The survey team recorded topography, vegetation associations, and cultural features along this transect, providing a well-studied cross-section of the entire depression (Fig. 3.1). At the start of the transect on the southeast end (0 m) the bajo forest was a dense monospecific stand of tall corozo palms. This end of the transect was adjacent to Survey Block 6 and the mouth of Drainage 3, which empties into the bajo here. Numerous berms that constituted a major part of Agricultural Zone 4 and that represented an important prehistoric water management technique were located nearby (Chapter 4). Elevation in the corozo stands was 111 m to 112 m above sea level. Nick Dunning explained to me in 2001 that the corozo forest had developed on alluvial soils associated with the delta of Drainage 3 and on colluvial soils derived from slope wash off the adjacent slopes. Thus, it represents a successional forest on land disturbed by a combination of natural forces and human activity. Such dynamism is typical of the bajo landscape and is explored below.

After a few hundred meters of flat land, the terrain rose sharply upward, forming a steep, isolated cone karst hill rising almost 20 m from the bajo floor. This hill proved to be the only significant topographic feature in the bajo and it became the focus of Survey

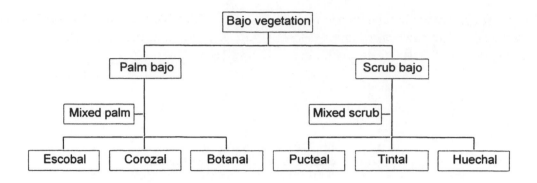

Figure 3.2. Schematic classification of bajo vegetation types.

Block 1. The Bajo Hill site, discussed in Chapter 5, was located atop this hill. As we ascended, the vegetation quickly changed to transitional forest on the hillslopes, followed by upland forest covering the hill crests. The hilltop was generally level for almost 100 m and provided ample flat terrain for several architectural groups of various sizes.

Our descent on the far side of Bajo Hill was equally sudden and steep, and at the base of the hill we entered the lowest part of the Far West Bajo. For almost 1 km (0.6 mile), elevation remained between 105 m and 109 m, and the ground surface attained a bumpy, hummocky character indicative of intermittent standing water. Such ground topography is related to the shrinking and swelling of the bajo's clayey soils as they alternately saturate and dry out. This long stretch of bajo was vegetated by low scrub forest, often accompanied by patches of sawgrass (*Scleria bracteata*). Canopy height rarely exceeded 10 m. At the 1,050 m mark, we encountered one of only two groups of cultural features found in the bajo interior (the other is located along Transect 4 near Survey Block 4). These rockpiles and the excavations in them are discussed in more detail below. After this point, the ground surface became more gently undulating, and elevation began to rise slightly. Starting at 1,500 m we encountered a band of escoba trees, easily recognizable with thick, long spines covering their trunks. Beyond this point we entered Survey Block 2, as the terrain continued to rise. Here a steady upward trend in elevation was complemented by vegetational changes from escoba bajo to mixed palm and transitional forests, to upland forest at almost 120 m above sea level at the far end of the transect.

Bajo Microenvironments

Interpretation of the microenvironmental variability within the Far West Bajo first requires the establishment of a classification of vegetation associations. Lundell (1933, 1937), whose vegetation studies remain landmarks in the field, recognized a basic dichotomy in bajo environments and made a distinction between escoba bajo and tintal bajo. In Lundell's usage, escoba bajo is a term describing areas dominated by palms, with a higher canopy and a more open understory than is found in other bajo areas. In contrast, tintal bajo refers to thick, low-canopied, scrub forest with an extremely dense understory. Lundell thought that escoba bajo was limited in distribution to the fringes of the more extensive tintal bajo. This basic dichotomy is generally accurate but obscures the existence of a larger variety of bajo subtypes. Moreover, the use of the species names "escoba" (*Crysophila argentea* Bartlett) and "tintal" (*Haematoxylum campechianum* L.) to refer to what are actually generic categories of vegetation is misleading. From walking across the bajo along Transect 1, it is clear that a fringe of escoba bajo does not encircle the depression, but is in fact only found in a narrow band on the northwest end of the bajo.

Recognizing the occurrence of many varieties of bajo vegetation, my colleagues on the Bajo la Justa project and I (see Chapter 2) refined Lundell's classification to distinguish two general categories of dominant vegetation: palm bajo and scrub bajo (Kunen and others 2000; Lanza 1996). Within each of these types a number of subtypes or habitats can exist in which a particular plant species dominates (Fig. 3.2). Corozal or corozo bajo is a species-specific type of palm bajo in which corozo palm (*Orbignya cohune*) dominates the assemblage. In this typology, escobal or escoba bajo refers to monospecific stands of the escoba palm, and not palm bajo more generally. Similarly, tintal bajo refers only to logwood bajo, and other types, such as huechal, refer to areas in which sawgrass (*zacate de hueche* in Spanish) dominates. In certain habitats, no single species dominates, but instead a mix of several palm species or several types of scrub co-exist. In these areas, then, a more accurate terminology is mixed palm bajo or mixed scrub bajo. Finally, mixed palm-scrub bajo refers to areas in which a mix of palms and low trees is present.

Vegetation Mapping Results

The Far West Bajo does not conform to the traditional understanding of bajo environments as described by Lundell (1937), but rather has a great variety of microenvironments (Fig. 3.3). Based on results from Transect 1, 59.2 percent of the bajo is covered in low scrub forest with a 6–m to 8–m high canopy and a dense understory of sawgrass. These parts of the bajo tend also to have undulating ground surfaces with many small hummocks of earth separated by shallow depressions. This type of ground surface is typical of areas that are seasonally inundated (King and others 1992: 220–221), and, unsurprisingly, these areas are located primarily in the bajo interior. A smaller portion of the sample (7.5%) is scrub bajo without sawgrass, which tends to feature a slightly higher canopy. A large part (25.8%) of the bajo is corozo bajo. Although generally growing in monospecific stands, corozo bajo also features isolated specimens of mature forest trees, such as ramon, sapodilla, tropical cedar, and mahogany. Corozo bajo completely surrounds the bajo hill in Survey Block 1 and grows exclusively on the east and southeast sides of the bajo at elevations of 106 m to 122 m above sea level. The terrain here undulates more gently and lacks the broken nature of scrub bajo terrain.

The remainder of Transect 1 features several different types of bajo. Mixed palm, mixed palm-scrub and corozo-scrub forests are all present in small patches. Escoba bajo is present in small amounts (5.4%) on the northwest side of the bajo. In contrast to the southeast side of the bajo, in which there is an

Table 3.1. Vegetation Zones of Residential and Agricultural Features

Vegetation Type	% Residential Features	% Agricultural Features
Upland Forest	47.7	36.6
Transitional Forest	13.5	10.0
Corozo Bajo	11.2	5.8
Mixed Palm-Transitional	3.9	26.0
Scrub Bajo	3.6	7.8
Mixed Palm Bajo	2.1	4.4
Mixed Palm-Scrub Bajo	1.1	3.0
Escoba Bajo	0.5	0.6
Disturbance*	8.1	5.8
Unclassified+	8.3	

* Disturbance growth is affected by modern activities.
\+ Unclassified indicates features located outside areas where vegetation was mapped.

abrupt transition from corozo bajo to scrub bajo, the northwest side features a more gradual transition from scrub bajo to escoba bajo to transitional forest, which contains many of the same species as upland forest but with more palms, a lower canopy, and denser understory. This transition corresponds to an equally gradual rise in elevation from 108 m above sea level to a peak of 135 m above sea level on the steep ridges of Survey Block 2, where upland forest dominates.

Table 3.1 presents vegetation mapping results from the eight survey blocks in relation to the distribution of residential and agricultural features. Almost 48 percent of residential features are located in areas of upland forest and only 13.5 percent are in transitional forest, indicating a distinct preference among the ancient inhabitants for settling on hills and ridgetops. In contrast, 36.6 percent of agricultural features are in upland forest, but almost as many (36%) are located in transitional or mixed palm-transitional forest zones, where the gentle slopes are conducive to soil management and intensive agriculture. Few residential features (11.2%) are located in areas of corozo bajo, but a system of berms implicated in water management is located in the corozo bajo portion of forest. The absence of abundant residential features in these areas strengthens the interpretation that they were reserved for cultivation. Only a few cultural features occurred in areas of scrub bajo, which today are certainly the least appealing parts of the landscape from a human perspective.

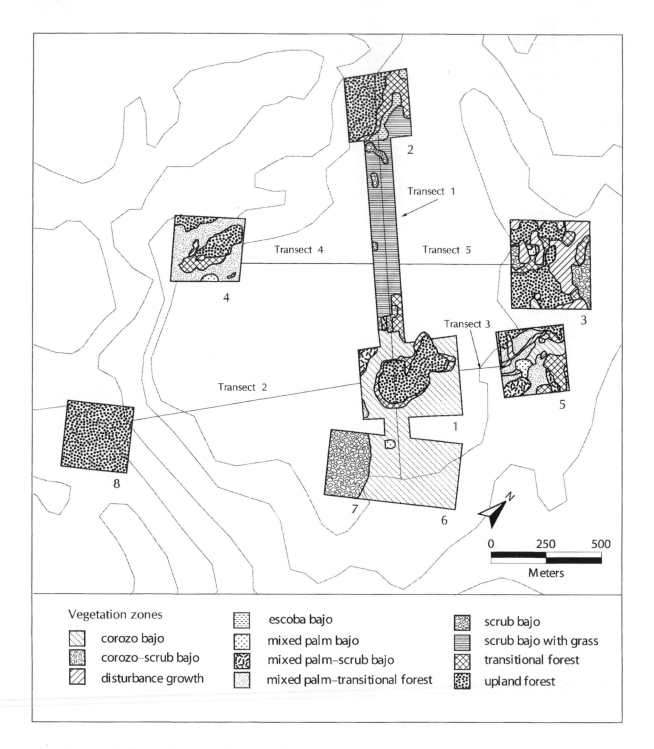

Figure 3.3. Vegetation map of the Far West Bajo, showing numbered survey blocks and transects.

Vegetation survey in the Far West Bajo has demonstrated two patterns that have implications for land use. First, the bajo itself is not a homogeneous area, but instead features patches of several different types of bajo forest that reflect differences in soil depth, drainage patterns, and longevity of inundation. Second, an elevational pattern exists in which the lowest areas feature bajo forest, sloping areas are marked by transitional forest, and ridges and hilltops are blanketed in upland forest. Because of the association among

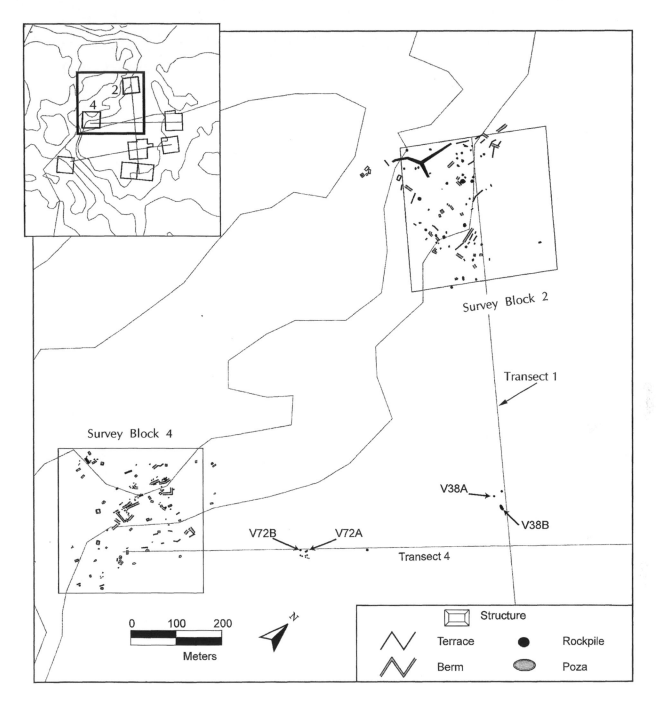

Figure 3.4. Locations of excavated rockpiles in the Far West Bajo interior. Rockpiles were mapped along Transect 1 near Survey Block 2 and Transect 4 near Survey Block 4. Rockpiles near the bajo edge in Survey Block 3 are not shown on this map.

vegetation type, soil type, drainage characteristics, and elevation, these patterns have corresponding parallels in land use, as demonstrated by the abundance or dearth of different types of cultural features in each vegetation zone.

Rockpiles in the Bajo Interior

Despite the stifling atmosphere and dense thicket of trees deep in the bajo interior, a cluster of rockpiles (Fig. 3.4) was located at the 1,050 m mark along

Table 3.2. Artifacts from Rockpile Excavations in the Bajo Interior

Op	Ceramics	Primary Flakes (>50% cortex)	Secondary Flakes (<50% cortex)	Tertiary Flakes (no cortex)	Bifaces	Cores and Tools*
V38A	7	31	66	100	2	19
V38B	127	13	45	28	1	5
V72A		7	9	15		
V72B		2	20	38		2
Total	*134*	*53*	*140*	*181*	*3*	*26*

* Tools include blades, flake tools, and core tools.

Transect 1, 450 m from the southeast edge of Survey Block 2. The rockpiles were in an area of scrub bajo and sawgrass where the surface topography was broken and marked by small hummocks of soil supporting tufts of grass and sedges. The rockpiles were in the lowest part of the bajo, where seasonal flooding was common. A second group of 11 rockpiles was located along Transect 4 just 220 m from the east edge of Survey Block 4 in an area where scrub bajo vegetation gradually grades into mixed palm-transitional forest as the terrain rises from the bajo floor. The ground surface here is flat, lacking the hummocks that indicate the presence of occasional standing water. A third group of 14 rockpiles was found at the edge of the bajo in Survey Block 3 below La Caldera, in an area of scrub bajo forest; unlike the other two groups, none of these features was excavated.

The discovery of cultural features in such inhospitable environments warranted investigation into their history of construction and potential function. The rockpiles in the bajo interior were amorphous concentrations of chert and limestone cobbles, roughly circular, ranging from 1 m to 6 m in diameter and 0.3 m to 1.5 m in height (Fig. 3.5). These features resembled those found in the agricultural zones on the bajo margins in size, shape, and fill composition. Test excavation in four of the rockpiles revealed, however, that their artifactual contents varied enormously (Table 3.2) and that they differed markedly from at least some of the agricultural zone rockpiles described in Chapter 4.

Op. V38A

A large rockpile located along Transect 1 consisted of an unstratified mound of small- to medium-sized chert cobbles (Lot 2) in a sparse soil matrix beneath a

Figure 3.5. A rockpile in the Far West Bajo. The top is outlined with a dashed white line. The small size of the feature demonstrates that careful pedestrian survey is necessary to identify rockpiles in heavily vegetated areas.

thin layer of humus (Lot 1). The crew detected no internal structure such as a basal or retaining wall in the 1–m by 5–m excavation. Beneath the cobble fill and beyond the edge of the rockpile was grayish brown clay (Lot 3) with a few chert cobbles overlying decomposing bedrock (caliche). The 7 sherds collected in the excavation date no later than the early Late Classic. Several hundred lithics were recovered, including flakes from throughout the reduction sequence, 2 bifaces, 14 flake cores, 3 core tools, and 2 flake tools.

Op. V38B

A 1.0–m by 2.5–m test trench on a small rockpile adjacent to the larger one tested in Op. V38A showed the mound was similar in composition. Beneath the thin humus layer (Lot 1) was a thick stratum of fill consisting of chert cobbles in a dark clayey soil matrix (Lot 2). Beneath the fill and beyond the edge of the rockpile was a dark, sticky clay with large chert inclusions (Lot 3). Artifacts were abundant in Lot 2, less so in Lot 3. More than 120 sherds were collected, but only 6 sherds could be dated, 2 to the early Late Classic period and 4 to the Late/Terminal Classic period. The approximately 100 lithics included primary, secondary, and tertiary flakes, a biface, 4 flake cores, and a flake tool.

Op. V72A

The fill of a 1–m by 2–m excavation on a large rockpile along Transect 4 was unusual, consisting of large chert boulders along with small- to medium-sized limestone and chert cobbles in a brown silty soil (Lot 2). The absence of a clayey matrix was unique among rockpile excavations. Beneath the cobble fill was sterile clay. No ceramics were present in the excavation, but a number of lithics, representing various stages of the reduction sequence, were collected in Lot 2. There were no bifaces or other formal tools.

Op. V72B

Excavation of a 1.0–m by 1.5–m unit on a small rockpile along Transect 4, only a few meters from Op. V72A, revealed a layer of large chert boulders and gravel in a reddish clay matrix (Lot 3) overlying sterile grayish-white clay. The boulders appeared to be a crude retaining wall, but no definitive structure could be discerned. Above the boulders was a thick layer of small- to medium-sized limestone and chert cobbles and gravel in a reddish brown clay matrix (Lot 2). This stratum was topped by a layer of humus with small rock inclusions (Lot 1). There were no ceramics. A moderate quantity of lithics came mainly from Lot 2,

representing all stages of the reduction sequence, and included a blade and a core (Table 3.2).

None of the four features tested in the bajo interior yielded clear evidence of a basal wall or an alignment defining the edge of the feature. The lack of internal structure argues against an interpretation of these features as substructures for pole and thatch buildings. Moreover, the scarcity of ceramic artifacts from three of the four rockpiles and the absence of any other domestic refuse such as groundstone or animal bones strengthens the interpretation that these features were not residential. With the low elevation of the bajo, its propensity for seasonal flooding, and the characteristic dense vegetation, the lack of residential features is not surprising. Even though the tangled vegetation of the bajo may well have obscured some features and others may have been destroyed by the shrink-swell cycle of the bajo soils, an abundance of cultural features hidden in the dense bajo vegetation seems highly unlikely.

Based on excavation data, it is probable that the two sets of rockpiles in the Far West Bajo, although morphologically similar, served different functions. The rockpiles along Transect 1 were probably locales for collecting, storing, and testing chert cobbles, which are abundant in the clayey bajo soil (see also Tourtellot and others 1994). As pointed out by John Olsen in 1999, tool production is indicated by the presence of substantial debitage from all stages of lithic reduction as well as by several broken formal tools and numerous cores. This interpretation, however, does not explain the presence of sherds in these rockpiles. The features at a slightly higher elevation along Transect 4 may have been foundations for ephemeral structures like fieldhouses, although these features lack ceramics. Proximity to Agricultural Zone 2 strengthens the fieldhouse interpretation. These features may also have been stockpiles of lithic raw material, but with the paucity of lithic artifacts encountered, this material was little utilized. The data are equivocal, at best.

A number of other scholars have offered interpretations of similar features found elsewhere in the Maya lowlands that may help clarify the function of these rockpiles. Pyburn and her colleagues (1998) excavated a number of features they call rubble mounds at Albion Island in northern Belize. Like the rockpiles in the Far West Bajo, these features are small, relatively uniform in size and shape, and present in dense clusters, often in proximity to larger structures or agricultural features. But the Albion Island mounds, unlike the ones in the Far West Bajo, also yielded evidence of burials, caches, plaster surfaces, and walls. Based on these elements of internal structure and on the utilitarian artifacts found within the features, Pyburn attributes permanent residential functions to the mounds. This interpretation is unlikely to apply to the Far West Bajo rockpiles, which lack such internal elements. Pyburn does note an important function served by the Albion Island rubble mounds that may apply to the rockpiles of the Far West Bajo. Small rocks create a basal surface that levels out uneven bedrock, provide stable foundations for floors and superstructures, and improve drainage in otherwise damp clayey soil. These benefits are consistent with the interpretation that some of the rockpiles in the Far West Bajo were bases for ephemeral fieldhouses. Pyburn rules out fieldhouses for the Albion Island features on the grounds that the mounds are too numerous and contain artifacts and internal features incongruous with such a purpose, but the fieldhouse interpretation for some of the features recorded here should not be eliminated. The clustering of these bajo features can be interpreted as evidence that their ephemeral superstructures were rebuilt frequently on new stone foundations.

Rockpiles may have served as small planting surfaces, using the cobbles as mulch. Such a system would have elevated crops above the level of any standing water remaining in the bajo. Folan and Gallegos Osuna (1999) offer this interpretation for similar features in the Bajo el Laberinto near Calakmul. Support for the idea of rockpiles as planting platforms also comes from the research of Kepecs and Boucher (1996), who suggest that rockpiles (*chich* mounds) in northeast Yucatan were used to grow tree crops. The rocks and dirt of chich piles served as mulch while simultaneously preventing the trees from toppling over in the wind. Interspersed among the chich mounds in Kepecs and Boucher's study area were slightly larger oval or rectangular cobble platforms. These larger platforms often featured a cobble retaining wall and Kepecs and Boucher (1996) suggest that they served as foundations for small houses. They envision small rural settlements with houses on the larger cobble platforms surrounded by orchards growing from the chich piles. This pattern is similar to that of the rockpiles in the agricultural zones of the Far West Bajo. In these zones, concentrations of rockpiles were interspersed with other agricultural features and with larger cobble platforms, which do seem to have supported perishable houses. The interpretation offered by Kepecs and Boucher (1996) may explain the function of the rockpiles located in upland and transitional forest zones, where 59 percent of all rockpiles I recorded are located, but may not be applicable to those in the bajo interior.

Several years ago, my colleagues on the Bajo la Justa project and I visited a farmer in Peten who was cultivating in a bajo. He stored much of his bean crop in a crib constructed of wood and thatch located in the midst of his fields (Fig. 3.6). Kepecs and Boucher (1996) suggest that some of the cobble mounds they documented in Yucatan could have served as stations for the collection of produce. It is possible that the rockpiles of the Far West Bajo are the stone bases of wooden cribs where farmers stored harvested ears of corn. The presence of maize pollen or phytoliths in the soil matrix of rockpiles would lend support for this interpretation. Soil samples were collected from each of the rockpiles tested, but unfortunately no analysis has yet been made.

RESOURCES OF THE BAJO INTERIOR

Considering the diversity of interpretations of the rockpiles, the presence of cultural features in the low bajo interior suggests that the Far West Bajo served as an important repository of resources for inhabitants of nearby residential zones. The four most notable resources provided by this zone are chert, clay, water, and organic soils. The off-mound portions of the excavations described above indicate that chert cobbles are found naturally in the bajo soils. This finding is corroborated by a description of the Jolja soil subsuite by King and his colleagues (1992), which characterizes bajo soils as clayey soils containing subsurface layers of flint. Tourtellot has proposed that rockpiles are the result of collecting activities, which created storehouses for lithic raw material (Tourtellot and others 1994). Such storehouses could have been visited intermittently for purposes of testing and selecting cobbles for stone tool manufacture. The lithic evidence from the excavations summarized above suggests that, at least in some cases, the entire manufacturing process took place at

Figure 3.6. A bean crib constructed of wood and thatch by a Maya farmer in Peten, Guatemala.

the rockpiles. Each of the four features tested yielded lithic artifacts ranging in quantity from a small number of pieces to several hundred flakes. In each case, the entire spectrum of the lithic reduction sequence was represented, as each rockpile contained primary, secondary, and tertiary flakes. Three of the features yielded formal tools such as bifaces and blades or flake cores. That some of the formal tools were broken may mean that they were used in situ, perhaps in clay collecting activities.

Bajo soils serve as a natural repository of clay. Laura Kosakowsky conjectured in 1999 that residents of nearby settlements may have traveled into the bajo to collect high-quality clay for ceramic manufacture. Unfortunately, this activity is unlikely to leave many archaeological traces. Tools for excavating the clay and vessels for carrying it might be the only lasting evidence. Perhaps the remains of stone tool manufacture described above reflect the expedient production of digging tools, and the few ceramics represent vessels used to carry the clay back to residences. Trace element analysis of finished vessels and raw materials might provide stronger evidence for such behavior, but no such analysis was done in connection with this research and the interpretation remains speculative.

More definitive evidence demonstrates that the bajo was a critical source of water for nearby settlers dwelling in a seasonally dry landscape. A medium-sized aguada (8 m in diameter) in the corozo bajo on the southeast side of the bajo and 20 small pozas located near residential structures on the slopes surrounding the bajo indicate a pattern of small-scale water storage (see also Weiss-Krejci and Sabbas 2002). Aside from hauling water to surrounding residential areas, inhabitants of the residential zones could have made use of the water in the bajo in two additional ways. First, although exceedingly labor-intensive, water could have been used in a form of "pot irrigation" to irrigate terraced fields on the nearby slopes. Second, as the water receded at the end of each rainy season, portions of the bajo could have been used for agricultural fields in much the same way that recessional agriculture is practiced in river floodplains. This kind of opportunistic, shifting cultivation would not leave archaeological traces, although the lithic artifacts found in the rockpile excavations may represent land-clearing activities in connection with field preparation.

A rich organic peat layer formed early in the bajo's history. Use of this material by the Maya as agricultural fertilizer is discussed below and in Chapter 4 on the development of the bajo margin agricultural system.

PALEOECOLOGICAL RESEARCH IN THE FAR WEST BAJO

Reconstruction of the changing Far West Bajo environment is based on paleoecological investigations of soils and sediments by Nick Dunning, hydrology by Sheryl Luzzader-Beach, geomorphology by Timothy Beach, pollen analysis by John Jones, and limited analyses of mollusks by Alan Covich. Fifteen pits were dug into the bajo and the lower reaches of Drainage 3 by a backhoe and several more were excavated by hand in various locations in the bajo. Here, I discuss results from the most significant trenches summarized in a recent article by Dunning and others (2002), to which the reader is invited to turn for more detailed information.

The Far West Bajo lies at the terminus of Drainage 3, an intermittent stream channel that drains the west side of La Milpa center, situated on a ridge some 70 m higher than the bajo. Dunning examined a hand dug trench that extended across this drainage (Op. V33A). The trench contained a buried topsoil (paleosol) whose soil humates date to about 1200–910 B.C. (calibrated; Dunning and others 2002: 273). After formation, this topsoil was buried several times by fluvial sediments and it underwent an episode of aggradation in which coarse alluvium choked the stream channel. Subsequently, erosion reopened the channel, flushing the alluvium out and creating a delta at the mouth of the drainage on the bajo floor: a wide fan of coarse sediment incised by meandering channels. One of the backhoe trenches, Op. BH6, was excavated in the deltaic fan and revealed two ephemeral channels later infilled with slackwater deposits of finer organic sediments. Soil humates in the lower of these two channel units yielded a calibrated date of 415–365 B.C., and the upper unit yielded a calibrated date of A.D. 330–440 (Dunning and others 2002: 273).

Beyond the delta several backhoe trenches were excavated on the bajo floor, revealing a general paleosol that once developed on the surface of the bajo. In the paleosol layer exposed in Op. BH9, some pollen was preserved and was identified by Jones based on a count of 200 pollen grains (Dunning and others 2002: 274, Table 2). The most prevalent pollen was cattail

(*Typha*), a plant common in perennial swamps and around the edges of lakes. Second in abundance were grasses (*Poaceae*), possibly including the aquatic grass *Olyra*. Other pollen included pine (*Pinus*) and oak (*Quercus*); these pollens travel long distances and are usually found when trapped in open stretches of water.

The buried paleosol extending throughout the backhoe excavations was dated in Op. BH9 to A.D. 15–110 (calibrated). Its composition shows that it represents an ancient peat layer that formed the surface of what was once a perennial wetland (Dunning and others 2002: 273). This interpretation is based in part on the isotopic composition of carbon found within the organic matter of the paleosol, which indicates that a combination of woody and herbaceous vegetation contributed to the signature. Such a combination is typical of vegetation within and on the edges of perennial swamps (Dunning and others 2002: 274). The isotope signature of organic material from the bajo paleosol is extremely significant because of evidence for the mining of bajo soils to fertilize nearby terraced fields. As part of Dunning's investigation of the Far West Bajo, carbon isotope analysis was conducted on soils recovered from Op. V26, an excavation across several terraces in a patch of mixed palm bajo in Agricultural Zone 3 (Chapter 4). Dunning reported to me in 2001 that his analysis revealed that much of the organic component of the soil is similar to that identified in Op. BH9 and it derived from aquatic plants such as grasses or cattail. Dunning postulated that the ancient farmers of terraces on the bajo margins collected peaty soil from within the bajo and deposited it behind the terrace walls as a means of intensifying production (Dunning and others 2003). Hansen and his colleagues (2002) have recently made a similar argument for terraces around the bajo south of Nakbe, and Chase and Chase (1998: 69) cite the presence of snail shells behind terrace walls as evidence for deliberate deposition of alluvial soils on agricultural fields at Caracol.

The stratigraphy of Op. BH9 revealed that a thick layer of sandy clay subsequently buried the peaty paleosol, probably as a result of widespread deforestation and subsequent erosion of the slopes surrounding the Far West Bajo. This sedimentation, whose rapidity facilitated the preservation of peat, dramatically affected the hydrology of the bajo. The elevation of the bajo floor was raised by the new clay layer, thus limiting groundwater seepage and recharge of the wetland. Severe deterioration of the watershed also resulted in reduced rainfall infiltration and evapotranspiration, leaving much more runoff to escape into seasonal channels (Dunning and others 2002: 274–275). The result of both these processes appears to have been the conversion of the perennial wetland into a drier seasonal swamp with scrub forest vegetation capable of adapting to severe fluctuations in moisture. Such wet-dry fluctuations were evident in the gross distortion of stratigraphy in the lower strata of Op. BH9. Based on the collected radiocarbon dates presented above, this transition apparently happened in response to deforestation and soil erosion associated with the activities of Preclassic (400 B.C.–A.D. 150) populations in the surrounding uplands (Dunning and others 2002: 275).

With this reconstruction in mind, I can make several inferences about the dynamic relationship between the Far West Bajo and the ancient Maya whose villages and fields surrounded it. It seems certain that the initial occupants of this landscape were drawn to it as a permanent source of water in an area that suffered several months of drought each year and had few permanent rivers or springs. Beginning in the Late Preclassic period, when the bajo was inundated year-round, small groups of people began to settle on ridges and hilltops in and around the wetland. Some of the activities undertaken by early inhabitants of this area had a devastating effect on the wetland, contributing to severe changes in its hydrology and leading to its conversion into a seasonally inundated swamp with little available surface water.

The most likely activity to cause such anthropogenic environmental change would have been the common lowland practice of slash-and-burn agriculture, which left hillslopes denuded of trees and vulnerable to erosion. Within the urban sphere of La Milpa, quarrying for the construction of masonry architecture also likely contributed to erosion and sedimentation. Thus, after many generations of farmers had pursued this traditional way of life, the inhabitants of the Far West Bajo would have had to develop new land-use strategies if their communities were to survive. Most critically, these new strategies would have required careful conservation and management of the dwindling soil and water resources of the landscape.

In response, the Far West Bajo inhabitants developed an intensive farming system that utilized terraces to conserve soil on the bajo margins and berms to manage surface runoff. This system took advantage of the silver lining in the erosive land-clearance practices that had so devastated the bajo's watershed: the sediments accumulated at the foot of slopes surrounding the bajo, creating a deep soil surface that, with careful management, was converted into productive agricultural land. As we see next, this system appears to have succeeded for several centuries before the ultimate abandonment of the bajo in the Terminal Classic period around A.D. 850.

CHAPTER FOUR

Agricultural Zones

Evidence for the development of agricultural practices designed to combat environmental degradation in the Far West Bajo comes from four distinct zones located around the margins of the depression. Each of these zones contained dense concentrations of features, including terraces, linear rubble piles known as berms, and rockpiles similar to those discussed in the previous chapter. Test excavations in a sample of these features demonstrated that the timing of construction of these features was consistent with that suggested for the sedimentation of the bajo. In many other regions of the Maya lowlands, agricultural terraces and ridged fields date to the Late Classic period and are thought to reflect pressure on agricultural production resulting from the tremendous population expansion throughout the Maya lowlands at that time. However, in the case of the Far West Bajo it appears that highly localized pressure on resources and farm production occurred far earlier, at the end of the Late Preclassic or beginning of the Early Classic period (A.D. 150–450). Most of the agricultural features around the Far West Bajo seem to have been constructed well before the Late Classic.

Agricultural zones are located in areas of bajo forest, transitional forest, or upland forest around the margins of the Far West Bajo. After discussing the distribution of terraces, berms, and rockpiles within these zones and their manner of construction, I describe each of the four agricultural areas in detail, providing summaries of the excavations in each area. Selected profiles are included with some summaries to illustrate typical features. There are patterns in the survey and excavation data from the agricultural zones, and I focus in particular on the chronology of agricultural developments and the function of agricultural features in relation to the paleoenvironmental reconstruction of the Far West Bajo.

I classified 384 of the 679 features mapped in the Far West Bajo study area as agricultural or land man-

Figure 4.1. An agricultural terrace on the edge of the Far West Bajo. The dashed white line outlines the top of the unexcavated feature, which measures approximately 3.5 m long.

agement features and tested 22 of them (5.7%). Of the 384, 61 were terraces, most extending roughly parallel to the slope contour (Fig. 4.1). They ranged in length from 2 m to 50 m. Some were dry slope terraces, but the majority were footslope terraces (Dunning and Beach 1994; Pohl and Miksicek 1995; Turner 1983). Both types were usually constructed in an area of naturally undulating bedrock or in a small excavation made in the bedrock immediately behind the terrace wall (Fig. 4.2). Often, the wall was anchored with large boulders that served as footings. One or two of the terrace clusters I mapped may have been box terraces (as described by Dunning and Beach 1994), which were constructed in a similar manner but formed enclosed rectangular plots on flat or gently sloping land.

Based on surface indications alone, terraces were not always easily distinguishable from rubble berms. I classified 101 features as berms, ranging in length from 3 m to 50 m (Fig. 4.3). Like terraces, berms were linear rubble features, but they usually did not

Figure 4.2. A terrace after excavation, showing a limestone cobble wall and underlying fill on bedrock. The measuring scale is extended 30 cm.

Figure 4.4. A berm during excavation, showing a layer of rocky fill that comprises the interior of the feature. The measuring scale is extended 50 cm.

Figure 4.3. A berm on the edge of the Far West Bajo. The dashed white line outlines the top of the unexcavated feature, which measures approximately 5 m long.

contain a wall built on footing stones. Instead, most berms were unstratified masses of chert and limestone cobbles in a clayey soil matrix. Frequently, single lines of cobbles demarcated the front and back edges of the feature, within which the fill was mounded (Fig. 4.4). Occasionally, a blanket of smaller stones overlay a core of larger stones, or vice versa, but this was the only interior structure discernible in berms. Unlike terraces, these features did not always run parallel to the slope contour; some did, but most ran at an angle to the contour and still others ran perpendicular to the slope. Often, they intersected or abutted terraces, forming V-shaped or rectilinear patterns. Moreover, flat plots of soil did not form upslope from berms as they did from terraces, and consequently the surface impression of a berm is different from that of a terrace.

Figure 4.5. A small rockpile during excavation, showing the cobble fill of the feature. The outer edge of the rocks defines the edge of the rockpile and the area of soil in the lower right corner is outside the feature.

Berms look like cobble "speed bumps" on the slope; because no soil collects upslope from a berm, a depression exists immediately behind the feature, creating an undulating profile.

Interspersed among the terraces and berms in the agricultural zones were 222 circular rockpiles. Usually an alignment of cobbles delineated the outer boundary of these amorphous features, within which the fill of limestone and chert cobbles was mounded (Fig. 4.5). Sometimes, a stone alignment served as an anchor around which the fill was blanketed, a morphological difference that distinguished these features from the rockpiles of the bajo interior. The mounds were similar to the chich piles described at Sayil, Yucatan (Sabloff and Tourtellot 1991: 13), except that those in the Far West Bajo contained chert as well as limestone rubble.

The final class of features in the agricultural zones were small cobble platforms, which looked like large oval or apsidal rockpiles. Some of these features had cobble retaining walls, while others did not. They were distinguished from circular rockpiles on the basis of their larger size and more formal shape, but the distinction was sometimes subjective.

Appendixes A through F present the quantities of materials from my excavations by lot for ceramics, lithic flakes, lithic tools, groundstone, obsidian, and fauna and shell. All lots are listed sequentially in Appendixes A, B, and C so that they appear in the same relative positions on pages in the different appendixes to aid in assessing the complete content of any particular lot. The majority of ceramics were surficially eroded, making their typological assessment difficult. However, the analysis by Kerry Sagebiel based on better preserved sherds, paste, and vessel form presents a chronological reconstruction of occupation in the Far West Bajo that I believe is accurate.

AGRICULTURAL ZONE 1

The first agricultural area, located on the northwest side of the bajo in Survey Block 2, is a 9.5 hectare square at the far end of Transect 1 (Fig. 4.6). In the eastern half of the block at the edge of the bajo, the elevation is low, ranging from 109 m to 113 m above sea level. Gentle slopes trending north-south give way to steep ridges in the western half of the block. Two ridges peak just outside the western boundary of the block at 143 m above sea level. A third ridge, slightly lower, peaks just beyond the southern boundary of the block at 125 m above sea level. Beyond the ridgetops the terrain flattens out and becomes relatively level.

Agricultural features, including 22 terraces, 17 berms, and 49 rockpiles, formed a dense band running across the block from southeast to northwest. In addition, four larger cobble platforms were dispersed among the other features. Most of the features were in upland forest or transitional forest; a few were located in a zone of escoba bajo forest on the edge of the depression. The majority of the agricultural installations extended along the base of and part way up the steep slope that defines the western corner of the block, from the 111-m to the 117-m contour lines. A second concentration of features was situated at the base of the slope just outside the block boundary on the northwest, between the 115-m and 119-m contour lines. A few terraces and rockpiles that were located higher up on the slope near Groups 2-A and 2-B were associated with a large, anomalous berm, discussed below. Many of the terraces and berms formed chains

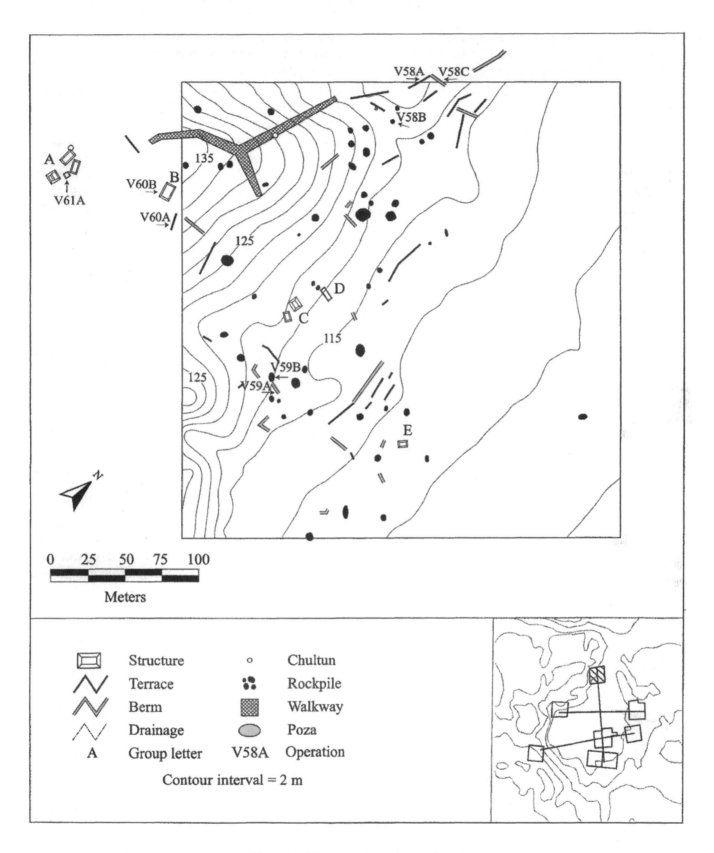

Figure 4.6. Map of Agricultural Zone 1.

in which several small features abutted to create long rows. In other places, terraces and berms adjoined at angles to form V-shaped units. Throughout these areas, rockpiles were clustered together among the other features.

A large feature in the western corner of Agricultural Zone 1 was a forked berm measuring 133 m in length and 7.5 m across at its widest point. The berm ran roughly perpendicular to the slope contour. The long arm of the feature was truncated by a modern logging road but appeared to be linked to a line of terraces on the northwest side of the survey block. The shorter arm jutted east toward several other concentrations of agricultural features. A chultun was constructed into the side of the feature about 50 m uphill from its downslope terminus. The feature appeared to link Groups 2–A and 2–B which were located just beyond the upslope end of the berm, with the agricultural lands below. The most likely interpretation of its function is as an elevated walkway that allowed residents of these groups to easily access their fields. The six features tested in Agricultural Zone 1 included two terraces, two berms, and two rockpiles.

Op. V58A

A 1–m by 4–m unit crossed a terrace along the northwest edge of Survey Block 2 (Fig. 4.7). The terrace was one of two that aligned with the large walkway in the western corner of the block. Excavation uncovered two lines of limestone cobbles that formed the footing for a wall. The cobbles were situated on a natural rise in the bedrock, and low spots in the surrounding bedrock were filled with small

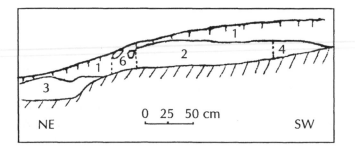

Figure 4.7. Op. V58A, an excavation on a terrace. The dashed area downslope from Lot 2 indicates the remains of the terrace wall.

rocks. Mounded around the footing stones was a matrix that formed the terrace retaining wall (Lot 6). Behind the wall was a layer of limestone cobbles, which increased in size immediately above bedrock (Lot 2). Farther upslope was a stratum of black, clayey soil without any rock inclusions (Lot 4). In front of the terrace wall was a stratum of light gray silty soil with limestone gravel inclusions (Lot 3). This stratum ended at the shallow bedrock in front of the terrace wall. The two sherds recovered in this excavation could not be dated. Lithic artifacts were abundant throughout the unit and included numerous flakes from all stages of the reduction sequence, five blades and two bifaces.

Op. V58B

Excavation of a 1–m by 2–m unit on a small rockpile near the northwest edge of Survey Block 2 revealed an alignment of unshaped chert cobbles defining the outline of a roughly circular feature. Within the alignment, large limestone boulders were on top of the bedrock and smaller cobbles of chert and limestone in a black, clayey matrix were mounded on top of the boulders (Lot 2). Many of the chert cobbles were thermally altered. Numerous flakes, core fragments, and sherds, as well as two biface fragments and a whole biface were in the cobble stratum. In contrast, outside the cobble alignment the matrix (Lot 3) was nearly sterile, containing only black clay with very few rock inclusions. Most of the sherds retrieved cannot be dated, but those few that are diagnostic are no later than early Late Classic.

Op. V58C

Excavation of a 1–m by 4–m unit designed to test the berm adjoining the terrace trenched in Op. V58A uncovered a line of unshaped chert cobbles delineating the front edge of the feature. In front of this line and above bedrock was a stratum of black, clayey soil with few rock inclusions and only a few lithic artifacts (Lot 3). Behind the cobble alignment was a mass of chert cobbles and pebbles with some unshaped limestone blocks in a black soil matrix (Lot 2). Larger cobbles were concentrated in the center of the feature where the mound was highest, with smaller cobbles blanketing the larger stones. Of the few ceramics, only two could be dated; they are Late Preclassic. One biface fragment was among the few lithics recovered.

Op. V59A

The crew excavated a 1-m by 4.5-m unit on a berm near the southwest edge of Survey Block 2 (Fig. 4.8). The berm was in a group of agricultural features near Group 2–C. Here, a layer of small chert and limestone cobbles in a black clayey matrix (Lot 2) sat beneath a thin humus layer. Below this was a layer of large unshaped limestone and chert blocks, first in a gray silty soil, then lower in a black clayey matrix (Lot 3). Bedrock lay underneath. Outside the downslope edge of the feature was a stratum of black clayey soil with frequent chert cobble inclusions (Lot 4). On the upslope side, the soil was much shallower and contained only a few chert cobbles (Lot 5). A moderate number of sherds and lithics were found throughout the excavation with fewer artifacts in the soil beyond the edges of the feature. Ceramics date from the Early Classic to the Late/Terminal Classic; the three sherds that can be dated from Lots 3 and 4 are Early Classic.

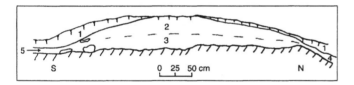

Figure 4.8. Op.V59A, an excavation on a berm.

Op. V59B

This unit was a 1-m by 2-m excavation on the rockpile located at the end of the berm tested in Op. V59A. No clear cobble alignment defined the edge of the feature, which consisted of an unstratified mass of small- to medium-sized limestone and chert cobbles with occasional large unshaped limestone blocks in a black clayey soil matrix (Fig. 4.9, Lot 2). Outside the feature, the same black clay contained fewer cobbles, most of which had tumbled from the rockpile fill (Lot 3). This stratum was culturally sterile except for two flakes. The few artifacts recovered in this excavation include some ceramics from Lot 2 that are Early Classic and Late/Terminal Classic and some flakes, two blades, and two flake cores.

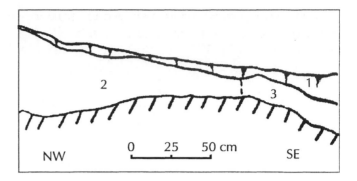

Figure 4.9. Op. V59B, an excavation on a rockpile. The dashed line between Lots 2 and 3 represents the edge of the feature, and Lot 2 is the cobble fill of the rockpile.

Op. V60A

Excavation of a 1-m by 3-m unit that was expanded to a 1-m by 5-m trench across a terrace adjacent to Group 2-B revealed that the terrace was constructed over naturally undulating bedrock. Atop one small bedrock rise were the remains of a chert and limestone cobble retaining wall. Only four cobbles remained in place; the remainder had tumbled forward into the fill downslope. Upslope from the wall was a black clayey soil with small- to medium-sized limestone and chert cobbles (Lots 2, 5, and 7), topped with a thick layer of humus that had built up behind the retaining wall (Lots 1, 4, and 6). Downslope from the wall, a similar matrix contained the larger cobbles that had tumbled from the wall (Lot 3). This stratum was capped by a thin layer of humus. Ceramics and lithics appeared throughout the unit, including one intact biface found upslope from the terrace wall in Lot 7. Ceramics cannot be dated with certainty, but probably are early Late Classic and Late/Terminal Classic.

AGRICULTURAL ZONE 2

The second agricultural zone in the Far West Bajo, located on the west side of the bajo in Survey Block 4, measures approximately 9 hectares and lies at the end of Transect 4 (Fig. 4.10). Within the block there is an upward trend in elevation from east to west. The extreme eastern corner of the block is in the bajo, at 106 m above sea level. From here, the terrain climbs steeply up to a large flat knoll in the center of the block, where the elevation is 130 m above sea level.

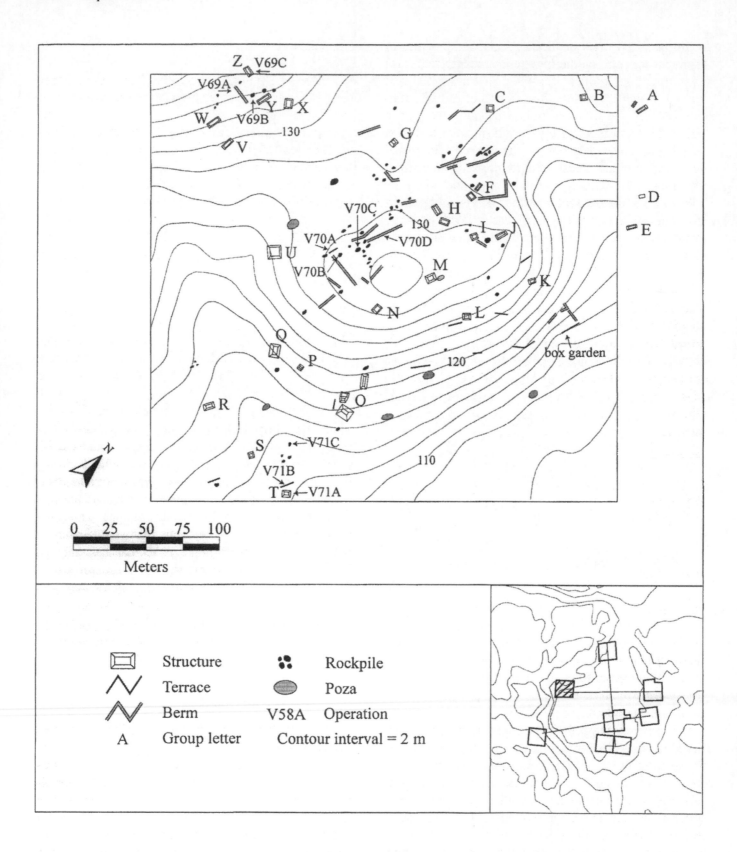

Figure 4.10. Map of Agricultural Zone 2.

Immediately west of the knoll is a flat expanse of land that forms a saddle between slopes on the north and west. The knoll is vegetated in transitional and upland forest; the saddle is in a zone of mixed palm-transitional forest. West of the saddle, the terrain slopes up again, more gently, to a maximum elevation of 140 m above sea level. The top of this slope, covered in upland forest, is outside the boundaries of the block.

The block contains 14 terraces and 19 berms interspersed with 22 cobble platforms and 6 more formal platforms or structures, along with numerous rockpiles. This agricultural zone is dominated by rockpiles and berms measuring from 6 m to 30 m in length. The majority of the features are located around the flat knoll and on the saddle behind it in the center of the zone.

A second cluster of cobble platforms and rockpiles is located part way up the gentle slope in the western corner. A unique cut-stone berm is also located in this area; it was tested in Op. V69A. The eastern half of the block contains six small pozas, thought to have once held water. Four of the pozas are located near Group 4-O, the most formal group of architecture in the block. A box garden is located in transitional forest to the northeast. It is a square space, almost completely enclosed on three sides by berms and a terrace, but it is not directly associated with any residential features.

Although numerous small platforms are interspersed among the agricultural features in this zone, few of them are masonry buildings like those in the upland residential zones. The platforms here are cobble constructions with no indications of plaster floors or features such as benches or burials and generally lacking in household debris. They are not arranged in formal patio groups as are many in the residential zones, and it is likely that they represent fieldhouses and not permanent residences.

Of the ten excavations conducted in this zone, two were in cobble platforms, one near the southern corner of the block (Op. V71A) on structure 4-T and one in the western corner (Op. V69C) on structure 4-Z. Because these structure excavations offer an important contrast to those in the more formal residential architecture of the Far West Bajo communities, they are included in Chapter 5. The remaining eight excavations are described here.

Op. V69A

A 1-m by 3-m excavation tested a cut-stone berm. Prior to excavation, three courses of a stacked cobble wall were clearly evident on the ground surface. Trenching revealed that the wall was constructed of a combination of medium- to large-sized chert and limestone cobbles with some dressed limestone blocks in a dark brown loamy soil matrix (Lot 3). The wall, roughly five courses high, sat directly atop bedrock. Behind the wall a mixture of small- to medium-sized unshaped chert and limestone cobbles in a dark clay-loam soil matrix was mounded atop bedrock (Lot 2). The cobble fill was reminiscent of that of a berm. To the outside of the feature, which I interpreted as a fieldwall, was a stratum of clay-loam soil with a few rock inclusions (Lot 4). Only two eroded sherds and a handful of small lithics were retrieved in this excavation, which therefore could not be dated.

Op. V69B

In a 1-m by 1.5-m excavation on a small rockpile adjacent to the fieldwall described above, an alignment of chert and limestone boulders formed a basal footing for the cobble fill of the rockpile (Lot 3). The alignment rested atop a stratum of black, clayey soil with chert cobble inclusions and small limestone pieces that underlay the entire feature (Lot 4). Within this stratum, a few large chert and limestone boulders were situated near the tallest part of the mound. Below the clayey layer, which was culturally sterile, was bedrock. The fill of the rockpile consisted primarily of thermally altered chert cobbles in a black clayey matrix (Lot 2). This fill was almost sterile. No ceramics were recovered and the feature could not be dated.

Op. V70A

A 1-m by 2.5-m excavation trenched a terrace that formed an L-shape with an adjoining berm. The terrace was located amid the dense concentration of features around the knoll in the center of the block. No definitive terrace wall was located in this unit. Instead, a concentration of large chert cobbles in the upslope end of the unit indicated that the retaining wall had collapsed. The terrace was built over a natural rise in the bedrock, and all four of the strata in the unit followed the contours of this rise. Immediately above bedrock was a thin stratum of reddish clay overlain by a mixture of small chert gravel in a black clayey matrix (Lot 3). Above this was a layer of small- to medium-sized chert cobbles and some limestone blocks in a black clayey soil (Lot 2) topped by a humus layer (Lot 1). There were no ceramics. Only a moderate number of chert lithics were recovered in this excavation, including three flake cores.

Op. V70B

A 0.50–m by 1.75–m excavation on a rockpile near the terrace described above revealed that the rockpile contained a footing wall of unshaped chert boulders in a clayey fill above bedrock (Lot 3). Mounded atop the wall was an unconsolidated mass of chert and limestone cobbles and boulders with virtually no soil matrix (Lot 2). In the humus layer that covered the feature were two larger chert blocks with signs of shaping (Lot 1). A small number of sherds, only one of which could be dated, were recovered. Lithics from Lot 2 included one biface and two flake cores.

Op. V70C

Excavation of a 1–m by 1.5–m unit on a rockpile in the same cluster of features as those tested in Ops. V70A, V70B, and V70D revealed a basal wall of unshaped chert cobbles and boulders in a reddish clay and gravel matrix (Lot 5). The wall sat atop a thick layer of marl (Lot 6), below which was the eroding bedrock. Surrounding the basal wall was a thin stratum of reddish-brown clay and gravel (Lots 3 and 4). Above this was the fill of the feature, consisting of chert cobbles in a clayey soil matrix (Lot 2). A small number of sherds (none dated) and a moderate number of lithics were collected in this unit, primarily from Lot 2. Lithics included flakes from throughout the reduction sequence, as well as a biface and five flake cores.

Op. V70D

A 1–m by 3.5–m unit trenched the berm adjacent to the rockpile described above. No formal construction was associated with this feature. Excavation revealed that a thick layer of sterile grayish white clay (Lot 4) lay atop bedrock, above which was a thin stratum of reddish gravelly clay (Lot 3). This layer was thickest at the center of the feature, where the mound was highest. Above it was a thick layer of medium- to large-sized chert cobbles in a clayey matrix (Lot 2). Many pieces of burned limestone appeared throughout the unit. The mound was capped by a thin layer of humus (Lot 1). Among the large number of lithics collected from this unit, especially from Lot 2, were two biface preforms and one blade. There were flakes from throughout the reduction sequence, as well as 15 flake cores. More than 100 sherds were retrieved, primarily in Lot 2; those that could be dated are predominantly Early Classic.

Op. V71B

The crew excavated a 1–m by 2–m unit on a terrace near the southern corner of Survey Block 4. The terrace was adjacent to Str. 4–T, tested in Op. V71A and described in the next chapter. A cobble retaining wall sat on bedrock near the center of the unit (Lot 3). Bedrock was not undulating as it was in most of the terrace excavation units, but instead was relatively flat. Downslope from the wall was a layer of medium- to large-sized limestone and chert boulders, which appeared to have slumped forward from the retaining wall (Lot 2). In the upslope portion of the unit, a layer of black clayey soil with small- and medium-sized limestone and chert inclusions (Lot 4) had accumulated behind the terrace retaining wall. Topping this was a layer of humus, much thicker in the upslope portion of the unit than below the retaining wall (Lot 1). Numerous lithics were recovered in this excavation, including 5 cores, 3 blades, and 200 flakes, mostly from Lots 2 and 3. In addition, 79 sherds were collected; those that could be dated are Late Preclassic through the Late/Terminal Classic.

Op. V71C

No formal alignment or basal wall was encountered in the excavation of a 1–m by 1.5–m unit on a rockpile near the terrace described above. Instead, cobble fill consisting of medium- to large-sized chert cobbles in a clayey matrix sat atop a thin lens of brown clay above bedrock (Lot 2). The frequency of large cobbles increased as the excavation approached bedrock. The cobble fill was capped by a thin layer of humus that contained no artifacts (Lot 1). A small number of undiagnostic lithics were recovered. Of the 48 sherds, only 6 from Lot 2 could be dated, and they are all Early Classic.

AGRICULTURAL ZONE 3

A band of agricultural features including 21 terraces, 23 berms, and 54 rockpiles extends across Survey Block 5 from south to north and constitutes the third agricultural zone (Fig. 4.11). Survey Block 5, which measures 9.2 hectares, is located only 110 m southeast of Survey Block 3 on the east side of the bajo. Terrain throughout the western half and the southern corner of the block is gently rolling, with a gradual increase in elevation from west to east. The lowest point, in the western corner, is 112 m above sea level. A well-entrenched arroyo meanders through the western half of the block. To the east, a small hill is separated by a narrow gully from a steep ridge. North of the gully, the terrain rises steeply to the top of the ridge, located just outside the eastern corner of the block and dominated by the large Group 5–B. The elevation at this high point is 138 m above sea level.

The agricultural features in this zone occupy ground intermediate between the bajo to the west and the steep ridge to the east. Most of the features are in mixed palm-transitional forest between the 112–m and 124–m contour lines. One concentration of features consists of a series of footslope terraces and berms at the base of a long, gentle slope in an area of mixed palm forest in the center and southern corner of the zone. These features are joined by a pair of berms that extend on opposite sides of a small platform, Str. 5–G–1. A similar configuration is on the western edge of the zone in upland forest, where two arms of a berm extend for 25–30 m to either side of a medium-sized platform, Str. 5–F–1. The southern arm ends at the bank of an arroyo and probably served to impound water from the stream or to divert its course away from the land behind the berm. Another set of terraces and berms forms V-shaped configurations in the northern corner of the zone, near an isolated platform (Str. 5–D–1) in an area of transitional forest. A unique, V-shaped wall forms a clearly artificial bank along the downslope edge of a large poza, which sits adjacent to the most imposing structure in this zone, the large, multiroomed building in Group 5–B that dominates the ridgetop.

Part of this steep ridge was mapped, but no terraces were located along its slopes.

Five excavations were conducted in the agricultural zone in Survey Block 5, which excluded the ridgetop. One was an excavation (Op. V75B) in Str. 5–D–1 and is described in the next chapter, as are the excavations in Group 5–B. I summarize the others here.

Op. V26

A 1-m by 10-m excavation across a series of three long terraces and berms in the center of Survey Block 5 was supervised and reported to me by Nick Dunning. Each of the three features contained an informal wall constructed of small limestone cobbles above a layer of limestone gravel (Lots 2 and 3). On the western (downslope) end, the cobble wall rested atop a stratum of larger limestone cobbles and boulders in a clayey matrix (Lot 4). On the eastern (upslope) end, the wall sat above an old topsoil layer consisting of small limestone cobbles and gravel in a dark reddish brown clay matrix (Lot 5). It is this buried topsoil that has the same organic isotope signature as the peaty paleosol found throughout the bajo in the backhoe trenches, suggesting to Dunning and his colleagues that the ancient bajo soils served as organic fertilizer on this and perhaps other bajo margin agricultural features (Dunning and others 2002). Beneath this layer was the same cobble stratum found in the western part of the trench. The central portion of the features was not excavated to bedrock. Only a handful of undiagnostic lithics and five sherds were recovered.

Op. V73A

Excavation of a 1-m by 2-m unit across a footslope terrace near the western edge of Survey Block 5 revealed a concentration of large unshaped boulders near the center of the unit where the slope rose. The boulders sat above a matrix of small chert and limestone cobbles, many of them burned, in gray clay (Lot 4). Beneath this layer was thick gray clay with a denser concentration of cobbles (Lot 5), followed by a sterile gray clay stratum with virtually no rock inclusions (Lot 6). Downslope from the boulder concentration was a stratum of reddish brown clayey soil with few rock inclusions (Lot 3). Upslope, large chert and limestone cobbles abounded in what appeared to be the cobble fill

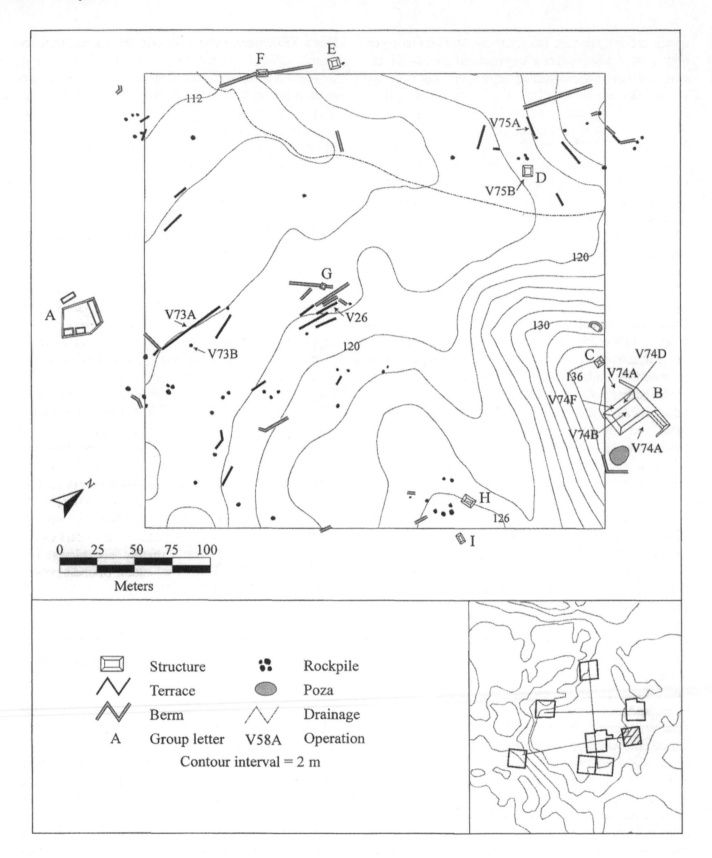

Figure 4.11. Map of Agricultural Zone 3.

of the feature (Lot 2). Surprisingly, the humus layer (Lot 1) was no thicker in the upslope portion of the unit than it was downslope. However, lithic artifacts were noticeably more prevalent in the upslope part of the unit. Among the lithics, two whole bifaces, three flake cores, and one utilized blade were collected from Lot 2, the area behind the boulder alignment. Four of the 45 sherds date to the Late Preclassic and the rest were eroded.

Op. V73B

Excavation of a 1-m by 2-m unit in a rockpile near the terrace described above revealed that the feature was clearly defined by a line of cobbles marking the edge of the mound. Inside this alignment was cobble fill (Lot 2), consisting of varying sizes of chert cobbles in a black clayey soil matrix. To the outside of the alignment, the soil was sticky black clay with few rock inclusions (Lot 3). Underlying the feature was a layer of sticky grayish brown clay with large cobbles (Lot 4), followed by a stratum of sterile gray clay with numerous angular chert cobbles (Lot 5), where excavation halted. The two datable sherds are Late Preclassic. A small number of lithics were collected, including four cores from Lots 2 and 4.

Op. V75A

No retaining wall or stone alignment appeared in a 1-m by 2-m excavation on a terrace in the northern corner of Survey Block 5 near Str. 5-D-1. The unit contained a layer of reddish brown clay with large chert cobbles (Lot 3) above yellow sterile clay (unexcavated). Above this was a layer of dark brown loamy soil with chert and limestone cobbles (Lot 2). A stratum of humus capped the cobble fill (Lot 1). Few lithics were recovered; most of them were undiagnostic, except for two cores from Lot 2. The four sherds also came from Lot 2, with one dating to the Early Late Classic; the others were eroded.

AGRICULTURAL ZONE 4

The last agricultural zone in the study area is located on the southeast side of the bajo in Survey Blocks 6 and 7 (Fig. 4.12). Survey Block 6 is the first of the blocks in the Far West Bajo study area mapped by

Hugh Robichaux (1995) as part of his doctoral research. In his dissertation it is designated Operation 20 survey area. This block, measuring 9 hectares, lies close to the terminus of Drainage 3. A section of the drainage channel travels along the western edge of the block (Robichaux 1995: 201). Survey Block 7 (Robichaux's Operation 21 survey area) abuts Block 6 on the southwest and is slightly lower in elevation. It, too, measures 9 hectares. The terrain is extremely flat. Survey Block 7 sits slightly inside the eastern edge of the bajo.

According to the Belize Ordnance Maps (Robichaux 1995: 307), the 100-m contour line passes through both blocks. My mapping, however, indicates about a 10-m discrepancy with these maps, recording an elevation of approximately 110 m on the western side of Survey Block 6 and a 107 m elevation in Survey Block 7. All of Survey Block 6 is vegetated in corozo bajo, as is the eastern half of Survey Block 7. The western, lower half is in scrub bajo.

Robichaux (1995: 307) mapped two dense clusters of berms and rockpiles in this agricultural zone, as well as numerous small cobble platforms and two more formal structures. No terraces were recorded in this block, which is not surprising considering the flat nature of the terrain. The first cluster of agricultural features, a group of five berms surrounded by rockpiles, is located in the northern corner of the zone. The second cluster is located south of a small, intermittent stream that enters the zone from the east. Here, two sets of three berms flanked a long U-shaped berm, which surrounded two small rockpiles. One trio of berms appeared to be positioned along the stream so as to impound water and direct it toward the other features. Robichaux also mapped a cluster of small platforms in the center of the block. These features appear to be equivalent to the cobble platforms mapped elsewhere in the Far West Bajo study area. The platforms share space with a small poza located west of the features. According to Robichaux, most of Survey Block 7 was devoid of features.

Robichaux excavated four test pits in this area (profiles of which are in his dissertation). One of the units (Op. 20A, which tested the patio between the two platforms in Group 16) is described in the next chapter. The others are summarized here. Data from these operations are not included in the Appendix compilations for my excavations.

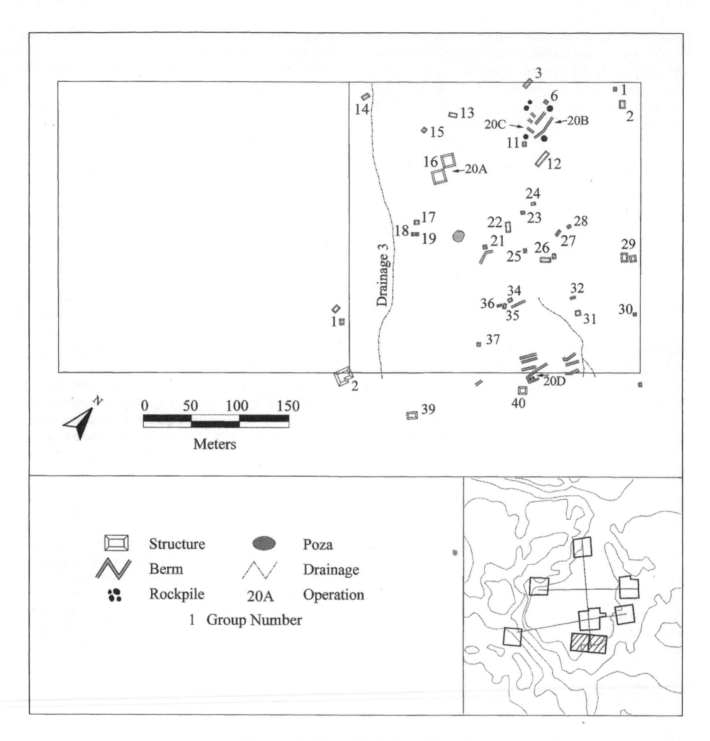

Figure 4.12. Map of Agricultural Zone 4.

Op. 20B

Robichaux uncovered no retaining wall or basal alignment of stones in a 1–m by 2–m unit placed across one of the long berms near the northern corner of Survey Block 6, but a layer of larger cobbles appeared to blanket an interior core of smaller cobble fill. Excavation revealed a thick layer of small limestone and chert cobbles with occasional large boulders in a brown soil matrix above bedrock. Above this was a stratum of medium-sized cobbles, predominantly limestone with some chert, in a similar soil matrix. This stratum was topped by a thin humus layer. A small number of ceramics dating to the Late Preclassic, Protoclassic, and Late Classic were collected. Lithics included two cores and three bifaces.

Op. 20C

Robichaux excavated a 1-m by 2-m unit in a small berm perpendicular to the one described above. The construction of this feature was similar to that of its neighbor. A thick stratum of small cobbles in a brown soil matrix was overlain by a layer of medium- to large-sized cobbles. This stratum was capped by a thin layer of humus. A moderate number of ceramics were recovered, dating to the Early Classic and early Late Classic. Lithics were numerous, including more than 150 unmodified flakes, a number of utilized flakes, 8 cores, and 3 bifaces.

Op. 20D

A 1-m by 2-m excavation was placed on a small rockpile enclosed by the U-shaped berm on the east boundary of Survey Block 6. The stratigraphy here was similar to that in agricultural features excavated in low-lying bajo areas of Agricultural Zone 3. Bedrock was overlain by sterile black clay that was covered with sterile gray clay with small stone inclusions. Above this was a stratum of small stones in a red clayey matrix. This layer was topped by a stratum of small cobbles in a brown soil matrix, above which lay a thin layer of humus. No ceramics and few lithics were recovered in this excavation. Lithics were all unmodified flakes, with the exception of one biface.

AGROTECHNOLOGY

The diverse array of linear agricultural features revealed throughout the Far West Bajo included dry slope terraces, footslope terraces, box terraces, berms, walkways, and barrier walls that appeared to have diverted water out of small streams for agricultural purposes. Interspersed among the linear features were cobble rockpiles that may have been fieldhouses, storehouses of lithic raw materials, or small planting platforms. These features were situated primarily at the base of long slopes around the margins of the bajo, but occasionally they were located higher up on gentle slopes and small hills and in flat terrain close to the bajo edge. No cross-channel terraces have been identified in the area, although they are prevalent elsewhere in the region (Beach and others 2002). Only in Agricultural Zones 1 and 3 were agricultural features directly associated with a formal residential compound. In all other instances associated platforms were small, isolated structures of cobble construction that were probably fieldhouses.

The distribution of agricultural features and the characteristics of each of the four agricultural zones in the Far West Bajo provide evidence for the timing of construction and utilization of agricultural features that has important implications for interpreting the development of intensive terrace agriculture as a response to environmental change in the bajo. The lithics recovered in the excavations help decipher the functions of terraces and berms when comparing these features to similar ones found elsewhere in the Maya lowlands. The distribution of different types of agricultural features throughout the various vegetation zones relates to issues of function. These patterns support an argument for the accretionary development of intensive agriculture in the Far West Bajo.

Chronology of Agricultural Zones

Agricultural features are notoriously hard to date because they usually contain few ceramics and those that are present are often too eroded to be diagnostic. The lack of floors to provide sealed contexts exacerbates the problem (Turner 1983). Yet, the dating of agricultural features is critical to discussions about the pace of development of intensive agriculture in the Maya lowlands. If all agricultural features in an area date to the same time period, they may be interpreted as indicating a very rapid inception of methods of intensive agriculture. This situation is especially true in the Late Classic, when population densities in most parts of the lowlands were at their maximum and many scholars infer that agricultural intensification reached its widest extent. In contrast, if the features date to several time periods, they may indicate a more gradual adoption of intensive methods of farming.

In many instances, the lack of diagnostic ceramics from agricultural contexts prompts scholars to date fea-

Table 4.1. Ceramics from Agricultural Contexts by Time Period

Agric. Zone	Op.	Context	Late Preclassic	Early Classic	Early Late Classic	Late/ Terminal Classic	Unknown	Total
1	V58A	Terrace					2	2
1	V58B	Rockpile	1		3		111	115
1	V58C	Berm	2				6	8
1	V59A	Berm		3	3	1	143	150
1	V59B	Rockpile		3		1	44	48
1	V60A	Terrace	1		4	2	97	104
2	V69A	Berm					2	2
2	V70B	Rockpile			1		6	7
2	V70C	Rockpile					11	11
2	V70D	Berm		22	4	1	103	130
2	V71B	Terrace	4	7	2	3	63	79
2	V71C	Rockpile		6			42	48
3	V26	Terrace					5	5
3	V73A	Terrace	4				41	45
3	V73B	Rockpile	2					2
3	V75A	Terrace			1		3	4
Total			14	41	18	8	679	760
Percent of dated sherds			*17.3*	*50.6*	*22.2*	*9.9*		

NOTE: Robichaux did not provide individual counts for each time period and his excavations in Agricultural Zone 4 are not included in this table.

tures by reference to the nearest datable residential structures on the grounds that there was likely an association between the local settlers and nearby fields (Turner 1983). In the Far West Bajo, however, the spatial segregation of terraced fields from substantial nodes of residential architecture precludes this option, except in Agricultural Zone 1. Here, a test pit in the smallest structure in Group 2–A yielded ceramics dating exclusively to the Late Preclassic, and a nearby isolated platform dates to the Late/Terminal Classic. To facilitate the discussion of chronology, all datable ceramics from all lots excavated in a single feature have been aggregated, resulting in a "bulk" range of dates for each feature tested. Because most of the agricultural features were single component, lumping the ceramics together does not unduly distort their construction history; however, in most cases only a handful of datable ceramics were excavated in any one agricultural feature (Table 4.1).

The agricultural features tested throughout the Far West Bajo are surprisingly early, with most ceramic material dating to periods prior to the Late/Terminal Classic. Of the six features excavated in Agricultural Zone 1, five yielded small numbers of datable ceram-

ics: Late Preclassic (4 sherds), Early Classic (6 sherds), early Late Classic (10 sherds), and Late/Terminal Classic (4 sherds). Eight features in Agricultural Zone 2 were excavated, but there were no ceramics in two of them (Ops. V69B and V70A). Four features date early; only four Late/Terminal Classic sherds were recovered. Moreover, one rockpile contained only Early Classic material. Early Classic and early Late Classic dates for the Agricultural Zone 2 features seem likely.

In Agricultural Zone 3, a pair of features (one terrace and one rockpile) yielded only Late Preclassic material, although admittedly in small amounts. A terrace yielded a single early Late Classic sherd. Again, early dates seem plausible for Zone 3. In Agricultural Zone 4, only two berm tests yielded ceramics. Robichaux (1995) reported that one contained Late Preclassic, Protoclassic, and Late Classic material. The other contained Early Classic and early Late Classic ceramics.

Based on the percentage of ceramics dating to each time period, it appears that most agricultural features were constructed in the Early Classic. However, half the Early Classic sherds came from one feature, which almost certainly dates to this time period. A more evenly distributed result derives from calculating the number of operations containing sherds representative of the four time periods. Six features contain Late Preclassic material, five contain Early Classic sherds, seven contain early Late Classic material, and five contain Late/Terminal Classic sherds. These numbers suggest that almost equal numbers of features were used during each of the four periods.

Another way to examine the ceramic data is to calculate the latest period represented in each excavation. For example, three features contain sherds dating no later than the Late Preclassic, and another three contain ceramics no later than the early Late Classic. Looked at in this manner, the ceramic data suggest early use of many of the features. This finding is corroborated by examining the total number of sherds dating to the Late/Terminal Classic. As the least well-represented time period, with only eight sherds, the Late/Terminal Classic represents just less than 10 percent of total datable sherds. In sum, the admittedly sparse ceramic data from the agricultural zones suggests that, although some features were used during each time period, many of them date earlier than expected, considering that more than two-thirds (69%) of datable sherds from residential features in the area date to the Late/Terminal Classic.

The results of these excavations point not to a sudden development of intensive agriculture in the Late Classic but to a more gradual development with an earlier inception than might have been anticipated without considering the occupational history of the Far West Bajo. These findings contrast with patterns documented in intensively farmed regions elsewhere in the Maya lowlands. By dating in association to nearby residences, Turner (1983) argued that agricultural terraces in the Río Bec region dated primarily to the Late and Terminal Classic. Through ceramic and radiocarbon dating, Healy and others (1983) and Chase and Chase (1998) determined that the terraces at Caracol in central Belize were largely Late Classic, although with an Early Classic component. Based on their excavations, Dunning and Beach (1994; Dunning and others 1997) reported that terraces in the Petexbatun area of the Peten were largely Late Classic. Fedick (1994) and Neff and others (1995) found that terraces in the upper Belize River valley were also Late Classic, based on the dates of associated residential structures.

Thus, the chronology of the Far West Bajo agricultural features is unusual.

Artifacts from Agricultural Contexts

The most striking observation about the collective artifact assemblage from agricultural contexts is how strongly it contrasts with artifact assemblages from the three residential zones, discussed in Chapter 5. Typically, residential function is attributed to a structure not only on the basis of architecture, but also on the presence of domestic artifacts such as cooking vessels, manos and metates, and obsidian blades (Haviland 1985). In agricultural features such domestic trash is scarce. Instead, bifaces, choppers, and flakes for clearing land, felling trees, digging soil, and harvesting crops are abundant. The agricultural features excavated fit this pattern (Table 4.2).

Lithics constitute 65 percent of the artifacts recovered from agricultural excavations, versus 21 percent from excavations in residential structures. Such a high percentage of lithics is indicative of an emphasis on activities where reliance on stone tools is high. Haviland proposed that an array of activities were indicated by lithics he excavated in small structures at Tikal (Haviland 1985): bifaces for chopping wood and loosening soil, flakes for woodworking and scraping, and blades for cutting. McAnany (1992) argued that bifaces were especially useful agricultural tools used principally for weeding and tilling. Lithics from bajo agricultural excavations included cores or core tools (4.3%), bifaces (1.2%), and blades (1.0%). In comparison, residential excavations yielded cores or core tools (1.0%), bifaces (1.3%), and blades (0.8%). The prevalence of flakes (93.7%) in the agricultural features suggests that cutting and digging tasks, such as harvesting and processing crops, predominated in these areas. Moreover, the presence of flakes from throughout the reduction sequence indicates that lithic tool production occurred in agricultural zones. The higher percentage of cores and core tools in agricultural contexts compared to residential contexts points to a greater emphasis on either flake production for cutting tasks or use of core tools as choppers or hoes. The nearly equal percentage of bifaces from both residential and agricultural contexts results in part from the presence of unused bifaces in caches in several of the residential groups and may also repre-

Table 4.2. Artifacts from Excavations in Agricultural Contexts

Agric. Zone	Op.	Context	Ceramics	Flakes	Cores	Bifaces	Blades
1	V58A	Terrace	2	299	9	2	5
1	V58B	Rockpile	115	114	3	3	1
1	V58C	Berm	8	7		1	
1	V59A	Berm	150	53	3	1	
1	V59B	Rockpile	48	35	2		2
1	V60A	Terrace	104	73	2	1	
2	V69A	Berm	2	23			
2	V69B	Rockpile		3			
2	V70A	Terrace		150	3		
2	V70B	Rockpile	7	44	2	1	
2	V70C	Rockpile	11	40	5	1	
2	V70D	Berm	130	79	15	2	1
2	V71B	Terrace	79	269	5		3
2	V71C	Rockpile	48	31			
3	V26	Terrace	5	22			
3	V73A	Terrace	45	59	6	3	1
3	V73B	Rockpile	2	11	4		
3	V75A	Terrace	4	18	2		
4	20B*	Berm	43	38	2	3	*
4	20C*	Berm	75	174	8	3	*
4	20D*	Rockpile		20		1	*
Total			878	1,562	71	22	13

NOTE: No groundstone or obsidian items were recovered in agricultural zones.
* Robichaux excavations; no information on blades available.

sent increased breakage of agricultural tools in near-residential contexts, an indication of agricultural intensification (Eguchi 2000; McAnany 1992).

The absence of substantial domestic trash in these excavations confirms the interpretation that the features were not residential. An average of only 42 sherds per excavation occurred in agricultural contexts, versus 716 sherds per similarly sized excavations in residential contexts. In addition, a complete lack of groundstone and obsidian means that typical domestic activities were not occurring in association with the features tested. The sample of agricultural features is too small, however, to draw many conclusions about differences in function among feature types on the basis of artifacts alone. For further insight, I turn to variation in the environmental signatures of terraces, berms, and rockpiles.

Vegetation Zones of Agricultural Features

There are some notable differences among the three classes of agricultural features in terms of distribution throughout vegetation zones (Table 4.3). These spatial patterns have implications for the functions of terraces, berms, and rockpiles. The vast majority of terraces occur in one of two vegetation zones. Almost 45 percent of terraces are located in upland forest and 25.3 percent are in mixed palm-transitional forest. Berms are more widely distributed, with 34.8 percent located in upland forest, 19.1 percent in mixed palm-transitional forest, and another 16.9 percent in corozo bajo forest. In contrast, only 1.5 percent of terraces occur in corozo bajo. Rockpiles are even more dispersed, with almost 35 percent in upland forest, 29.3 percent in mixed palm-transitional forest, 12.7 percent in scrub bajo, and 10.2 percent in transitional forest, but only 2.4 percent in corozo bajo forest.

The concentration of terraces in upland and transitional or mixed transitional forests that grow on slopes indicates that these features had a specialized function as erosion control mechanisms. Although many berms served in concert with terraces, which explains their prevalence in these vegetation zones as well, they also had other functions. The high percentage of berms in corozo bajo, which is a forest type that is known to be

Table 4.3. Agricultural Features in Vegetation Zones

Vegetation Type	Terrace		Berm		Rockpile	
	Number	%	Number	%	Number	%
Upland forest	30	44.8	31	34.8	71	34.6
Mixed palm-transitional	17	25.3	17	19.1	60	29.3
Transitional	7	10.4	8	9.0	21	10.2
Mixed palm-scrub bajo	4	6.0	1	1.1	6	2.9
Mixed palm bajo	4	6.0	8	9.0	4	2.0
Corozo bajo	1	1.5	15	16.9	5	2.4
Escoba bajo					2	1.0
Scrub bajo			2	2.2	26	12.7
Disturbance *	4	6.0	7	7.9	10	4.9
Total	67	100.0	89	100.0	205	100.0

* Disturbance growth is forest of any type that has been disturbed, and thus altered significantly, by modern activities.

amenable to cultivation (see Chapter 2), suggests that water control activities took place in these areas even in the absence of terraces. The variety of vegetation zones in which rockpiles were built suggests that they served multiple purposes (Chapter 3).

Construction and Function of Agricultural Features

A primary line of evidence supporting the idea that the agricultural zones of the Far West Bajo were loci of intensively cultivated fields is found in the design of the features themselves. The terraces around the margins of the Far West Bajo are primarily footslope terraces, but others are linear dry slope terraces. Footslope terraces are situated at the base of long or steep slopes that are left otherwise unprotected and capture slopewash (colluvium), creating large planting surfaces at the foot of the slope. Dry slope terraces trap eroding soil from upslope areas behind a rubble retaining wall positioned on the slope itself. Both types were constructed in the manner described by Turner (1983) for the Río Bec area of Mexico. A typical terrace on the slopes around the Far West Bajo contained a front wall made of unshaped, dry-laid limestone rubble. The wall was constructed directly atop bedrock, indicating the removal of the ancient soil surface, perhaps for placement behind the wall. The front wall was sometimes secured by large anchor stones placed on the bedrock. Behind the front wall or sometimes blanketing the anchor stones was mounded a thick layer of smaller rubble fill. Other types of terrace construction described elsewhere in the low-

lands (Dunning and Beach 1994; Healy and others 1983; Turner 1983), such as double-wall terraces and slab terraces, were not evident in the Far West Bajo.

Terraces are used by farmers to overcome the problems inherent in cultivating slopes (Donkin 1979: 2). In the Maya lowlands, hillslope soils are generally well-drained and fertile, but shallow and subject to erosion, especially when cleared of vegetation (Turner 1979: 106). Through time, cultivation of these soils reduces nutrient levels, which must be artificially maintained if successful cropping is to continue. Regulation of soil moisture levels is also necessary, and includes both management of runoff during heavy rains and conservation of soil moisture during periods of dryness. Agricultural terraces can ameliorate these problems. Terraces impede erosion by trapping downward-moving soil behind walls. As soil accumulates, a deep and often level planting surface is created. Deeper soils increase the amount of moisture available to plants by slowing the velocity of runoff (and consequent soil erosion) during rains, allowing water to absorb into the soil and allowing better root development (Treacy and Denevan 1994: 95).

Soils may also be carried from bottomlands and redeposited behind terrace walls (Turner 1979: 109-111), a practice that adds vital nutrients to the fields. The walls distribute slopewash, often redirecting it so that sediment and soil nutrients are deposited behind other terraces. The rubble fill of terrace walls is porous, facilitating drainage and reducing the possibility that planting surfaces will become waterlogged (Treacy and Denevan 1994; Turner 1983).

In contrast to terraces, which have been extensively researched, berms are less well-known and, consequently, more difficult features to interpret. With few exceptions, berms contained no formal walls, although occasionally they contained footing stones. Nevertheless, their rubble construction, angle in relation to hillslope, and position in relation to terraces indicated that their primary purpose was one of water management. Many berms ran roughly parallel to the slope contour and served to slow the speed of water coursing downhill, thus reducing soil erosion (Dunning and Beach 1994). Other berms ran at an angle to or perpendicular to the slope contour and may have diverted soil and water toward or away from selected areas, depending on need (Hughbanks 1998). The porous rubble construction of berms seems particularly conducive to slowing the flow of water, while still allowing it to permeate the feature and continue with reduced velocity downslope. Support for the interpretation of berms as water management features designed to alter the flow of water comes from the Yalahau region of northern Yucatan. There Fedick and others (2000: 144) mapped linear arrangements of limestone boulders and slabs that helped control runoff during heavy rains and protected cultivated areas. Other interpretations of berm function include their use as property walls, elevated walkways, or stockpiles of lithic material (Fedick 1994; Hughbanks 1998; Tourtellot and Hammond 1996; Tourtellot and others 1993). Because of the variety of configurations berms can take, they should be considered "all purpose landscape features" (Hughbanks 1998: 112).

ACCRETIONARY DEVELOPMENT OF INTENSIVE AGRICULTURE

The extent to which the presence of agricultural features such as terraces and berms is necessarily an indicator of intensive agriculture is open to question. The crops grown in terraced fields and the degree to which cropping was continuous cannot be assessed from an examination of the features alone (Pohl and Miksicek 1995). Likewise, debate exists as to whether terracing represents the introduction of cultivation into otherwise marginal lands or whether it represents the intensified use of lands already under cultivation (Fedick 1994; McAnany 1995). Fedick thinks that terracing represents intensification of farming in areas

of high population density and proposes that terracing occurs not in marginal areas but in highly fertile zones. In contrast, McAnany suggests that terracing of infields represents reclamation of marginal lands. Turner (1983) argues that terraces can represent both the expansion of cultivation into marginal areas and the intensification of production in areas with high population density. He also notes that terraces were associated with yearly cultivation, or at most, only short fallow periods. According to Turner, fallow periods were not likely to be lengthy, because the development of tree roots in fallow-field vegetation would damage or destroy the stoneworks. Moreover, if terraces were not used annually, they would have been economically unfeasible, because they represent a substantial investment of time, labor, and material.

Each terrace and berm in the Far West Bajo area required not only the initial effort and material of construction but maintenance and repair to prevent damage to agricultural fields. The current state of many of these features indicates that substantial soil loss and potential flooding could occur if the installations were not maintained. These requirements must mean that cultivation of terraced fields was permanent rather than shifting. Through soil and water management strategies effected by the agricultural installations, fields could have been kept in permanent cultivation without the erosion and nutrient loss that otherwise characterize upland fields. It is doubtful that individual farmers would have invested such efforts if the fields were to be used only once every several years. The interpretation of some berms as property walls or field markers may reflect a heightened consciousness of ownership and a desire to control improved parcels of land. In short, there seems to be no question that terraced and bermed fields indicate that intensive production was taking place around the Far West Bajo. It is possible that double-cropping occurred, with both a dry-season and a wet-season crop, especially in light of the water control features that existed in the corozo bajo zone (see also Turner 1983).

The establishment of terrace agriculture around the Far West Bajo was not a purely Late Classic phenomenon. In areas such as Río Bec and the Petexbatun, slope management through terracing is viewed as a largely Late Classic development in response to increased population density and pressure on production systems (Dunning and Beach 1994; Turner 1983).

In contrast, in the Far West Bajo terracing apparently started before or in the Early Classic period in response to localized pressure placed on production because of the deteriorating natural resource base. As the populations of bajo settlements grew, the agricultural zones likewise expanded and areas already in cultivation were re-engineered to ensure their continued productivity.

As Turner (1983) notes, it is difficult to evaluate the economic system within which agricultural features participated, because they could have served as components in any number of farming strategies. Many scholars debate whether terraced fields represent the incremental spread of intensification throughout a long period of time (Dunning and Beach 1994; Fedick 1994; Turner 1983) or rather the large-scale, centrally planned construction of agricultural fields (Chase and Chase 1998; Healy and others 1983). One way to address this question is by examining the spatial patterning of terraces. In some locations, the irregular, discontinuous pattern of terraces reveals an incremental or piecemeal intensification of agriculture and likely represents the small-scale responses of individual farmers or smallholder families to the demands of production within their localized resource base (Fedick 1994: 124). In other cases, the orderly, uniform appearance of terraces indicates a well-coordinated program of planning and labor investment; here, the formality and scale of the fields portray the implementation and control of agricultural intensification by a centralized entity (Chase and Chase 1998; Healy and others 1983).

The spatial patterning of the residential and agricultural features of the Far West Bajo stands in marked contrast to both these patterns. The arrangement of features does not support the interpretation that intensive agriculture was centrally planned and implemented. The terraces and berms are not carefully interspersed among residential groups and are not large, uniformly spaced, or regular in shape or size. Nor do the features seem to represent localized, small-scale levels of production. They are not directly associated with houses and do not delimit small farmsteads or house lots. Box terraces, usually interpreted as seed beds or house gardens and associated with individual residential units, are rare in the area. Rather,

the agricultural features of the Far West Bajo are spatially discrete from residential areas and constitute concentrated zones of resource exploitation. As this pattern represents neither the centralized control of agriculture nor autonomous household decision making, I argue that it represents management of critical resources by agriculturally specialized communities.

I interpret evidence for the development of intensive agriculture in the Far West Bajo as an accretionary transformation of the landscape as bajo communities implemented multiple strategies of production designed to utilize the varied resources of the local landscape and cope with environmental change. Whereas residents' initial agricultural adaptation of shifting cultivation led to severe environmental degradation, it also provided an unanticipated new resource in the form of deep colluvial soils at the base of the eroded slopes. The Maya then exploited this new environment through innovative use of terraces around the bajo margins and of berms to manage increasingly limited water supplies in the once-perennial wetland. Limited evidence for the redeposition of organic muck from inundated portions of the bajo to areas behind terrace walls (as demonstrated in Op. V26) provides an additional indicator of the level of intensification of agriculture around the Far West Bajo.

Such intensive use of a bajo's immediate environs has not previously been emphasized in other studies of bajo agriculture. Earlier research on bajos focused on the possibility of intensive wetland cultivation through the use of ridged fields and drainage canals (Culbert and others 1990; Culbert and others 1995; Culbert and others 1996; Fialko 1999; Gliessman and others 1983; Harris and Hillman 1989; Harrison 1977; Kunen and others 2000). This study yielded no evidence of intensive cultivation of this type within the bajo, but it is now clear that terrace agriculture and, to a lesser degree, nonterraced forms of farming using berms to manage runoff on slopes and in small arroyos in flat areas at the bajo's edge formed an important strategy designed to utilize the resources of the dynamic bajo environment. Although the abandonment of the Far West Bajo, along with most of the southern lowlands, at the end of the Terminal Classic period demonstrates that even this strategy was ultimately unsuccessful, it persisted locally for several centuries prior to failure.

CHAPTER FIVE

Bajo Communities

I n previous chapters the description of the Far West Bajo and its environmental and cultural history has been curiously devoid of the people who once populated it. There are good reasons for this, such as the notable absence of any permanent residences in the bajo interior and the heavy utilization of the bajo margin slopes for farming but not for habitation. Here I focus on three bajo communities located in upland areas in and around the Far West Bajo. Two of them, the Bajo Hill site and La Caldera, I studied in depth from 1997 to 1999. The third, Thompson's Group, was investigated by Hugh Robichaux (1995) as part of his research along a nearby transect in the La Milpa sustaining area. Fortuitously, Thompson's Group was situated not only within one of Robichaux's survey blocks but also at the end of my Transect 2 and was thus included in my study.

The three bajo communities investigated share several important patterns. First, ceramic data from each reveal an occupational history in which a small number of settlers colonized each area and founded a community that expanded and prospered through time. Settlement began in the Late Preclassic or Early Classic and increased dramatically until the Late/ Terminal Classic period, after which time the area was abandoned. Second, almost all of the residences in each settlement were more elaborate than the most basic household architecture built in the Maya lowlands. The structures I tested made use of masonry blocks, lime plaster, and furniture such as benches and buttresses, and several incorporated special deposits such as caches into their fill. Even substructural platforms generally featured masonry as opposed to cobble retaining walls and plaster instead of packed earth surfaces. Most structures witnessed multiple construction episodes indicative of expansion and refurbishment through time. Third, each of the three residential zones contained a principal architectural group that was different in size, configuration, and history from the other groups at each site. My interpretation is that the principal groups housed community founders, who played pioneering and central roles in the management of land and other critical resources. I attribute the longevity and prosperity evinced by the three bajo communities to the successful adaptations developed by Far West Bajo residents through generations of occupation.

Of the 679 features mapped in the 8 survey blocks, including the 3 blocks studied by Robichaux, 258 are platforms or walled structures and therefore are considered residential in nature. Another 37 associated features include chultuns, patio walls, walkways, or residential terraces. Throughout the residential areas, the crew placed excavations in structures, platforms, plazas and other extramural spaces, and patio walls. Excavations in residential features served two primary purposes. First, they provided information about architectural style and subsurface construction phases that offered a much more refined understanding of structure types than did assessments based on surface remains alone. Second, they yielded ceramics with which the occupational history of groups and settlements could be determined. Such chronological control provided insight into how settlements developed through time. Together with mapping and survey, these two lines of data contributed to a discussion of patterning both within and among settlements in the Far West Bajo area. In total, 54 excavations were undertaken in residential areas: 34 in 29 individual structures or platforms, 17 in plazas or extramural areas, 1 in a residential terrace, and 2 in patio walls. A set of shovel tests was placed in Survey Block 5 near the large Group 5–B, which dominates the tall ridge in the eastern half of that block. Robichaux excavated an additional seven test pits in the survey blocks he investigated.

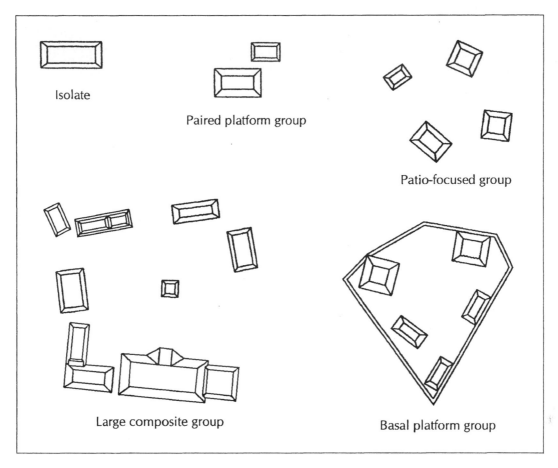

Figure 5.1. Laura Levi's typology of residential compounds (after Levi 1994; reproduced with permission of Laura J. Levi).

Residential features existed in all of the survey blocks, but excavators identified three especially dense concentrations: at the Bajo Hill site in Survey Block 1, located within the bajo; at La Caldera in Survey Block 3, on the gentle ridges northeast of the bajo; and at Thompson's Group in Survey Block 8, atop a steep slope south of the bajo. Below, I describe these settlements using a typology for residential group classification developed by Laura Levi (1994, 1996). A typology like this is designed to facilitate comparison of architectural groups within and among sites by identifying common patterns in the spatial arrangements of structures (Fig. 5.1). Levi's approach contrasts with other typologies of settlement used in the Maya area, which often focus on the layout of whole sites (Adams and Smith 1981; Ashmore 1991) or, at the other end of the spectrum, the specific functions of individual structures (Haviland 1981, 1988).

RESIDENTIAL GROUP AND STRUCTURE TYPOLOGIES

At the site of San Estevan, in northern Belize, Levi (1994: 5) focused on households as economic units and sought to understand the various means used by such groups to integrate both personnel and social space into viable domestic units. In her residential classification, she placed greatest emphasis on detecting architectural mechanisms that served to meld individual residential structures into larger groups. Levi attributed differences in the size and complexity of residential groupings to differences both in the number of participatory household members and in the diversity of household production strategies; larger groups housed more members and engaged in correspondingly more diverse economic strategies, whereas smaller groups reflected smaller households with fewer economic options.

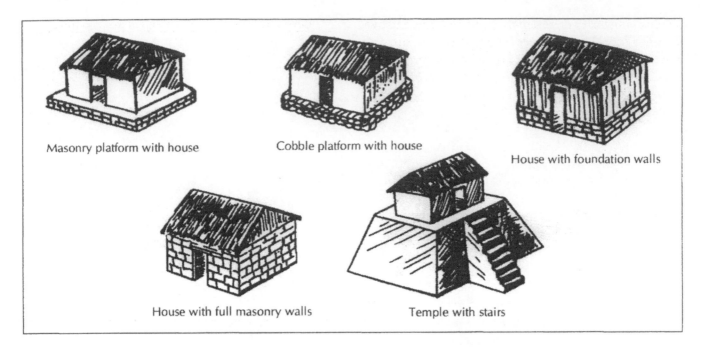

Figure 5.2. Typical forms of prehistoric buildings in the Maya lowlands. (Drafted by Marcia Bakry and Ron Redsteer.)

Levi's (1994) initial classification recognized five classes of residential architecture (Fig. 5.1). Isolates were single structures or platforms that may or may not have served residential purposes. Paired platform groups consisted of two structures that may have abutted or merely shared spatial proximity. In focus groups (patio-focused groups) the constituent structures were integrated by placement around a central plaza or patio area. The patio space may or may not have been formally constructed. Basal platform groups consisted of at least two structures sitting atop a substructural platform and arrayed around a central space. Large composite groups featured a number of structures integrated by a variety of mechanisms, including basal platforms and central patios.

In an effort to distinguish both intrasettlement and intersettlement patterns in the Far West Bajo area, and because I wished to study households as differentially productive economic units, I adopted Levi's typology. In a later publication, Levi (1996: 101–104) simplified her residential classification into three groups: isolates and paired platform groups remained the same, but focus groups, basal platform groups, and large composite groups formed a single, plaza-focused category. Because the composite groups of the bajo communities were markedly larger and more complex than any

other groupings in the bajo and played unique roles in bajo settlements, I continue to use the initial five-class categorization developed by Levi.

For the description of individual structures (Fig. 5.2), I generally follow the categories distinguished by Tourtellot and Sabloff (1989) in their study of community organization at the site of Sayil in Yucatan.

1. Buildings with full-height masonry walls, which may or may not have vaulted roofs.
2. Structures with masonry foundation walls, with upper walls and roofs made of perishable materials such as wood and thatch.
3. Platforms, which presumably supported houses built completely of perishable materials, with either cobble or masonry facing.
4. Temples (or shrines) built on substructural platforms that were squarer and taller than those of other structures. This category is not distinguished as a discrete type by Tourtellot and Sabloff, but is recognized as unique by Becker (1971).
5. Cobble mounds, called chich mounds at Sayil (discussed in Chapter 3, not illustrated in Fig. 5.2).

Usually structure descriptions are based on the surface remains of the feature, which represent the last phase of construction and therefore may not be representative of earlier construction phases buried below the surface. However, whenever possible I base the descriptions on knowledge gained from test excavations. Selected profiles represent excavations of various features and illustrate the more complex stratigraphic examples.

THE BAJO HILL SITE

An isolated cone karst hill known as Bajo Hill is located in Survey Block 1, which measures 13 hectares and is of irregular shape because it was expanded to accommodate the hill's topography (Fig. 5.3). The surrounding land is low and flat, about 108 m above sea level, and covered in corozo bajo vegetation. The hill, which trends north-south, rises more than 20 m to its highest point at 130 m above sea level. It features three distinct crests that increase in height from north to south. The crests are separated by slightly lower saddles. Most of the hill is vegetated in upland forest, save for a thin band of transitional forest at the base of the hillslopes. Two short and ephemeral drainages descend the hill to the east and west. On the east, a berm is positioned perpendicular to the end of the stream, suggesting control of its flow, perhaps for household purposes. Two small pozas sit on the slopes of the hill, one on the north and one on the south. In the western corner of the block, in flat terrain covered in mixed palm-scrub bajo, is an aguada into which three small, intermittent drainages flow.

A cluster of residential features, known as the Bajo Hill site, extends across the slopes and crests of the bajo hill. The settlement consists of 38 structures arranged in 17 groups and structure isolates (Table 5.1). The numbering system begins with the block number, followed by the group letter, then the structure number. For example, Str. 1–M–3 refers to the third numbered structure of Group M in Block 1. Excavations in the Bajo Hill site were located in 16 structures (19 pits), plazas and extramural spaces (8 pits), and patio walls (2 pits).

Group A

Located atop the northern crest of the bajo hill, Group A is the largest and most complex group in the settlement. It is a composite group, consisting of five structures, a low platform, and a set of patio walls cen-

Table 5.1. Description of Groups in the Bajo Hill Site

Group	Number of Structures	Group Area (square meters)	Group Type
A	5	1,058	Composite
B	2	117	Pair
C	3	171	Patio-focused
D	1	49	Isolate
E	2	152	Basal platform
F	3	291	Patio-focused
G	1	39	Isolate
H	2	397	Patio-focused
I	3	150	Patio-focused
J	1	23	Isolate
K	1	21	Isolate
L	1	19	Isolate
M	4	61	Patio-focused
N	2	69	Pair
O	4	144	Patio-focused
P	2	68	Pair
Q	1	15	Isolate

tered around a small plaza. In configuration, this group is a Plaza Plan 2 (Becker 1971), with structures ranged around the plaza on the cardinal axes and a pyramidal structure (Str. 1–A–2) located on the east side of the plaza. The pyramid was disturbed by a looters' trench on the northeast side. A set of low cobble walls connects the three structures on the north and east sides of the plaza, and two walls form an "L" shape between the northern structure and the eastern pyramid. Their effect is to separate a portion of the plaza between these two structures from the remainder of the plaza space. A small opening between the walls forming the "L" served as a doorway on the west side and would have allowed restricted access to this space. A low platform juts out in front of the west structure (Str. 1–A–5) and extends almost to the west edge of the north structure (Str. 1–A–4). Three chultuns are associated with Group A. Nine excavations were located in Group A in three structures and four plaza or extramural areas.

Op. V27

The purpose of a 1–m by 1–m excavation adjacent to a chultun on the saddle immediately south of Group A was to determine if any formal plaza surface characterized this area. Undulating bedrock appeared about 10 cm below the surface. No formal surface existed here, but the shallow bedrock may indicate artificial

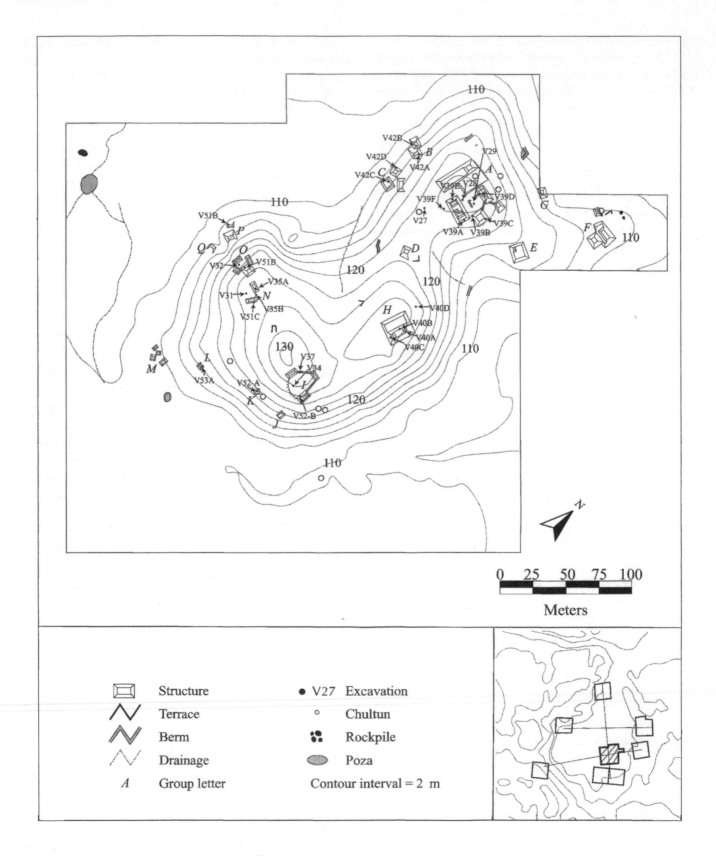

Figure 5.3. Map of the Bajo Hill site.

leveling of the hilltop. The presence of chipping debris, including primary, secondary and tertiary flakes, could represent either flaking activities or sheet midden. All of the 75 sherds recovered were too eroded to be identified.

Op. V28

No formal floor was encountered in a 1-m by 1-m unit located within the plaza of Group A in front of Str. 1-A-1. The excavation ended at bedrock approximately 50 cm below the surface. From chert and limestone cobbles in Lot 3 it appeared that a floor had been prepared, but had since eroded. Most of the sherds were badly eroded; the remainder date from the Early Classic to the Late/Terminal Classic.

Op. V29

A 1-m by 1-m operation was located within the low stone walls that enclose part of the plaza of Group A. The presence of medium-sized chert and limestone cobbles (Lots 2 and 3) above a stratum of even larger rocks (Lot 4) may indicate that a now-eroded plaza floor existed in this area. Two deeper strata, Lots 5 and 6, contained small sherds and lithics above bedrock. In marked contrast to the nearby Op. V28, bedrock was nearly 140 cm below the surface. Many of the almost 800 sherds were eroded, but those that can be dated point to a series of stratified deposits. The top two strata (Lots 1 and 2) contain material from the Late Preclassic to the Late/Terminal Classic. In contrast, the lowest level (Lot 6) contains only Late Preclassic sherds and eroded material. Again, this is markedly different from what was encountered in Op. V28 and suggests a different occupational history for the plaza area enclosed within the low stone walls. This unit is central to the interpretation of Group A as the residence of the founders of the Bajo Hill settlement. The early date of this well-defined patio is an important piece of evidence offered in support of this argument.

Op. V39A

A 2-m by 2-m unit with a 1-m by 2-m extension to the west revealed that Str. 1-A-1 was a large platform constructed of densely compacted limestone fill with a retaining wall of carefully squared limestone blocks built directly atop bedrock. The extant portion of the retaining wall stood 90 cm high. There were surface indications that two superstructures stood atop this platform, but they were not excavated. Ceramics from outside the platform edge (Lot 3) as well as above the platform (Lot 2) date construction to the Late/Terminal Classic; the platform fill itself (Lot 4) contained no sherds. Other artifacts included chert, obsidian, and groundstone, but cultural material was generally sparse.

Op. V39B

A 2-m by 2-m excavation on the southwest corner of Str. 1-A-2, the east pyramid, was extended twice, first with an L-shaped strip 0.5 m wide and finally with a 0.5-m by 1-m extension, resulting in a 2.5-m by 2.5-m unit with a small projection on the northwest side. The excavation revealed an inset corner of the pyramid, defined by a single-course stone alignment atop a plastered plaza floor. Beneath the floor was cobble fill (Lot 4), ending at bedrock. The floor continued under the pyramid, thus predating it. The interior of the building consisted of compact limestone fill (Lot 3). Among the lithics were two high-quality chert bifaces, one ovoid (Fig. 5.4) and one stemmed, located close together near the top of the building fill. I interpret these bifaces as a cached offering placed on or beneath the now-eroded steps of the pyramid. Ceramics recovered from this excavation indicate at least two phases of construction. The earlier version of the pyramid (Lot 3) dates to the Early Classic and a later version (tumbled construction material in Lot 2) is Late/Terminal Classic. These two phases are also distinguishable in Op. V39C.

Op. V39C

Operation V39C involved removing the backdirt from a looters' trench located on the back of the Group A pyramid and screening it for artifacts (Lot 1). Two plaster floors were visible inside the cleared trench (Fig. 5.5); the higher floor had been cut through by the looters, and the lower floor was intact, forming the base of the looters' trench. A 1-m by 0.5-m unit excavated through this floor revealed it to be a thick, hard plaster surface (Lot 2). Beneath the plaster was a layer of loose earth and small limestone cobbles (Lot

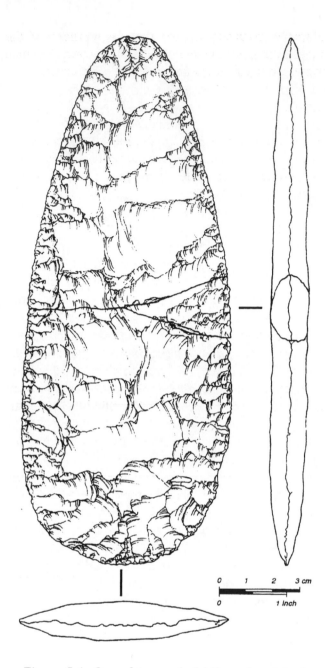

Figure 5.4. One of two cached bifaces found in the Group A pyramid. (Drawing by Sarah Stoutamire; reproduced courtesy of the Programme for Belize Archaeological Project.)

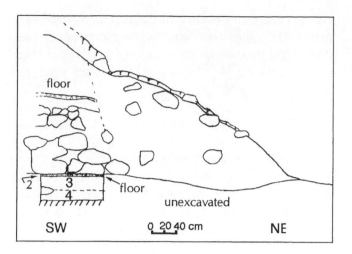

Figure 5.5. Profile of Op. V39C, which cleaned out the looters' trench in the Group A pyramid. The trench revealed two floors, an upper floor broken through by the looters and an intact lower floor.

(which includes two phases of construction) includes a mix of ceramics, the latest being Late/Terminal Classic, whereas material associated with the lower floor in Lot 2, which was not intruded into by looters, indicates that it dates to the Early Classic.

Op. V39D

A 1-m by 3-m excavation on the front of Str. 1-A-4, on the north side of the plaza, was placed at the juncture of the structure and a low patio wall that juts into the plaza. Excavation uncovered badly decayed remains of the plastered plaza floor (Lot 3). This floor led to a small step or narrow terrace at the front of the structure (Lot 4). The terrace was formed by a single course of faced limestone blocks. Beyond the terrace, shaped limestone blocks, perhaps indicating the front wall of the structure, were visible in the north baulk of the excavation. In front of the plaza floor was a compact, mounded lens of earth and charcoal (Lot 5) with abundant artifacts in the fill immediately beneath (Lot 6). This feature may represent (1) a packed earth floor that continued at the same level as the plaster floor, (2) a lens of trash deposited at the foot of the building, or (3) the remains of the patio wall, which was constructed of cobbles, earth, and trash. Ceramics from the building fill date the construction of the structure to the Late/Terminal Classic. Ceramics from

3), ending at sascab (Lot 4), with bedrock approximately 40 cm beneath the lower plaster surface. Cultural material recovered from the backdirt includes human skeletal remains from minimally two individuals (Appendix G). Ceramics corroborate the findings of Op. V39B: material above the lower plaster floor

the lowest layer of cobble fill beneath the packed earth surface (Lot 8) date its construction earlier, perhaps to the early Late Classic.

Op. V39E

The space between Structure 1-A-1 and the west Structure 1-A-5 was the lowest point within this grouping, and a 2-m by 2-m unit was placed on the west end of Str. 1-A-1 in the hope of encountering midden or trash washing into the area. The excavation revealed the other end of the large platform that charaterizes the base of this structure (Op. V39A). In the upper portion of the unit, the veneer stones have fallen off, revealing a core of unshaped limestone rubble in a brown, silty matrix. Lower down, the veneer of carefully faced limestone blocks is still extant. The platform retaining wall sits directly on top of undulating bedrock. In one location, a low portion of bedrock was leveled out with cobble fill and the wall constructed on top. Ceramics from within the platform fill and from the area immediately outside the platform edge (Lot 2) date construction to the Late/Terminal Classic.

Op. V39F

A 1-m by 2-m unit located in the extramural space behind Str. 1-A-1 was positioned closer to the structure than the nearby Op. V27 in the hope of discovering trash discarded off the back of the structure. The fill of the unit, a dark, clayey soil dug in two lots (1 and 2), was rich in artifacts. More than 600 eroded ceramics were recovered, eight times the number from Op. V27 (which measured 1 m by 1 m). The lots yielded many small lithics, including flakes, blade fragments, and two pieces of gray obsidian. I interpret this cultural material as having been utilized within Group A, then discarded behind the south structure. The few sherds that could be identified date to the Late/Terminal Classic.

Group B

Group B is located approximately 40 m downslope from Group A. This paired-platform group consists of two small squarish structures positioned at right angles to each other. The upslope structure (Str. 1-B-1) has slumped considerably, so that the corners of the mounds representing the two buildings overlap in plan view. Both structures in this group were tested.

Op. V42A

Excavation of a 1-m by 3-m unit on the back of Str. 1-B-1 (Fig 5.6) revealed four phases of construction. In the earliest phase, a low plastered platform of faced limestone blocks was built atop bedrock. In the second phase, foundation brace walls were added to the platform, creating an interior room with a plaster floor. In the third phase, the room floor was raised 60 cm, and a second foundation brace wall was built atop the new floor. Lastly, the room was filled with compact limestone fill (Lot 2) and a living surface was created atop the fill. An intact granite metate was upside-down at the level of this now-destroyed surface (Lot 1). The position of the metate in relation to the walls indicated that it may have been left in an outdoor workspace, under the eaves of the structure. Ceramics recovered from each of the subfloor levels (Lots 5 and 6) date construction of all phases of the building to the Late/Terminal Classic.

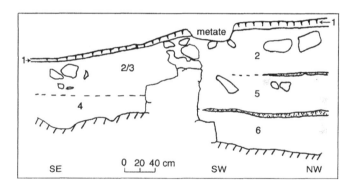

Figure 5.6. Profile of Op. V42A. An intact turtle-back granite metate was found near the surface of the excavation.

Op. V42B

An excavation located on the corner of Str. 1-B-2 began as a 1-m by 2-m unit during the 1998 season. It was completed, after extension to almost 2 m by 5 m, in 1999. The southeast portion of the excavation revealed the corner of a room created by limestone foundation brace walls. In front of one wall was a

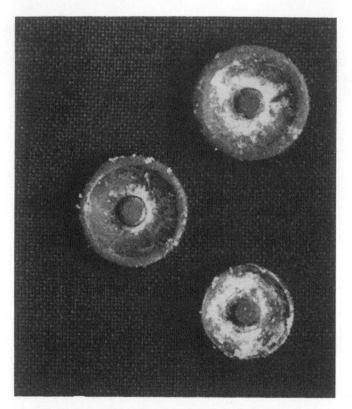

Figure 5.7. Hematite discs associated with Burial 2 in Group B. The disc in the upper right corner is approximately 2 cm in diameter. (Photograph by Heather Knustrom, reproduced courtesy of the Programme for Belize Archaeological Project.)

plaster floor, presumably defining a patio space in front of the structure. The patio floor lips up to the wall, indicating it is a later construction. The interior of the room had a plastered floor as well. At some later date, a large masonry bench, plastered on the top and at least one side, was added to the room. The bench abuts the south and east walls that define the exposed corner of the structure. Two primary burials were inside the bench (Appendix G). The uppermost, Burial 1, was located on the room floor underneath the bench. The skeletal remains were fragmentary, but were identified as a young, adult female lying on her back in a flexed position, with the head facing to the west. A vertical limestone slab was placed as a headstone just west of the head. No other grave goods were associated with the remains. Below and slightly west of Burial 1 was Burial 2; the skeletal remains were on bedrock inside a shallow hole cut into the room floor. The remains were of a young adult, probably male, lying on his left side

in a flexed position, with the head to the south. Again, a vertical headstone marked the location of the cranium. Grave goods included an obsidian blade fragment, a miniature pot, and three highly polished hematite discs (Fig. 5.7). Ceramics from under the room floor (Lot 11), which runs underneath the bench, date the original construction of this building to the Early Classic. Subsequent modifications to the building, including the construction of the bench and the placement of the burials, appear to date to the Late/Terminal Classic.

Group C

Just south of Group B is focus Group C, consisting of three structures facing onto a shared patio space. The crew tested two of the three structures in this group.

Op. V42C

A 1-m by 3-m unit on the front of Str. 1–C–1, the southern mound, revealed two phases of construction (Fig. 5.8). The initial construction was a low platform defined by a double row of rounded limestone cobbles and containing limestone rubble fill (Lot 7). The platform sits on bedrock and has a plastered surface. In the second phase of construction, a trash-rich layer of fill was laid down on top of bedrock in front of the platform (Lot 3) and capped with a plaster floor. This

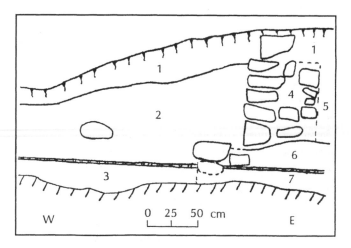

Figure 5.8. Profile of Op. V42C, showing a masonry foundation brace wall built atop an earlier platform.

floor is at the same elevation as the original platform surface, and forms a patio for the structure that was built next. Atop the platform, cobble fill was added (Lot 6) and topped with a foundation brace wall of squared limestone blocks (Lot 4). No additional room surface was created; instead it appears that the original plastered platform surface continued to serve as the living surface in the newly defined room. Of the more than 1,000 sherds collected, most came from the trash-rich fill beneath the patio floor and most were highly eroded. The sherds that are diagnostic date the construction of the original platform (Lot 7) and the patio fronting it (Lot 3) to the Early-Late Classic transition. The subsequent renovation, which transformed the 'platform into a walled building, dates to the Late/Terminal Classic.

Op. V42D

Excavation of a 1-m by 3-m unit on the back of Str. 1-C-2, the small squarish mound on the north side of the group, revealed the rear foundation brace wall of the building. It consisted of several courses of squared limestone blocks sitting atop a layer of clay fill, which in turn was sitting on bedrock. About two courses below the extant top of the wall the stones stepped out, perhaps indicating that the wall was built in two phases. Excavation in the remainder of the unit outside the rear wall yielded tumbled construction material atop a thick layer of bajo clay above bedrock. Of the several hundred ceramics recovered from this stratum (Lot 2), the handful that could be identified date primarily to the Late/Terminal Classic.

Groups D-G

No excavations were conducted in Groups D, E, F, and G. Their features were as follows. Group D was a single isolated structure located on the saddle separating the northern and central crests of the bajo hill. A small residential terrace lies adjacent to the structure on the east.

Group E was located downslope and east of Group A. It is classified as a basal platform group although it is an unusual example of one. The group consisted of a large square platform with a small superstructure sitting atop its southwest corner. There was no surface evidence of additional structures atop the platform.

Group F, located on the slope of the bajo hill near its northern edge, is difficult to classify, but I consider it a focus group. On the north, a rectangular structure (Str. 1-F-1) sat atop a larger platform. A narrow, L-shaped alley of space atop the platform separated this structure from a smaller building (Str. 1-F-2) that faced it on the south side of the platform. A third, small structure (Str. 1-F-3) sat in an offset position on the northwest corner of the platform. A chultun was directly behind this structure, along with a small cobble berm, a terrace, and two small rockpiles.

Group G was an isolated platform located at the base of the bajo hill on the north side. It was 57 m to the west of Group F.

Group H

Atop the central crest of the bajo hill was patio-focused Group H, consisting of two small platforms facing each other across a patio. The two structures were linked by low cobble walls that defined the sides of the patio. To the west, adjoining the western patio wall, was a large platform. I tested both structures in this group, as well as a patio wall and an extramural area.

Op. V40A

A 2-m by 2-m excavation on the front corner of Str. 1-H-1, the northern structure, revealed the southeast corner of a structure, faced with two courses of squared limestone blocks. The alignment was badly disturbed by tree roots. Excavation did not determine whether this feature was the retaining wall of a platform or the front face of a foundation brace wall. The wall was built atop a layer of limestone cobbles (Lot 3) that lay above bedrock. The bedrock in front of it was uneven. It appears that the builders of this structure leveled the bedrock with small cobbles and pebbles, then plastered over this material to form a patio surface. Patches of plaster remained, particularly in the southwest corner of the unit. Excavation also revealed part of the wall that ran along the east edge of the patio. As in Op. V39D, it was a low, mounded feature of unshaped cobbles and earth. A posthole dug into bedrock was uncovered 25 cm off the corner of the structure. The hole, approximately 15 cm in diameter and 20 cm deep, probably held a post that supported the perishable roof of the building, thus creating a shaded patio adjacent to the structure. Abundant cultural material was recovered from outside the corner of the structure, including more than 500 ceramics (Lot 2). Although most sherds are undiagnostic, they indicate occupation during the Late/Terminal Classic. The density of artifacts, which also included three bifaces and two pieces of obsidian, may indicate that the shaded patio served as a work space for residents of the structure.

Op. V40B

A 2–m by 3–m excavation was designed to test the west patio wall of Group H and to locate any trash that might have been dumped outside or at the edges of the patio. After uncovering the outlines of the wall, which consisted of unshaped or semishaped poor-quality limestone cobbles roughly stacked in a matrix of loose brown earth (Lot 1), we bisected the unit and excavated half the wall down to bedrock (Lot 2). Abundant ceramics and a moderate quantity of lithics, as well as five pieces of obsidian and one piece of groundstone, were recovered from the soil outside the patio wall, indicating probable dumping of trash from the neighboring structures. Ceramics date largely to the Late/Terminal Classic.

Op. V40C

A 1–m by 3–m excavation on the back of Structure 1-H-2 revealed a two course alignment of squared limestone blocks sitting directly atop bedrock. Small cobbles and chinking material served to level bedrock and fill the spaces between the wallstones. This alignment represented either the retaining wall of a platform or the outer face of a foundation brace wall for a structure with rooms. Excavation did not proceed far enough toward the front of the structure to determine which it was. Scant cultural material was recovered from this unit, with all but one sherd too eroded to date.

Op. V40D

A 1–m by 2–m excavation placed in a large flat area directly north of Group H was designed to uncover either a midden area or evidence of a kitchen garden.

The flat space behind the mound group seemed suitable for these purposes, but no evidence supporting either activity was discerned. The unit ended 50 cm below the surface at bedrock, having yielded 71 sherds, 6 dating to the Late/Terminal Classic, but no lithics. This quantity of artifacts may be indicative of a midden, but not an especially dense one. The soil was not rich in organic material, as would be expected of a garden plot, but instead was a thin, light brown color (Lot 2).

Group I

Group I, atop the southern crest of the bajo hill, was a patio-focused group consisting of three structures arranged around a medium-sized patio. The three structures were linked by two low cobble walls that marked the edges of the patio on the northwest and northeast sides. The southern edge of the platform was defined by a natural incline. Two chultuns were located behind the eastern structure, which was tested, along with the northwest patio wall and the patio.

Op. V34

No formal surface was encountered in a 1–m by 1–m unit in the patio of Group I, which was dug in three 10–cm lots. The excavation terminated at a large limestone boulder, too big to remove from the pit. Most of the approximately 200 sherds recovered were too eroded to date; the remaining few range from the Late Preclassic to the Late/Terminal Classic. Some 174 pieces of chipped stone were recovered, suggesting that knapping activities took place in the patio.

Op. V37

A 1–m by 3–m excavation extended across the patio wall linking Str. 1-I-1 and Str. 1-I-2. The wall consisted of a dense but shallow layer of chert and limestone cobbles paving the space between the two structures. The unit was bisected lengthwise, and one half was excavated to bedrock 25 cm below the surface. Traces of plaster (Lot 2) indicated that the wall may have served as a low causeway or rampart defining the edge of the patio. A large shell pendant made of a piece of conch (*Strombus* sp.; identified by Alan Covich in 1998) was recovered near the surface. Almost 1,000 sherds were collected from throughout the unit; most are too eroded to date and the rest are predominantly Late/Terminal Classic. Such a density of sherds, along with abundant lithics indicative of flintknapping activities, serves as evidence of trash dumping or sweeping along the edges of the patio.

Op. V52B

Several phases of construction were uncovered in a 1–m by 2–m excavation on the front of Str. 1–I–3 (Fig. 5.9). The structure originated as a low platform with a plaster surface (Lot 8) fronted by a plastered patio surface over cobble fill (Lot 9). A second construction episode raised the height of the platform by half a meter (Lot 6), expanded it forward (Lot 7) and extended the patio fronting it (Lot 3). In the next phase, the platform was again raised slightly (Lot 5). Finally, the landing was filled in and raised to the height of the third-phase platform (Lot 2), and a foundation brace wall defining a room (Lot 4) was constructed on top of the platform. Based on recovered ceramics, the first phase (Lots 8 and 9) of the building dates to the Early-Late Classic transition, with some Late Preclassic fill. Subsequent construction dates to the Late/Terminal Classic.

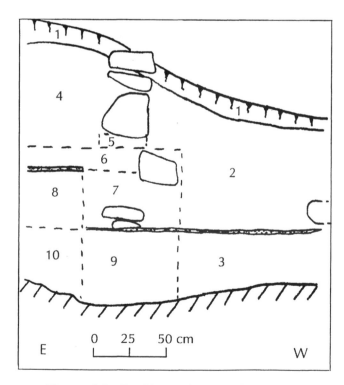

Figure 5.9. Profile of Op. V52B, showing multiple construction levels.

Group J

Group J is an isolated platform located immediately south of Group I. It was not excavated.

Group K

Group K is formed by a small platform adjacent to an unusually large chultun. It is located just south of Transect 1, close to Groups I and J.

Op. V52A

A 1–m by 2–m excavation located on the west side of Str. 1–K–1 revealed a small platform with an ill-defined cobble retaining wall enclosing limestone cobble fill (Lot 3). No platform surface was encountered.

Although the unit was less than 1 m deep, almost 1,000 sherds were recovered, along with three blades, a biface, and a moderate number of flakes. Most of the artifacts came from the topsoil stratum (Lot 1). Many of the sherds were pieces of large water jars, a vessel form that is congruous with the location of this platform next to a chultun; it was probably used as a water collection station (see also Scarborough and Dunning 1995). The few datable ceramics are predominantly Late/Terminal Classic.

Group L

Group L is an isolated structure with a single room. The building is located on the southern slope of the bajo hill near a chultun.

Op. V53A

Excavation of a 1–m by 2–m unit uncovered the northeast corner of the structure, consisting of low foundation brace walls built of roughly shaped limestone blocks. A layer of cobble fill that served to level bedrock underlay the walls. Inside the space defined by the walls was a plaster room floor. More than 200 sherds were collected in this small unit, including 108 from below the floor (Lot 3). Most are too eroded to date; the remaining are primarily Late/Terminal Classic. Other artifacts include a biface and a few flakes.

Group M

A patio-focused arrangement of four structures located near the base of the southern slope of the bajo hill forms Group M. Three structures on the northwest (Str. 1-M-3), southwest (Str. 1-M-2), and east (Str. 1-M-1) share a central patio space. A fourth structure (Str. 1-M-4) is located behind the northwestern building, but does not actually share the common patio space. A small poza is nearby. No excavations were conducted in this group.

Group N

Group N is a paired platform group consisting of two rectangular structures at right angles to each other. The group is located west of the southern crest in a flat area adjacent to the juncture of Transects 1, 2, and 3. Both structures in this group were tested, as well as the space between the two structures and the patio defined by the buildings.

Op. V31

A 1-m by 1-m unit was excavated in the patio defined by the two structures. No formal patio surface was encountered, and bedrock was reached 40 cm below the surface. Aside from 76 flakes, little cultural material was recovered, and with few exceptions the ceramics are too eroded to date.

Op. V35A

A 1-m by 3-m excavation on the front of Str. 1-N-2 was extended at the top to the east and west by two 1-m by 1-m units, resulting in a T-shaped excavation. This unit remained unfinished at the end of the 1997 season and was not continued in later seasons. A well-preserved plaster floor extended throughout the unit. An oval depression in the floor might have indicated the presence of a subfloor burial, but time constraints precluded further investigation. The floor ended at the back of the unit at a short wall, consisting of a single course of squared limestone blocks. The wall defined the back edge of the structure, but neither the floor nor the wall were excavated. Scant cultural material was recovered; the few dated ceramics are Late/Terminal Classic.

Op. V35B

The purpose of a 1-m by 2-m unit in the small space between Str. 1-N-1 and Str. 1-N-2 was to ascertain if any floor or formal doorway existed between the two structures in Group N. This unit remained unfinished at the end of 1997 and was not continued in later seasons. No architectural features were encountered, and cultural material was meager.

Op. V51C

A 1-m by 3-m excavation on the back of Str. 1-N-1 was expanded to a large L-shaped unit with a final width of 4 m. The first of two phases of construction consisted of a well-made wall forming the rear of the structure. This wall, of squared limestone blocks, sat atop a large, rectangular shelf cut from bedrock. At a later time, the room space defined by this wall was filled and a much rougher wall was built to retain the fill. This more poorly constructed wall sat atop the well-made one. At the top of the later wall was a plaster surface, indicating that the structure was converted into a tall platform. Ceramics from this unit indicate that both the original platform and later addition (Lots 3 and 4) may date to the Early Classic.

Group O

The patio-focused Group O, of Plaza Plan 2 type, consists of four structures arranged on the cardinal axes around a shared patio. A pyramidal building (Str. 1-O-1) defines the east side of the patio. Smaller square structures abut the pyramid on the north (Str. 1-O-2) and south (Str. 1-O-4) sides. A rectangular structure (Str. 1-O-3) defines the west side of the patio. Excavations in this group included a test pit into the plaza and a unit on the front of the east structure.

Op. V32

A 1-by 1-m excavation in the patio did not uncover any formal patio floor, and bedrock was reached 60 cm below the surface. Ceramics are too eroded to date.

Op. V51B

A 1.5-m by 4.0-m unit located on the front of the pyramidal structure was designed to confirm the identification of this building as a temple pyramid and to uncover any steps on the front of the structure. Despite excavating to bedrock, this structure remains an enigma. There were two plaster floors; the patio floor (Lot 6) lay directly atop bedrock, and the other was just 10 cm above it, forming a shallow platform (Lot 5). Both floors appeared to lip up to a bedrock shelf that ran along the southern edge of the unit, forming the side wall of the structure. Above this shelf was a ramplike arrangement of roughly shaped limestone blocks, which may have been a badly decaying set of stairs. If so, these stairs were a later addition, placed on top of a deliberate layer of fill (Lot 3) that overlay the platform floor. An intact, stemmed biface and three pieces of obsidian were associated with this floor, possibly as a cache (Lot 4). Both the presence of these objects and the stairs support the identification of the structure, at least in its second phase, as a pyramid, but the evidence is not conclusive. Several hundred ceramics were recovered from the excavation, with diagnostic sherds dating construction to the Late/Terminal Classic.

Group P

At the base of the western slope of the bajo hill is paired platform Group P, consisting of one large structure (Str. 1-P-1) and one small structure (Str. 1-P-2) facing each other with a small alley of space between them. The smaller of the two structures in this group was tested.

Op. V51A

Three phases of construction were revealed in a 1-m by 2.5-m excavation on the side of Str. 1-P-2. The structure featured a foundation brace wall consisting of two courses of limestone masonry resting atop a thick stratum of loose chert cobble fill above clayey soil and then bedrock. Two room floors were associated with this wall. Beneath both of the floors was extremely trash-rich, loose cobble fill (Lots 3 and 6). At some later date, the room defined by these sequential plaster floors appears to have been filled with compact limestone fill (Lot 2). A living surface associated with this final phase of construction was not preserved. A dense concentration of sherds and lithics was on the upper room floor. A small cache of objects, including a

limestone ball and three bifaces, was located directly underneath in association with the lower room floor. Other exotic artifacts included a greenstone axe near the surface (in Lot 1) and a large piece of unworked conch (*Strombus* sp.; in Lot 3). Of the 13 bifaces that were recovered, 7 came from Lot 3 alone. Abundant ceramics were retrieved from both subfloor levels, indicating that all phases of construction date to the Late/Terminal Classic.

Group Q

Group Q consists solely of a structure isolate at the base of the western slope of the bajo hill. The structure is a short distance south of, and faces toward, Group P. It was not excavated.

LA CALDERA

The second concentration of residential features in the Far West Bajo area forms the settlement of La Caldera. It is in Survey Block 3, located on the northeastern edge of the bajo (Fig. 5.10). In this survey block there is a general upward trend in elevation from west to east. The lowest elevations are along the southwestern edge of the block, where the bajo ends and there is a large cluster of rockpiles, and in the northern corner where the terrain descends again toward the bajo. In the western corner, a gentle slope rises up to a saddle and an area of relatively level terrain. Elevation here peaks at 120 m above sea level at a pair of nearby knolls. Several areas of relatively flat ground of intermediate elevation are located in the center of the block. In one of these areas are several berms associated with small clusters of rockpiles. Then, the terrain rises gently to a flat ridgetop in the eastern corner, peaking at 126 m above sea level.

There are 75 structures arranged in 32 groups and isolates throughout this survey block (Table 5.2), primarily on the flat ridgetops and knolls of the east and west corners. At La Caldera, 16 excavations tested 7 structures and 5 plaza areas, as well as a residential terrace, a cache, a berm, and an extramural space.

Group A

Composite Group A consists of eight structures arranged around a formal plaza and is atop one of the

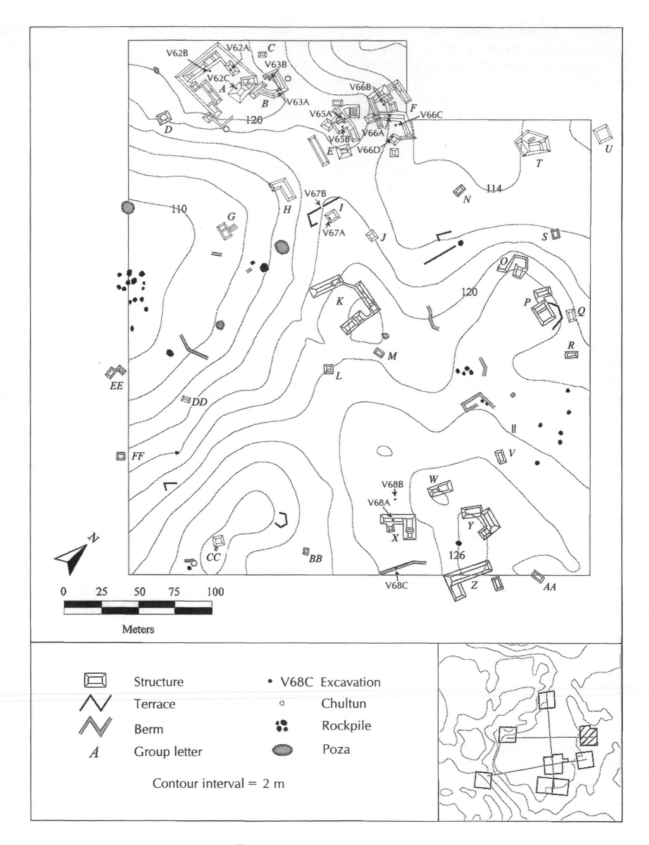

Figure 5.10. Map of La Caldera.

Table 5.2. Description of Groups in La Caldera

Group	Number of Structures	Group Area (square meters)	Group Type
A	8	855	Composite
B	7	226	Composite
C	1	14	Isolate
D	1	64	Isolate
E	8	543	Composite
F	13	671	Composite
G	2	75	Pair
H	1	133	Isolate
I	1	50	Isolate
J	1	33	Isolate
K	3	481	Patio-focused
L	1	37	Isolate
M	1	26	Isolate
N	1	33	Isolate
O	1	113	Isolate?
P	2	242	Pair
Q	1	37	Isolate
R	1	33	Isolate
S	1	31	Isolate
T	3	306	Basal platform
U	1	103	Isolate
V	1	47	Isolate
W	1	116	Isolate
X	2	280	Pair
Y	2	261	Patio-focused
Z	3	401	Patio-focused
AA	1	44	Isolate
BB	1	16	Isolate
CC	1	41	Isolate
DD	1	19	Isolate
EE	2	54	Pair
FF	1	25	Isolate

flat knolls in the western corner of the block. A pyramid (Str. 3–A–1) is on the east side of the plaza, conforming with a Plaza Plan 2 arrangement. Unfortunately, this structure was badly looted, although the looters' trenches revealed details of the structure's architecture, including the presence of two vaulted rooms. A partially looted cache was discovered in front of the building (discussed below). A smaller, rectilinear structure (Str. 3–A–2) is positioned next to the pyramid at a 45° angle. This structure, also looted, is at the northeast corner of the plaza. Along the north and west sides of the plaza are long rectilinear structures (Strs. 3–A–3 and 3–A–4). Three buildings line the south side of the plaza. The three westernmost structures along the plaza are linked by low cobble walls. Just outside the plaza is a small platform (Str. 3–A–8)

directly behind Str. 3–A–7 and a chultun located in the southeast corner. One structure excavation, a plaza pit, and the excavation of a cache took place in Group A.

Op. V62A

Several extensions increased both the length and width of a 1-m by 3-m unit on the front of Str. 3–A–3 on the north side of the plaza. As architectural features were uncovered, the unit was enlarged to approximately 2 m by 5 m (Fig. 5.11). The earliest of several phases of construction was represented by a plastered plaza floor extending throughout the unit, just above bedrock (Lots 10, 18 and 22). A 5–cm step was carved into bedrock below this floor so that, although it was a continuous surface, the effect is of a short terrace stepping up from south to north. In the second phase of construction, a small plastered platform was constructed over part of the lower section of the floor, which then served as a patio in front of the platform (Lots 17 and 21). At some time prior to the next phase of construction, both the platform and underlying patio surface were broken through, and a burial cist (Lots 25–27) was constructed on the underlying bedrock. The cist consisted of seven limestone slabs standing vertically in a shallow groove carved into the bedrock to accommodate them. The slabs were capped by a horizontal capstone. Plaster and chinking stones solidified the construction. Inside were the badly preserved remains of a middle-aged adult male in a tightly flexed position, with the head to the south (Burial 4, Appendix G). No grave goods were associated with the burial, which was badly affected by root

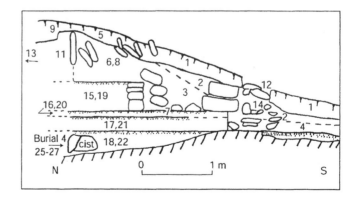

Figure 5.11. Profile of Op. V62A, showing the location of a cist containing Burial 4 and plaster-topped bench constructed above.

Figure 5.12. A plaster-topped bench with masonry veneer stones exposed during excavation of Op. V62A.

action. The patio floor was replastered around the cist, and the platform surface above it was repaired with a plaster patch.

The platform was later raised slightly by a resurfacing episode (Lots 16 and 20), with the new floor about 5 cm above the older floor and transformed into a walled structure. A roughly constructed wall of stacked limestone blocks aligned with the slight bedrock step transformed the structure from a platform into a walled building (Lot 14). The doorway of a room was defined by squared limestone blocks sitting on the floor; they formed door jambs on either side of the excavation. Inside the newly created room, a plastered masonry bench was built against the rear wall, over the burial cist (Lots 15 and 19; Fig. 5.12). The rear wall formed the spine of the building, which had a set of rooms in front and a set in back. In the final renovation, the bench height was raised to the base of a set of large vertical stones, which formed an even higher rear room wall (Lots 11 and 13).

The excavation was not rich in cultural material. Several hundred sherds were recovered, dating to a variety of phases. Ceramics indicate that the first phase of construction took place during the Late Preclassic. Subsequent phases date to the Early-Late Classic transition (Lot 21) and Late/Terminal Classic. Ten pieces of obsidian were collected; flakes were abundant, but tools were scarce.

Op. V62B

There was evidence of a recent campfire (new charcoal, burned batteries) near the surface of a 1-m by 1-m unit located on the west side of the plaza of Group A. Excavators reached bedrock 40 cm below the surface without encountering any indication of a formal plaza surface, a surprising observation considering the formal nature of the group's architecture. A substantial quantity of cultural material, including more than 400 sherds, 61 lithics, and one piece of obsidian were collected, presumably representative of activities taking place in the plaza. Ceramics range from the Early Classic to the Late/Terminal Classic.

Op. V62C

A salvage operation removed the vessels and the remaining contents of a partially looted cache found in front of the large eastern pyramid (Str. 3-A-1). Two parallel looters' trenches penetrating the pyramid clipped portions of the two cache vessels situated in front of the structure. Both vessels had been broken into by looters, and most of their contents presumably removed. Some material, and the cache vessels themselves, remained in situ. Each of the cache vessels carried a lid. Vessel 1 was a large gray, striated cauldron (Tu-tu Camp Striated type), with an unmatching lid of a large Rubber Camp Brown plate. It was situated on bedrock, braced against a large, square limestone block. The vessel was plastered into place by a floor surface that surrounded the vessel. Inside the cauldron were two human femoral shafts, a few small human bone fragments, two pieces of greenstone, three pieces of marine shell, and five pieces of obsidian. One piece of greenstone, of a light green color, was polished, but uncarved. The second piece, dark green, was part of a broken bead. Two obsidian blades were whole; the other three were broken. In addition, lying on the floor and wedged beneath the cauldron was an intact chert biface. A second biface piece was located in the fill above the vessel on the east side. Finally, below the plaster floor under the vessel was a piece of obsidian, a broken biface, and a biface blank fragment. Vessel 2 was a small matte orange bowl with lid (both Pedregal type) above the plaster floor into which Vessel 1 was set. Vessel 2, located west of Vessel 1, was empty. Both vessels were broken, but almost wholly reconstructible. They date to the Late/Terminal Classic.

Group B

Seven structures are arranged around a patio with an extremely constricted entrance in composite Group B, located just beyond the northeast corner of Group A. Two structures (Str. 3–B–1 and 3–B–6) jut toward each other and form the narrow space on the west through which the patio is entered. A third structure (Str. 3–B–7) forms the "tail" of the otherwise U-shaped group and is located directly behind the Group A pyramid. Other structures define the north (Str. 3–B–2), east (Str. 3–B–3 and 3–B–4), and south (Str. 3–B–5) sides of the patio. A chultun, which had a stone lid beside it, lies just outside the patio, behind the northern structure. Two units, one in a structure and one in the patio, were excavated in Group B.

Op. V63A

A 1–m by 3–m unit was later extended to 1.0 m by 4.2 m on the front of Str. 3–B–3. Excavation revealed a number of renovations to this structure (Fig. 5.13). The building began as a substructural platform in the north end of the trench, constructed of loose chert cobble fill (Lot 8) held in place by a cut stone retaining wall. The platform, which was topped by a plaster surface, served as the base for some type of walled structure, as shown by the remains of cut stone walls above the plaster surface. Below the platform was a lens of burnt limestone with abundant charcoal and artifacts (Lot 10). This lens was capped by a plaster floor (Lot 9), which probably formed a patio in front of the platform.

In another construction episode, the plaster surface of the platform was broken through, perhaps for a bur-

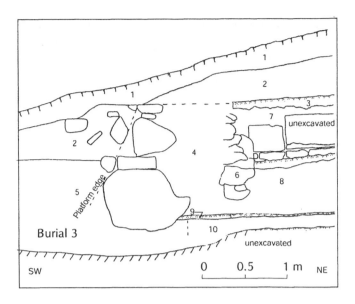

Figure 5.13. Profile of Op. V63A, showing the location of Burial 3 in construction fill.

ial, although none was encountered. Following this, a retaining pen of large limestone blocks was constructed to hold the fill of a higher platform (Lot 6). The platform height was raised to the level of the stone walls that had stood atop the earlier platform, and the surface was plastered (Lot 3). Finally, the entire platform was expanded significantly to the south (although its height remained the same) by the addition of a masonry retaining wall and the placement of compact limestone fill behind it (Lot 4). The expanded platform was presumably plastered, although the surface is no longer present.

In front of the retaining wall was a low stone step, also of limestone masonry. In front of that was a packed earth surface or lens of dense trash at the patio level (Lot 5). Below this stratum a child had been buried in a flexed position, with head to the south, in the construction fill (Burial 3; Appendix G). An obsidian blade fragment accompanied the bones.

Abundant artifacts were collected from this excavation, including almost 2,000 ceramics, 14 bifaces or biface fragments, 16 pieces of obsidian, groundstone, and shell. Much of the material came from the packed earth lens in which the burial was found (Lot 5) or from the burned limestone layer at the bottom of the unit (Lot 10). Ceramics date all the construction phases to the Late/Terminal Classic.

Op. V63B

Slightly below the surface of a 1–m by 1–m unit in the patio, and running diagonally across it, was a limestone cobble wall three courses high. Plaza fill was evident to one side of the wall (Lot 2), but no extant surface was discerned. Beneath the wall was a second stone alignment, running almost perpendicular to the first. The alignment, consisting of three large limestone boulders resting on bedrock, appeared to be a retaining pen for plaza fill (Lot 4). At least two patio construction episodes were represented, with abundant artifacts, including ceramics, flakes, and obsidian. Ceramics date from the Late Preclassic to the Late/Terminal Classic.

Groups C and D

A small isolated platform (Group C) located slightly downhill and to the west of Group B was not excavated. Group D is a platform isolate located south of Group A; it was not tested. A looters' trench disturbed the east side of the structure.

Group E

Group E is the first of two composite groups defining three almost completely enclosed patios. These groups are located on flat terrain northeast of Group A. A long rectilinear structure defines the southern edge of the group (Str. 3–E–1). To the east is a small pyramid (Str. 3–E–2). The west and north sides of the patio are defined by an L-shaped agglomeration of structures and platforms. The southernmost of these buildings (Str 3–E–3), together with a tall L-shaped structure (Str. 3–E–4), are fronted by a large, low platform that juts out from these structures into the patio. A long platform (Str. 3–E–8) extends along the northern edge of the patio. On the northwest side of the group are two small platforms (Str. 3–E–5 and 3–E–6) leading to a low wall. At the other end of this wall is a large platform with a masonry superstructure (Str. 3–E–7) that forms the northernmost structure in the group. One structure and one platform were tested in Group E.

Op. V65A

A 1–m by 3–m excavation was later extended to an irregular cross shape, approximately 4 m long and 2 m wide at the widest part. The excavation was located on Str. 3–E–4, which appeared on the surface to be an L-shaped building. Excavation revealed two phases of construction, along with several floor replastering episodes. The structure was a tall platform, defined by two six- to eight-course high limestone masonry walls retaining construction fill. These walls, one of which ran north-south and the other east-west, abutted to form the right angle of the L-shape that characterized the structure. The east-west wall, although constructed first, did not continue beyond its juncture with the north-south wall. A plaster floor at the base of the walls ran underneath them, defining a patio surface. The rear (north side) of the platform was adorned by a large square buttress or pilaster, constructed of squared limestone blocks, which were then plastered. A large patch of plaster remained on the front of this feature. Beneath the buttress was a series of three plaster floors separated by only a few centimeters of fill (Lots 6–8) that represent floor resurfacings and were not associated with any new architecture. Sometime after the plastering of the uppermost floor, the buttress was enlarged toward the north by the placement of additional squared limestone blocks along the east edge of the buttress. The space behind these veneer stones was filled with compact limestone fill. It is possible that a series of these buttresses, which appear to be decorative, line the rear façade of the platform. Aside from a few flakes and one piece of obsidian, scant cultural material was recovered in this excavation; the fill was rocky, with little soil matrix and many fallen wall stones. Most of the ceramics recovered could not be dated.

Op. V65B

A 1–m by 2–m excavation was later extended to 1.5 m by 2 m. It was located on the platform that extends in front of Str. 3–E–4 into the Group E patio. Excavation revealed a large platform retaining wall built in three stages. The earliest stage consisted of two courses of cut limestone blocks sitting on a layer of fill (Lot 8) above bedrock. The wall is associated with the lower of two plaster floors (Lot 6) found on the inside (upslope side) of the wall. Ceramics from the wall and floor date to the Early-Late Classic transition. A layer of fill (Lot 5) separated this floor from a later one, which may have been associated with a vertical extension to the wall. Finally, a much rougher construction, consisting of approximately five courses of poorly shaped limestone blocks capped by a line of enormous limestone boulders (Lot 7), sat atop the original masonry wall. The boulders appeared to define the edge of the platform (Lots 2 and 3) in front of the L-shaped building. Any surface associated with it, however, had eroded. These later construction episodes date to the Late/Terminal Classic.

The fill above the two plaster floors (Lot 2), the soil matrix between the rocks of the latest phase of the wall (Lot 7), and the tumbled material outside the wall (Lot 4) contained large quantities of lithics (almost 3,000 flakes) and ceramics. Many of the lithics were biface trimming flakes. Other lithics identified by John Olsen included retouched tools and flakes, blade fragments, and unexhausted flake cores. This evidence points to substantial lithic production activities nearby, most likely in the patio of Group E. Residents of this group appear to have specialized in the production of bifaces and other stone tools, probably for agricultural purposes.

Group F

Large composite Group F, located just north of Group E, contains 13 structures and platforms that define a pair of patios linked by a shared structure (Str. 3–F–10) that connects both the east side of Patio 1 and the west side of Patio 2. Patio 1 is almost completely enclosed, with two small platforms (Str. 3–F–6 and 3–F–9) forming a narrow entrance on the north side. The west side of Patio 1 is defined by a tall structure (Str. 3–F–5), and the south side is enclosed by a lower platform (Str. 3–F–4). To the north of Str. 3–F–5 is a short, low platform connecting to a long structure (Str. 3–F–8) that extends east-west and is located to the north of Patio 1.

The entrance to Patio 2 is defined by a small structure (Str. 3–F–2) on the southwest and a low, square structure (Str. 3–F–13) on the southeast. The latter structure is at a 45° angle to the patio. Immediately behind it, east of the patio, is another low square structure (3–F–14). Although square in plan, neither of these eastern structures is pyramidal. The north and northeast sides of Patio 2 are defined by long platforms (Str. 3–F–11 and 3–F–12). A small platform (Str. 3–F–1) on the south between Patio 1 and Patio 2 juts

toward Group E. Two structures and two patio spaces were tested in Group F.

Op. V66A

A 1-m by 3-m excavation was placed on Str. 3–F–10, which separates Patio 1 and Patio 2. Several phases of construction converted the original platform into a walled building with multiple rooms. The excavation revealed part of one of these rooms. The structure began as a small plastered platform with a retaining wall of limestone cobbles (Lot 10). In the second phase of construction, full masonry walls (Lot 4) and a plaster floor were added (Lot 9). A third stage was marked by a resurfacing of the room with a new plaster floor (Lot 8). In the fourth phase, a step or terrace was constructed in front of the front wall. Under one of the large limestone blocks in the terrace, two intact bifaces were cached (Lot 11). Some time later, the terrace was expanded to the west with a plaster surface that covered the original step (Lot 7). A sixth phase was marked by a later resurfacing episode (Lot 6). Finally, the entire structure was filled with compact limestone rubble (Lots 3 and 5), with a presumably now-eroded surface at the top. Reanalysis of ceramics by Sagebiel now suggests that Lots 6, 7, and 11 may date to the Early-Late Classic transition. This tentative interpretation would mean that the west terrace and its two associated plaster surfaces might in fact be the remains of the first incarnation of this structure.

As excavation reached bedrock below the lowest plaster surface on the east side of the building, part of an oval depression cut into the bedrock beneath the structure became visible. The pit measured 2.1 m by 1.6 m and was 1 m deep. On the north end, two steps carved out of bedrock led to the bottom. Each step was between 10 cm and 20 cm high. On the east side of the pit was a small niche carved into the wall; it was empty. A layer of large boulders capped the deposit inside the pit (excavated in multiple lots). Beneath it was a dark, compact fill with abundant charcoal and a diverse array of artifacts (Lots 18–31). In fact, the fill was essentially all cultural, with practically no "dirt" in it. More than 5,000 sherds (many of them polychrome), 19 bifaces, 47 broken obsidian blades, 7 pieces of groundstone, 10 pieces of marine shell, and 44 pieces of animal bone, many of them worked, were recovered from the dark pit fill. The midden inside the pit appears to have contained elite household trash and possibly some sacred or religious items, supporting a ritual interpretation of the placement and design of the pit (Kunen and others 2002). The pit and associated construction date to the Late/Terminal Classic.

In the cobble fill between the middle plaster floor and the pit (Lot 15) were three human interments (Appendix G). Burial 5 was a young adult male in a flexed position, with head to the south. The body was accompanied by a tooth offering, a canine with decorative filing and root carving. Burial 5 intruded on an earlier interment, Burial 6, which was a young adult male, also in a flexed position, with head to the south. Burial 7 was a young to middle-aged adult of unknown sex. The body was flexed, with head pointing north. All three interments were placed in construction fill through holes cut into the floor, which were then patched with plaster. The presence of multiple burials, and at least two holes in the floor, indicate that the pit was visited repeatedly during different stages of the overarching building's construction.

Op. V66B

Unexpectedly, excavation in a 1-m by 1-m unit in Patio 1, the western patio in Group F, uncovered a two-course cut stone wall (Lot 4) with a plaster floor lipping up to it. The feature may represent a step leading into the patio, but no surface was found atop the wall. It may have eroded, as the wall is close to the ground surface. Surprisingly, the wall continued beneath the level of the floor, but no lower surface indicative of a prior construction episode was detected. Beneath the wall was a line of large boulders (Lot 5) resting on bedrock. A large linear cut in the bedrock extended across the unit and was filled with large tabular limestone slabs laid flat in the cut. This cut may have been a quarry scar that was later refilled to make a flat area for construction of the patio. Ceramics from this unit, primarily from the surface layer, are largely eroded. The small number of datable sherds found in the subfloor fill (Lot 3) and in association with the wall date to the Early Classic and early Late Classic.

Op. V66C

Beneath topsoil in a 1-m by 1-m unit in Patio 2, the eastern patio, were several strata of plaza fill, consist-ing of dark, clayey soil with limestone inclusions ranging in size from pebbles to boulders. Bedrock was approximately 65 cm below the surface. No patio surface was encountered. More than 1,000 ceramics were recovered, mostly eroded, but diagnostic sherds date primarily to the Late/Terminal Classic. Lithics were abundant, including several broken bifaces and flake tools and cores, indicating the presence of a work area nearby, probably in the patio itself.

Op. V66D

Excavators placed a 1-m by 2-m unit on Str. 3–F–13 on the east side of Patio 2 to elucidate the relationship of this structure to other buildings (Fig. 5.14). The structure was offset 45° from others in the group, so that the corner of the building pointed into the patio. Excavation revealed that two structures originally existed, but were later joined into one, whose surface remains are now visible. The first of the two structures was represented by a limestone block wall (unexcavated); its face was visible in the east baulk of the excavation. Directly in front of the wall was a second, lower wall (Lot 13) that served as a step leading to the higher one. The two walls were built as a unit, because the face of the taller wall did not continue behind the shorter wall. The structure was separated by a packed earth surface (Lot 8) from the second building. This structure was represented by a badly preserved plaster floor (Lot 9), which was visible in the unit profile but not in the course of excavation.

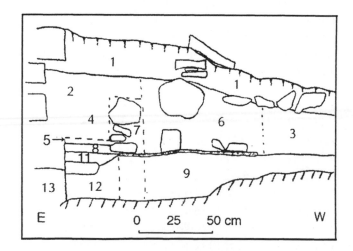

Figure 5.14. Profile of Op. V66D, showing multiple construction episodes.

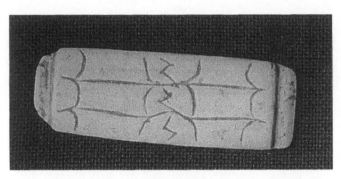

Figure 5.15. A shell pendant found during excavation of Op. V66D. Length is approximately 4.5 cm. (Photograph by Heather Knustrom; reproduced courtesy of the Programme for Belize Archaeological Project.)

Sitting atop the floor, facing the first structure, was a three-course limestone block wall (Lot 7). It appears to have served as a foundation brace wall for a small room, whose floor is represented by the now-eroded plaster surface. At a later stage, a large, thick, roughly constructed retaining wall of semishaped limestone blocks (Lot 6) was constructed abutting the foundation brace wall. The retaining wall served to contain the fill (Lot 4) that transformed the two buildings into a single platform. The surface of this platform is now eroded.

Artifacts from this unit were especially interesting. Abundant ceramics, lithics, obsidian, and some groundstone were recovered, as well as a shell pendant (Fig. 5.15). Much of the cultural material came from the levels that witnessed the joining of the two structures into one platform (Lot 6 in particular). Ceramics date the construction of all phases of the buildings to the Late/Terminal Classic. Chert lithics and obsidian, including numerous flakes, flake cores and one obsidian blade core, suggest manufacturing activities. As in Op. V66C, it appears that residents of Patio 2 in Group F engaged in stone tool production. Several whole manos and fragments of a mano and metate may point to use of the final platform as a kitchen.

Groups G and H

The crew did not test Groups G and H. The T-shaped, paired-platform Group G contains two structures at right angles to each other. The larger structure is a platform (Str. 3–G–1) with a superstructure atop its east half; the building runs east-west. The smaller structure (Str. 3–G–2) is a small platform just north of the larger one. Group H is a large L-shaped platform located between Group G and Group E.

Group I

Group I features a medium-sized, square platform associated with a long, L-shaped, residential terrace. The platform sits atop the level ground created by the terrace. Both of these elements were tested.

Op. V67A

A 1.0-m by 2.5-m excavation on Str. 3–I–1 revealed two phases of construction (Fig. 5.16). The earlier phase was represented by a small platform visible in one corner of the excavation. It was defined by three courses of squared limestone blocks running across the unit at a sharp angle (Lot 11). In the later phase, the platform was reoriented and significantly expanded. A new platform retaining wall, consisting of three courses of squared limestone blocks (Lot 8), was constructed to hold the fill of the enlarged structure (Lot 7). The platform was then topped with a plaster surface (Lot 10) that covered the earlier structure. A one-course step was built in front of the new platform retaining wall (Lot 9). Fronting it was a plastered patio floor (Lot 5). Substantial numbers of ceramics indicate that the earlier platform dates to the Early Classic. The later version also appears to date to the Early Classic and may have remained in use until the Late/Terminal

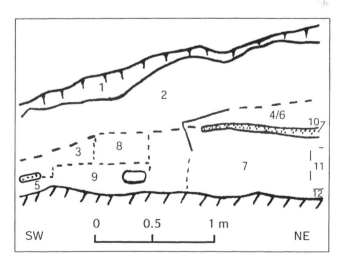

Figure 5.16. Profile of Op. V67A, a platform with at least one phase of construction dating to the Early Classic.

Classic. Nearly 300 lithics from all stages of manufacturing suggest that flintknapping took place nearby, as the debris was incorporated into construction fill.

Op. V67B

A 1.0–m by 2.5–m unit on the residential terrace in front of Str. 3–I–1 revealed that a single-course terrace wall of unshaped limestone blocks (Lot 4) was constructed atop a naturally undulating portion of bedrock. The wall sat in a matrix of dark, clayey soil (Lot 1). Behind the terrace wall was a layer of rocky fill (Lot 2), which served to create the flat land surface upon which Str. 3–I–1 sat. No formal surface was encountered, although one may have eroded. In front of the wall the ground slopes downward. Cultural material was abundant throughout the unit, including nearly 1,400 sherds, approximately 300 lithics, and a number of bone fragments, probably human. Ceramics indicate that the terrace was constructed in the Early Classic and was contemporaneous with the adjacent structure. Much of the debris in the topsoil layer above the terrace wall is Late/Terminal Classic in date.

Groups J–W

No excavation occurred in Groups J through W. Group J is a structure isolate, a small square platform located northeast of Group I. Group K is a patio-focused group, consisting of three tall rectilinear structures linked by low walls. The west (Str. 3–K–1) and north (Str. 3–K–2) structures are lower, and feature at least partial masonry superstructures atop platforms. The east structure (Str. 3–K–3) is exceptionally tall and consists of two masonry buildings atop a platform.

Group L is an isolated platform located southeast of Group K. Group M is an isolated platform a short distance east of Group K. Group N is an isolated platform located east of Group F.

Group O consists of a small, rectilinear structure atop an irregularly shaped platform or residential terrace. The terrace is roughly J-shaped, with the small structure located on the east side.

Group P is a paired platform group. The larger structure (Str. 3–P–1) features a low platform atop which sits a masonry structure. Abutting this structure on the west side is a smaller, L-shaped platform (Str. 3–P–2). To the north of the larger structure is a residential terrace that curves around the north and east sides of the building.

Group Q is a platform isolate situated just northeast of the residential terrace in Group P. Group R is an L-shaped platform isolate located east of Group P. Group S is a small platform isolate located north of Group O.

Group T is near the base of the ridge in the northern part of Survey Block 3 as the terrain descends again into the bajo. It is a basal platform group, with three structures occupying the east side of a large pentagonal platform. The northernmost structure (Str. 3–T–1) is notably tall. The middle structure (Str. 3–T–2) slopes down from the edge of the tall structure to the third, low platform (Str. 3–T–3). The west half of the basal platform is vacant save for a long cobble wall or berm running north-south.

Group U is an isolate, consisting of a large, low square platform located just outside the northern corner of Block 3. Group V is a structure isolate located near a low area marked by agricultural features, including several berms and rockpiles and a small poza. Group W is the first of four groups on the east side of Survey Block 3 notable for their height; it is a structure isolate, a tall building with two masonry superstructures.

Group X

A large structure, an extramural space, and a berm were tested in Group X, a paired platform group consisting of a large L-shaped building and a smaller platform. The L-shaped building (Str. 3–X–1) is tall and features three masonry rooms atop a platform. The structure is oriented so that the apex of the "L" points north. A small, much lower platform (Str. 3–X–2) abuts the southeast side of the larger building.

Op. V68A

A 1–m by 3–m excavation on Str. 3–X–1 uncovered several phases of construction (Fig. 5.17). In its original form, the structure had full masonry walls and perhaps, judging from the presence of large limestone slabs in the construction tumble, a vaulted roof. The front structure wall (Lot 11) featured a lower step or landing in front of the full height wall. A ceramic curtain rod holder was found in situ in the front wall (Fig. 5.18). The walls defined a room space with a

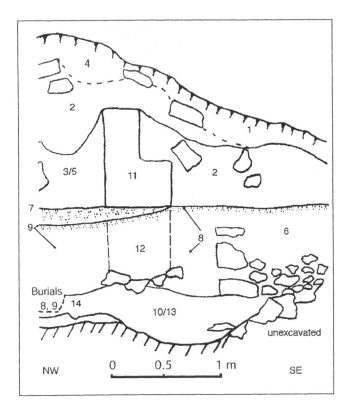

Figure 5.17. Profile drawing of Op. V68A, showing the location of Burials 8 and 9 in subfloor construction fill.

Figure 5.18. A ceramic curtain rod holder in situ in a masonry wall exposed during excavation of Op. V68A. Diameter of holder is approximately 10 cm.

plaster floor, which was resurfaced once (Lot 7). The two plaster floors pinch together under the wall and continue to the front of the building, forming a terrace or patio in front of the structure. At a later time, a cut stone retaining wall (unexcavated) was constructed on top of the terrace floor, and the entire structure was converted into a tall platform by infilling. The surface associated with this platform is now eroded. There is evidence for an early, small platform in front of the original structure, which was later incorporated into the terrace or patio fronting the building. This platform was not excavated.

Underneath the lower room floor inside the building were two burials (Appendix G). The skeletal remains were in the subfloor fill (Lot 9); there was no evidence of a cut through the floor. Burial 8 was a young adult male in a flexed position with the head to the south. Burial 9 was that of a young child represented only by teeth and may have been a secondary burial. No grave goods were associated with the remains, other than the artifacts found in the surrounding fill. Ceramics date

the construction of all phases of the building to the Late/Terminal Classic.

Op. V68B

A 1-m by 1-m excavation was placed in the large, open area northwest of Str. 3-X-1 to determine if any formal plaza had been constructed. No evidence of either plaza fill or a prepared surface was encountered. Bedrock was shallow, only 40 cm below the surface. A moderate number of ceramics and lithics were recovered, but the ceramics cannot be dated. The presence of primary, secondary, and tertiary flakes suggests that flintknapping activities took place nearby.

Op. V68C

A 1-m by 3-m excavation was located on a berm a short distance from Str. 3-X-1. The southeastern edge of Survey Block 3, where the berm is located, is only 25 m from the cluster of features in Agricultural Zone 3 that occupy the northern corner of Survey Block 5. Excavation revealed that a single line of squared stone blocks formed a footing wall atop reddish sterile clay. Constructed above this alignment was a rough cobble wall, approximately three courses high, across the center of the mound (Lot 3). Surrounding the wall was a stratum of small chert cobbles with very little soil matrix (Lot 4). Above this layer was a blanket of larger chert cobbles mixed with black clayey soil (Lot 2). This stratum was surmounted by a thick layer of humus with a high clay content (Lot 1). The berm was extremely trash-rich, and excavation recovered some 1,700 ceramics and 600 lithics, including 7 bifaces and 17 cores. Most of the datable ceramics are Late/Terminal Classic and come from Lots 2 and 4. This berm was near several large residential structures and was unlike agricultural berms in construction and contents; it was likely a trash berm filled with refuse from the nearby structures.

Groups Y–FF

No excavations were placed in Groups Y through FF. Group Y is a patio-focused group consisting of two buildings arranged around the west, north, and east sides of a patio. The north building (Str. 3–Y–2) is the tallest, and forms an L along the north and east sides of the patio. The west building (Str. 3–Y–1) abuts the north structure, but is much lower.

Group Z is a patio-focused group consisting of three structures arranged around the west, north, and south sides of a patio. The longest building (Str. 3–Z–1) defines the west side of the patio. A smaller, lower platform (Str. 3–Z–2) abuts it and forms the southern edge of the platform. The northern platform (Str. 3–Z–3) is spatially separated from the other two buildings, but defines the north edge of the patio.

Group AA is a platform isolate located just north of the north building in Group Z. Group BB, a small platform isolate, is one of five small structures or groups in the lower terrain of the southern corner of Survey Block 3. Nearby are several agricultural features. Group CC is a square platform isolate connected at its southern corner to a low, rocky berm. A chultun a short distance south of the platform is adjacent to a small terrace and a single rockpile.

Group DD is a small platform isolate southeast of a rockpile, berm, and small poza. Group EE is a paired platform group consisting of two platforms at right angles to each other. It is located slightly outside the boundary of Survey Block 3 on the edge of the bajo. Nearby is a large concentration of rockpiles. Group FF is a platform isolate located just outside Survey Block 3.

THOMPSON'S GROUP

The third residential community in the Far West Bajo area is Thompson's Group, located in Survey Block 8, Robichaux's Operation 22 survey area (Fig. 5.19). It is a 9–hectare block south of the bajo but, unlike the other blocks, it is situated away from the bajo edge and therefore occupies much higher terrain. Steep slopes mark the southern and eastern portions of the block, peaking at over 160 m above sea level (180 m above sea level, according to Robichaux 1995: 207). Three stream channels cut down steep ravines defined by high ridges on the north and east. A large berm is at the head of one of the northern channels. The flat ridgetop above the slopes in the southern corner of the block is one of the highest in the vicinity, similar in elevation to the ridge on which La Milpa center is situated (Robichaux 1995: 207). Robichaux did not map topographic relief in his survey blocks, but instead relied on estimated elevations from the British Ordnance Survey Maps. As these maps have a low level of resolution and as there is some discrepancy between these maps and the baseline data from LaMAP to which my topographic mapping is tied, I do not present detailed topographic data for Thompson's Group, nor are contour lines present in the figure.

Robichaux excavated six test units in Thompson's Group as part of his doctoral research. I summarize them here; the original data are in his dissertation (Robichaux 1995: 134–142, 390–402). To facilitate comparison with the data collected by Robichaux, I use his group numbers and structure letter designations, although the survey area number (Op. 22 survey area) has been replaced by the Far West Bajo survey block designation (Block 8).

Thompson's Group consists of 53 mounds arranged in 24 groups and isolates (Table 5.3). Robichaux summarizes the architecture of Thompson's Group by noting that the "largest, best constructed, most formally

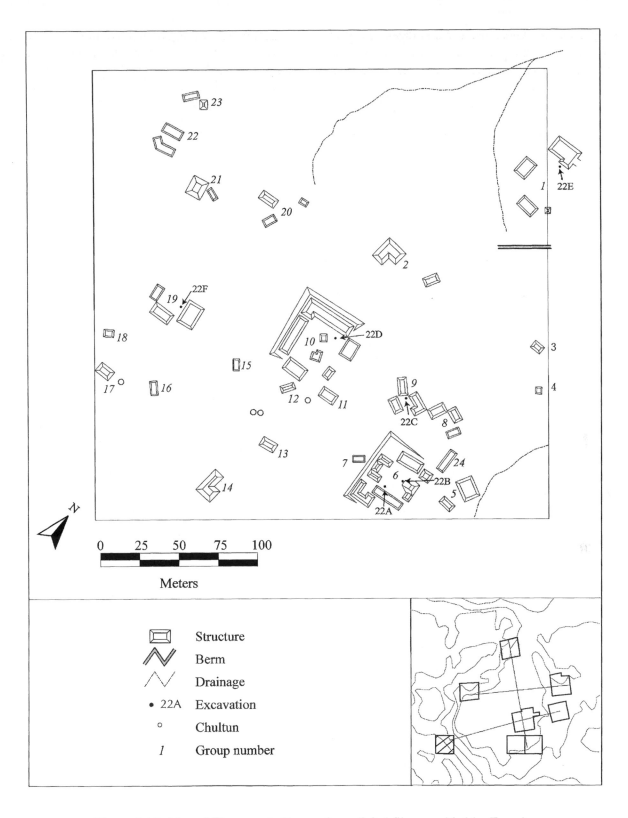

Figure 5.19. Map of Thompson's Group, from digital files provided by Francisco Estrada Belli, courtesy of the La Milpa Archaeological Project. (After Robichaux 1995: 309, Map H; reproduced with permission of Hubert R. Robichaux.)

Table 5.3. Description of Groups in Thompson's Group

Group	Number of Structures	Group Area (square meters)	Group Type
1	5	482	Patio-focused
2	2	280	Pair
3	1	45	Isolate
4	1	21	Isolate
5	2	219	Pair
6	7	820	Composite
7	1	38	Isolate
8	3	190	Patio-focused
9	3	245	Patio-focused
10	7	1201	Composite
11	1	90	Isolate
12	1	47	Isolate
13	1	73	Isolate
14	1	191	Isolate
15	1	36	Isolate
16	1	51	Isolate
17	1	78	Isolate
18	1	34	Isolate
19	3	372	Patio-focused
20	3	153	Patio-focused
21	2	178	Pair
22	2	196	Pair
23	2	87	Pair
24	1	45	Isolate

organized structures [encountered in his survey] ... were present here" (Robichaux 1995: 268). This formality of construction includes a large Plaza Plan 2 group, masonry construction, vaulting, and the alignment of most buildings to the cardinal directions.

Group 6

Group 6, one of two large composite groups, is the principal group of this community, "apparently serv[ing] as the religious/ritual focus of the site" (Robichaux 1995: 268). This interpretation is based on the presence of a pyramid (Str. 6–c) on the east side of the plaza, which is shared by six other structures. Two C-shaped structures (Strs. 6–f and 6–g) define the west side and southwestern corner of the plaza. Longer structures (Strs. 6–a, 6–b, and 6–e) line the north and south ends of the plaza. Two smaller structures flank the pyramid. The presence of the east pyramid defines Group 6 as a Plaza Plan 2 arrangement. Two test units were excavated in this group.

Op. 22A

No formal plaza fill was encountered in a 1.3–m by 2.0–m unit at the base of the east pyramid (Str. H–6–c); it appeared that level bedrock served as the plaza surface. A large ceramic cache vessel was discovered in a cavity carved into bedrock to accommodate it. The vessel, which originally had a lid, contained many cache items, including marine shell, pyrite, obsidian, mother of pearl, coral, and quartz crystals. Other artifacts found in the unit include ceramics, dating to the Late Classic; lithics, including a number of chert cores and flakes; and a carved limestone object of indeterminate function.

Op. 22B

Excavation of a 1.3–m by 2.0–m unit at the base of Str. H–6–e revealed the presence of a low terrace or platform in front of the structure, indicated by an alignment of rounded limestone blocks resting on bedrock. The structure itself was not tested. Ceramics from above the plaza, whose surface is interpreted to have been plastered bedrock, date from the Early Classic to the Late Classic.

Group 10

Group 10 is the other large composite group in this settlement. Two long rectilinear structures (Strs. 10–d and 10–e) border a formal plaza on the west and north sides. Three smaller platforms (Strs. 10–a, 10–b, and 10–c) define the east and south sides, along with two small structures (Strs. 10–f and 10–g) situated at odd angles in the middle of the plaza. One unit was excavated in this group.

Op. 22D

Robichaux placed a 1.2–m by 2.0–m unit in the plaza adjacent to a small structure (Str. H–10–g) that sits in the center of the plaza. No plaza fill or surface was encountered, and it appears that bedrock, which was shallow, served as the plaza surface in this group. Only a few ceramics were recovered, which date to the Late Classic (Robichaux used a different ceramicist and a slightly different ceramic chronology, which distinguished Late Classic from Terminal Classic and also recognized a Protoclassic period between the Preclassic and Early Classic). Three cores were also recovered.

Patio-focused Groups

Several other architectural clusters, including Groups 1, 8, 9, 19, and 20 are patio-focused groups consisting of three or more structures arranged around central spaces. Group 1 consists of five structures and a poza in the north corner of the survey block, adjacent to one of the drainage channels. One of the structures and the poza are far enough outside the survey block boundary as to be excluded from Robichaux's map. Groups 8 and 9 are adjacent to each other and just north of Group 6. Each consists of three small structures facing each other to form a small patio. Group 19 is a similar configuration located in the western half of the block, consisting of three slightly larger structures arranged on the east, south, and west sides of a shared patio. Group 20 also consists of three small buildings facing onto a less well-defined patio space just upslope from one of the northern drainage channels. Three test-pits were excavated among these groups.

Op. 22E

A 1.2-m by 2.0-m excavation in Group 1 in front of the northern structure (Str. H-1-a) revealed a low platform extending in front of the building, which, based on evidence from a looters' trench, had masonry walls. The platform was constructed of cobble fill, but no retaining wall was encountered in the excavation. Ceramics date to the Protoclassic and Early Classic periods. Other artifacts include three chert bifaces and a number of chert flakes.

Op. 22C

A 1.2-m by 2.0-m unit in the patio of Group 9 revealed patio construction fill above bedrock, but no formal surface survived. A packed earth surface may have been present in antiquity. Ceramics date from the Early Classic through the Late/Terminal Classic. The stratigraphy indicates a great deal of mixing, perhaps as a result of tree falls. The construction fill itself appears to date to the Late/Terminal Classic.

Op. 22F

Robichaux placed a 1.2-m by 2.0-m unit on what appears to be a low platform extending in front of Str. H-19-a in Group 19. No construction fill was encoun-tered, however, and bedrock was only 20 cm below surface. Only a few ceramics, dating to the Late Classic period were recovered.

Platform Pairs and Isolates

Groups 2, 5, 21, 22, and 23 are paired platform groups. Group 5 is adjacent to the principal Group 6. Groups 21, 22, and 23 cluster together in the western corner of the block. Groups 3, 4, 7, 11 through 18, and 24 are structure isolates scattered throughout the survey block, especially in the southern corner (see Table 5.3). No excavations were undertaken in either paired platform groups or isolates.

OTHER RESIDENTIAL GROUPS

In addition to the three bajo communities described above, small numbers of residential structures were scattered throughout the other survey blocks of the study area (Table 5.4). With few exceptions, no formal groups of structures were present.

Survey Block 2

Only nine residential structures are located in Survey Block 2 (see Fig. 4.6). Group A is a patio group consisting of four structures arranged around a small patio, with a chultun located behind the north-west structure (Str. 2-A-4). Technically, Group A is located outside the survey block boundaries, but it is clearly linked spatially to the large berm or walkway described in Chapter 4. Groups B, D, and E are platform isolates; Group C is a paired platform group. All are interspersed with the agricultural features so prevalent in this block. Two structures were tested.

Op. V61A

Excavation in a 1-m by 3-m unit on the smallest of the four mounds in Group A (Str. 2-A-2) revealed the retaining wall of a platform in the upslope portion of the unit. It was constructed of an alignment of lime-stone boulders, which served to level the uneven bedrock, atop which were two courses of faced lime-stone blocks. Few ceramics were recovered, but all that could be dated are Late Preclassic. A number of lithic artifacts, including chert blades, blade cores, and

Table 5.4. Description of Other Residential Groups

Group	Number of Structures	Group Area (square meters)	Group Type	Group	Number of Structures	Group Area (square meters)	Group Type
2-A	4	168	Patio-focused	5-G	1	14	Isolate
2-B	1	77	Isolate	5-H	1	37	Isolate
2-C	2	84	Pair	5-I	1	26	Isolate
2-D	1	36	Isolate	6-1	1	14	Isolate
2-E	1	30	Isolate	6-2	1	49	Isolate
4-A	2	30	Pair	6-3	1	51	Isolate
4-B	1	16	Isolate	6-6	1	17	Isolate
4-C	1	18	Isolate	6-11	1	20	Isolate
4-D	1	8	Isolate	6-12	1	90	Isolate
4-E	1	19	Isolate	6-13	1	38	Isolate
4-F	2	34	Pair	6-14	1	38	Isolate
4-G	1	19	Isolate	6-15	1	20	Isolate
4-H	2	52	Pair	6-16	2	351	Pair
4-I	1	20	Isolate	6-17	1	22	Isolate
4-J	1	26	Isolate	6-18	1	10	Isolate
4-K	1	15	Isolate	6-19	1	12	Isolate
4-L	1	17	Isolate	6-21	1	17	Isolate
4-M	1	35	Isolate	6-22	1	56	Isolate
4-N	1	21	Isolate	6-23	1	15	Isolate
4-O	3	138	Patio-focused	6-24	1	16	Isolate
4-P	1	10	Isolate	6-25	1	16	Isolate
4-Q	1	49	Isolate	6-26	2	75	Pair
4-R	1	30	Isolate	6-27	1	21	Isolate
4-S	1	16	Isolate	6-28	1	14	Isolate
4-T	1	23	Isolate	6-29	2	109	Pair
4-U	1	63	Isolate	6-30	1	12	Isolate
4-V	1	25	Isolate	6-31	1	31	Isolate
4-W	1	33	Isolate	6-32	1	15	Isolate
4-X	1	30	Isolate	6-34	1	20	Isolate
4-Y	1	33	Isolate	6-35	1	17	Isolate
4-Z	1	27	Isolate	6-36	1	29	Isolate
5-A	4	563	Basal platform	6-37	1	18	Isolate
5-B	2	647	Pair	6-38	1	77	Isolate
5-C	1	25	Isolate	6-40	1	68	Isolate
5-D	1	46	Isolate	6-49	1	16	Isolate
5-E	1	45	Isolate	7-1	2	69	Pair
5-F	1	33	Isolate	7-2	1	243	Isolate

flake cores were collected, suggesting that flintknapping took place in the vicinity.

Op. V60B

Excavation of a 1–m by 3–m unit on the large isolated platform of Group B began in 1998, but was postponed until 1999 because of heavy rain. A platform retaining wall was revealed, consisting of a row of boulders sitting on bedrock (Lot 5) that provided a footing for two upper courses of rounded limestone boulders (Lot 4). Ceramics range from the Late Preclassic to the Late/Terminal Classic, with the highest percentage of diagnostic sherds from the Late Preclassic. Other artifacts include four chert bifaces and biface fragments and a thick, rectangular piece of shell incised with parallel grooves, which may be a rasp (Fig. 5.20).

Survey Block 4

Block 4 contains 26 groups of structures; with one exception they are all structure isolates or paired platform groups (see Fig. 4.10). Group O, a patio-

Figure 5.20. A shell rasp found during excavation of Op. V60B. Length is approximately 12 cm. (Photograph by Heather Knustrom; reproduced courtesy of the Programme for Belize Archaeological Project.)

focused group, is the only group in the block with any architectural elaboration. It features three platforms, one of which (Str. 4-O-2) has a masonry superstructure. Groups A, F, and H are paired platform groups. All the other structures in the block are isolates. Many of the buildings in Survey Block 4 likely represent fieldhouses, as they are distributed throughout an area dense with berms, rockpiles, and terraces. Two platforms were tested in this block, revealing the kind of cobble construction and paucity of artifacts one might expect in nonresidential structures.

Op. V71A

A 1-m by 2-m unit was excavated on Str. 4-T-1, a cobble platform on the east edge of the block. No clear retaining wall marked the construction of this structure. Instead, the mound contained two strata of cobble fill (Lots 2 and 3) atop a layer of sterile, red clay (Lot 4) above bedrock. The scant cultural material included only a few sherds and about 90 flakes. Ceramics cannot be securely dated, but may be earlier than Late/Terminal Classic.

Op. V69C

Excavation of a 1.0-m by 1.5-m unit on the corner of Str. 4-Z-1, a cobble platform in the western corner of the block, revealed a retaining wall consisting of a single line of unshaped chert cobbles (Lot 4) in clayey fill (Lot 3) atop bedrock. Upslope from this alignment, structure fill consisted of chert cobbles in a similarly clayey matrix (Lot 2). Many of the chert cobbles looked fire-cracked. No ceramics were recovered, so the platform cannot be dated. Secondary and tertiary flakes with signs of retouch and usewear and a number

of conjoinable flakes point to stone tool manufacture nearby.

Survey Block 5

Nine groups of structures are located in or near Block 5 (see Fig. 4.11); all but two are platform isolates. Group A is a basal platform group located in the bajo slightly south of Block 5. Three structures sit atop a large platform, with a fourth structure (Str. 5-A-4) just off the platform to the west. Group B is just outside the block boundary atop the high ridgetop in the eastern corner of the block. Structure 5-B-1 is a large, tall structure sitting on a leveled expanse of the hill, with a low platform (Str. 5-B-2) bordering it on the east and a low wall on the west. A looters' trench is on the west side of the large structure. A large poza with an artificially squared embankment is just off its southeast corner. A short distance downslope is Group C, a structure isolate. Groups D through I are small structures associated with agricultural features. Excavations in this block included two units on Str. 5-B-1, one on a platform, two plaza pits, a series of shovel tests, and the cleaning and profiling of the Group B looters' trench.

Op. V74A

No formal plaza surface or construction fill was encountered in a 1-m by 1-m excavation in the eastern plaza of Group B. There were no ceramics and few lithics were retrieved.

Op. V74B

A 1.5-m by 2.0-m excavation on top of Str. 5-B-1 was placed on the flat upper portion of the building where surface remains indicated a pair of rooms. The unit uncovered part of a large wall extending along the spine of the building. The wall divided the structure into two halves, with rooms to either side of the centerline. The wall was not built of limestone blocks but of compact marl (Lot 5). At the base of the wall was a plaster floor (Lot 3) that formed a landing or hall between the two rows of rooms. A second phase of construction was evident as the rooms were later filled with compact limestone rubble (Lot 2), converting the structure into a high platform. The surface associated with the second phase of construction is no longer extant. The fill of the building was almost sterile, with only a few ceramics and a moderate number of lithics. The ceramics date from the Late Preclassic to the Late/Terminal Classic.

Op. V74C

Just as in Op. V74A, no plaza surface or construction fill was encountered in a 1–m by 1–m unit in the western plaza of Group B. Few artifacts were retrieved and the ceramics cannot be securely dated.

Op. V74D

A 1–m by 4–m excavation on the west flank of Str. 5–B–1, later extended to 1.0 m by 5.1 m, was designed to determine whether stairs or a set of terraces facilitated access to the rooms of this tall structure. The excavation did not proceed to bedrock, but was a stripping operation that removed topsoil and construction tumble. Although construction fill consisting of compact limestone and marl was encountered, excavators could not identify any definitive features such as stairs, doorways, or landings. There were only a few artifacts; ceramics date from the Late Preclassic to the Late/Terminal Classic.

Op. V74E

The crew excavated a set of 40 shovel tests in a regular pattern of lines radiating from Str. 5–B–1 (not shown in Fig. 4.11). The shovel tests were placed at 5–m intervals in eight lines on the cardinal and intercardinal directions, forming a radius of 25 m around the structure. The units were designed to locate trash deposits, because the fill of the plazas and the structure was almost sterile. The excavators were unsuccessful in locating any midden deposits, despite testing terrain that slopes steeply downhill from the crest on which the structure sits. The tests yielded only a handful of artifacts and the few ceramics cannot be securely dated.

Op. V74F

Cleaning out the looters' trench on the west side of Str. 5–B–1 revealed the corner of a room with a plaster floor. The back wall of the room and a doorway that was later blocked were visible. It appears that the wall encountered in Op. V74B forms the back of this room and others in line with it. All backdirt from the trench was screened and all artifacts collected, yielding a moderate number of ceramics and lithics. Ceramics date from the Late Preclassic to the Late/Terminal Classic.

Op. V75B

A 1–m by 2–m excavation on a small platform (Str. 5–D–1) in Group D showed that the platform fill consisted of chert cobbles in a dark, clayey matrix (Lots 2 and 4). No retaining wall was encountered, although slight differences in the cobble strata may indicate the edge of the feature (Lot 3 may be outside the platform edge). The excavation terminated at a layer of sterile clay (Lot 5). The unit yielded numerous lithics and a few sherds that cannot be dated.

Survey Blocks 6 and 7

Survey Block 6 is similar to Survey Block 4; the 35 structures present are arranged in 32 groups, most of them isolates (see Fig. 4.12). Only Groups 16, 26, and 29 are paired platform groups. Of these, Group 16 is the most substantive, with two large, square structures adjacent to each other, their corners almost touching. The remaining residential features in the group are small, simple platforms. Block 7 constitutes an extension to Block 6, as the two are adjoining. Only three structures are present in this block, a pair of small platforms (Strs. 7–1–A and 7–1–B) and a larger L-shaped structure (Str. 7–2). Robichaux conducted one residential excavation in Survey Block 6.

Op. 20A

A 2–m by 2–m unit in the courtyard between the two structures in Group 16 revealed a plastered patio beneath which was construction fill. Many artifacts were recovered. Ceramics are mixed, with sherds dating from the Late Preclassic to the Late Classic found beneath the floor. Nine bifaces and a number of cores were also collected, as well as a mano fragment and a piece of obsidian.

OCCUPATIONAL HISTORY OF THE RESIDENTIAL ZONES

The test excavations summarized above provide ceramic data that support a common occupational history for the three residential communities in the Far West Bajo. In each community, one or at most two groups were founded early in the settlement's history, atop hills or ridges. In subsequent periods, new residences were built close by, often slightly downslope from the pioneer residences. Later, population increased substantially, and the communities thrived. By the Late Classic, the pioneer residences had become the largest and most impressive architecturally of any of the settlement components, containing shrines that were also established early in each group's history. The communities continued to expand, adding new residential groups and refurbishing older ones until a sudden, regional collapse in the Terminal Classic period.

Before presenting the occupational history, a number of cautionary statements are necessary. First, the total area surveyed was 0.798 square kilometers, not a large area, which means that it may not be possible to extrapolate my findings to a larger region. Second, although 14 percent of structures mapped were tested, they were not a stratified random sample and inferences made about a larger settlement area may not be valid. Moreover, the number of excavations sampling structures varied dramatically from block to block. In presenting the general patterns in settlement history for the entire surveyed area, I break down the data by block so that any biases present in the sample are obvious to the reader. Third, more than 80 percent of ceramics recovered were not diagnostic as to time period and the conclusions drawn about the dating of particular structures must be viewed as tentative and sometimes based on extremely small samples. In 2001, Kerry Sagebiel, who was the ceramicist for the project, indicated that identification of ceramics dating to the early Late Classic was still preliminary, and no secure separation of Late Classic and Terminal Classic was yet possible. In spring 2003, Sagebiel reported an improved ability to distinguish Early Classic (Tzakol 2 and 3) ceramics from early Late Classic (Tepeu 1) sherds, but Late/Terminal Classic (Tepeu 2 and 3) ceramics remain together in a single category (Appendix A). Finally, Robichaux's excavations in Block 6

and Block 8 did not penetrate structures but only plaza spaces and platforms fronting buildings, so dating of construction in those areas is based on limited evidence. Despite these caveats, I present a summary of the occupational history of the study area based on what we do know and provide projected calculations of structure densities per square kilometer derived from findings in the sample area.

To calculate structure densities for each cultural period I began with the 258 structures (a category already distinct from agricultural features) mapped in an area of 0.798 square kilometers (corrected to account for structures mapped outside survey block boundaries). From this number, I removed any structure smaller than 20 square meters on the grounds that such small structures were likely to be nonresidential ancillary buildings, such as kitchens or fieldhouses. Most of those removed were cobble platforms in the agricultural zones that probably did not represent permanent habitations. Other scholars working in the area of La Milpa have also removed small structures (usually less than 15 square meters in area) from their samples (for example, Robichaux 1995; Rose 2000; and as Tourtellot communicated to me in 2002). However, I did not follow their practice of also removing from the sample nonresidential structures such as pyramidal shrines because my goal was not so much calculation of the number of people living in the landscape, in which case nonhabitations such as shrines ought to be excluded, as it was documentation of the spread of communities throughout the region. Thus, I was interested in when such religious architecture became a component of the communities included in the study.

Following these adjustments, 233 structures remained in the sample. From this number, I subtracted 10 percent to cover disuse and lack of contemporaneity among structures. Although somewhat arbitrary, I chose this number because other scholars working at La Milpa used it as well and one of my goals was to seek comparability among data sets from various scholars. Unlike my colleagues, however, I added back to the sample a small percentage (5.5%) to account for buried structures that were not visible on the surface. The question of "invisible" housemounds remains contentious in Maya settlement pattern studies, but I made this correction to the raw data because 3 of the 54 residential zone excavations revealed evidence of mounds that were not visible on the surface. In two cases (Op. V65A and Op. V66D), excavation showed the presence of two structures where only one was apparent on the surface, and in one case (Op. V66B) a buried platform was revealed in a plaza test pit. With these two corrections, the sample contained 222 structures in 0.789 square kilometers, or 278 structures per square kilometer. From this maximum, I calculated the percentage of structures present on the landscape during each chronological period. The presence of diagnostic ceramics (minimally one sherd) in structure fill or associated midden is interpreted as indicating occupation of that or a nearby structure during that period (since the material was produced somewhere and is not likely to have traveled far). Only diagnostic ceramics in subfloor or otherwise sealed contexts are interpreted as dating construction episodes. By presenting projected structure densities based on both occupation and construction, I provide liberal and conservative estimates for the reader to assess. These estimates are based on 61 excavations (including Robichaux's) in residential groups that tested 29 individual structures and additional associated features.

Late Preclassic
400 B.C.–A.D. 250

Twenty-eight test excavations, including 21 in individual structures, contained Late Preclassic ceramics in construction fill, suggesting occupation at this time. These structures were widely dispersed throughout Blocks 1 through 6. Only two structures (6.9%) and one patio had construction phases dating to the Late Preclassic: the walled patio in Group A in the Bajo Hill site, Str. 3-A-3 at La Caldera, and Str. 2-A-2 in Survey Block 2, indicating the presence of early settlers in each of these locations. Interestingly, Str. 2-A-2 was occupied only during this period and contained no later ceramic material. All other structures that contained Late Preclassic material also contained later ceramics. If a figure of 72 percent of structures mapped (21 of 29 structures tested) is used to calculate Late Preclassic structure density, then a total of 200 structures per square kilometer may be estimated for this period. A much more conservative estimate is based on the percentage of structures with Late Preclassic construction. Using the 6.9 percent figure, 19 structures per square kilometer would have

been built during this period, dispersed throughout the area on ridgetops, knolls, and hilltops.

Early Classic
A.D. 250–600

Thirty-eight test excavations (62% of the total), including those in 24 structures, contained Early Classic ceramic material, indicating denser occupation than in the preceding period. Early Classic material is most common at the Bajo Hill site and at La Caldera. At the Bajo Hill site, the small pyramidal shrine (Str. 1-A-2) in Group A has an Early Classic construction phase. The construction of the shrine during this time indicates both the development of nonresidential architecture at the settlement and the beginning of construction that distinguished Group A (which in final form was a large composite group) from the other groups. Structure 2 in Group B and Structure 1 in Group N were also built at this time. At La Caldera, a small Early Classic platform in Group I was a short distance from Group A. The accompanying residential terrace also had an Early Classic component. One structure (Str. H-1-a in Group 1) tested by Robichaux in Thompson's Group reportedly had an Early Classic construction date, and Early Classic material occurred in Str. H-6-e in Group 6, a Plaza Plan 2 group, suggesting to Robichaux construction of the group in the Early Classic.

If the figure of 83 percent is used (24 of 29 structures tested), a total of 230 structures per square kilometer may be postulated for occupation during the Early Classic. If a more conservative number is used based on datable construction episodes (4 of 29), then 38 structures per square kilometer may have been built at this time. Some structures would represent continued occupation of Late Preclassic settlement locations, particularly those groups on hilltops and knolls, and others would indicate establishment of new groups a short distance away from the pioneers. A few Late Preclassic structures may have been abandoned during the Early Classic, based on the example from Survey Block 2. The estimates for Early Classic occupation are somewhat surprising, as previous discussions of settlement in the La Milpa sustaining area have noted a decline in population following the Late Preclassic, before a sharp increase in the Late Classic (Tourtellot and others 1997). Based in part on a refined understanding of the ceramic sequence at La Milpa, sherds diagnostic of the Early Classic are now more easily classified, and occupation dating to this period is more accurately identified (Appendix A; see also Kosakowsky and Sagebiel 1999).

Early Late Classic
A.D. 600–750

Populations in the Far West Bajo area maintained themselves during the transition from the Early Classic to the Late Classic period. Of structures tested, 83 percent (24 of 29 structures) contained early Late Classic ceramic material in construction fill. Three new structures at Bajo Hill contain early Late Classic construction: the north structure (Str. 1–A–4) in Group A, Structure 1 in Group C, and the east structure (Str. 1–I–3) in Group I. La Caldera and Survey Block 4 each featured units with early Late Classic construction levels: a version of La Caldera's Str. 3–A–3 in Group A and Patio 1 in Group F date to this period, and in Block 4 a small cobble platform (Str. 4–T–1) near the edge of the bajo may have been constructed in the early Late Classic. When extrapolated, calculations indicate 230 structures per square kilometer with occupation in the early Late Classic or 48 structures per square kilometer constructed during this period. This number suggests the continuation of populations from the preceding periods, the enlargement and rebuilding of existing settlement nodes, and the establishment of new residential groups.

Late/Terminal Classic
A.D. 750–850

As in most areas of the Maya lowlands, the Late/Terminal Classic period marks the greatest extent of structures occupied and, by inference, the densest population. More than 93 percent of structures in the study area contain Late/Terminal Classic material, and 19 of 29 structures (65.5%) tested feature sealed Late/Terminal Classic construction levels. All structures tested at the Bajo Hill site and La Caldera were occupied at this time, and this pattern is likely to be prevalent elsewhere. The percentage of structures constructed is lower than expected, because eroded surfaces in many buildings prevented definite identification of sealed Late/Terminal Classic deposits, even

though ceramics of this period were abundant in the upper levels of most excavations. Calculations estimate that 258 structures per square kilometer would have been in use during the Late/Terminal Classic period in this area. Alternatively, based on the 65.5 percent figure I calculate for construction levels, 182 structures per square kilometer would have been built during this period. This number seems large, but it is corroborated by Robichaux's surveys along the PfB border, which estimated 100 Late Classic residential structures in seven survey blocks of 0.09 square kilometers each. This calculation includes the three survey blocks incorporated into this study, but the 65.5 percent figure above is calculated only on my excavations and excludes those by Robichaux (since they were not in structures), hence the two samples do not overlap. For Robichaux's (1995) work, this yields an estimate of 161 residential structures per square kilometer, similar to the number I project. Rose (2000) calculated almost 160 dwellings per square kilometer (excluding shrines) for the La Milpa sustaining area during the Late/Terminal Classic, also similar to the figure I derive. These numbers indicate that settlement in the Far West Bajo area reached its fullest extent, with groups at maximum size, during the Late/Terminal Classic. This period witnessed the establishment of many small residential groups near the larger, earlier groups. Most residents continued to occupy ridges, hilltops, and knolls, although some lived on lower slopes. No ceramics have been recorded dating later than the Late/Terminal Classic, signifying a total abandonment of the Far West Bajo area at the end of the Terminal Classic.

The occupation and construction data for residential structures according to survey block are in Table 5.5. Figure 5.21 presents a summary of three related calculations. The first is the percentage of all my excavations in residential features, including those in structures and in associated features such as plazas and patio walls, that contain ceramic material dating to each of the four ceramic periods. The second and third calculations focus on excavations in structures only. The second provides the percentage of structure excavations that yielded evidence for occupation in each of the four periods. The third presents the percentage of structures that featured construction episodes dating to each of the four periods. Then, based on Figure 5.21 and the 0.798-square-kilometer sample

Table 5.5. Occupational History of Residential Structures

Survey Block #	Total no. of structures	Structures tested	Late Preclassic Occupation	Construction	Early Classic Occupation	Construction	Early Late Classic Occupation	Construction	Late/Terminal Classic Occupation	Construction
1	38	16	11	(+1)	13	3	14	3	16	10
2	9	2	2	1	1		1		1	1
3	75	7	5	1	7	1 (+1)	7	1 (+1)	7	6
4	31	2	1		1		1	1	1	1
5	13	2	2		2		1		2	1
Total	166	29	21	2 (+1)	24	4 (+1)	24	5 (+1)	27	19 (+7)

NOTE. Numbers in parentheses indicate additional contexts in which ceramics came from construction of a terrace, plaza, or patio wall.

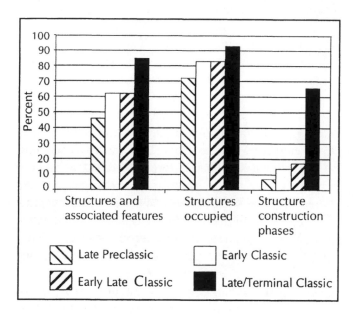

Figure 5.21. Residential occupation by chronological period.

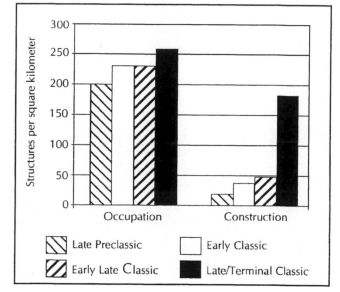

Figure 5.22. Projected structure density by chronological period.

area, Figure 5.22 extrapolates the structure calculations and projects structure occupation per square kilometer and structure construction per square kilometer. In both of these figures, the numbers for structures constructed are by far the more conservative and are likely to be the more realistic representation of the settlement history of the Far West Bajo.

Measures of Architectural Complexity

The next pattern I explore concerns comparative measures of architectural complexity among residential groups in the three bajo communities. To assess residential architecture, I follow Haviland (1985; see also Arnold and Ford 1980), whose excavations in small structures at Tikal revealed residences that lacked the richness in luxury items and elaborate architecture of the large buildings of the city center, but featured solid construction, a moderate quantity of luxury goods, and some evidence for artisanal specialization. Haviland concluded that residents of the structures he studied were neither members of the Tikal elite nor occupants of the bottom of the social scale; rather, they occupied a middle position. I examine several measures of architectural complexity that describe the construction present in the residential zones that lead me to conclude that, as at suburban Tikal, residents of the bajo communities, while not political elites, devoted some of their economic resources to embellishing their homes with furnishings, structural improvements, and exotic goods. The architectural measures of complexity

Table 5.6. Types of Groups in Far West Bajo Residential Zones

Group Type	Bajo Hill Site (N, 17)	La Caldera (N, 32)	Thompson's Group (N, 24)	Other (N, 74)
Composite	1	4	2	
Paired Platform	3	4	5	10
Patio-Focused	6	3	5	2
Basal Platform	1	1		1
Isolate	6	20	12	61

NOTE: N is the number of residential groups in each settlement.

Table 5.7. Architectural Features Among Excavated Residential Structures

Feature	Bajo Hill Site (N, 16)	La Caldera (N, 7)	Other (N, 6)
Masonry Platform	2	1	
Partial Walls	7	3	
Full Walls		3	1
Vaulting		2	
Plastering	10	7	1
Furniture	1	2	
Special Deposit	5	5	

NOTE: N is the number of structures tested in each settlement.

demonstrate both a marked degree of elaboration among the residential zones as a class, as well as important variability within them.

The architectural complexity of the three bajo communities can be assessed in several ways. First, the group typology that I constructed for each settlement based on survey data not only evaluates the degree of integration of each residential group (which was Levi's intended use in 1994 and 1996) but also measures the presence or absence of multiple residences, exterior workspaces, public areas, and shrines. These features are all indicators of the number of residential members in the group and of investment of economic resources in domestic spaces (Table 5.6; see also Arnold and Ford 1980). As illustrated here, many groups in the residential zones are classed as composite, paired platform, patio-focused, or basal platform groups. Approximately 65 percent, 38 percent, and 50 percent of the groups at the Bajo Hill site, La Caldera, and Thompson's Group, respectively, integrated more than one structure and a variety of other features like patios, basal platforms, and patio walls. In contrast, only 18 percent of residential groups elsewhere in the study area featured such additional elements, and 82 percent were structure isolates.

Second, architectural complexity can be examined through excavation data by looking at investment in construction elements such as masonry walls and vaulting, furniture like benches and buttresses, decorative additions (plastering and painting), and special deposits such as burials and caches. Each of these features represents a labor and material investment beyond the level of basic subsistence. As such, each provides evidence of the ability of residents to marshal economic resources and display them in a conspicuous manner. Arnold and Ford (1980) noted that, together,

group size and architectural complexity measure the total labor investment in residential construction, thereby reflecting social status. Similarly, Haviland (1985) wrote that construction style and structure plan are important criteria for comparative analysis of residential features. He focused particularly on floors, walls, and the contents of fill to evaluate the status of the residents of structures he tested at Tikal. Haviland's use of structure volume, area, height, details of architecture, and presence of caches and burials to identify structures that may have housed family leaders or other administrators is similar to the evaluations in Table 5.7.

Of the 16 structures tested at the Bajo Hill site, the most common type had partial masonry walls (foundation brace walls) and a plaster floor. At La Caldera, of the seven structures tested, one was a tall multiroomed structure with a decorative marl buttress, and six others had either partial or full masonry walls. Two provided evidence of vaulted roofs and all featured plaster floors. No quantitative assessment can be made of Thompson's Group, because Robichaux did not excavate structures, but based on surface indications he reported the presence of partial masonry walls, full masonry walls, or vaulting for 32 of the structures at the site. In contrast, of the six structures tested in other parts of the Far West Bajo study area, only one, the large, looted Str. 5–B–1, provided evidence of any architectural elaboration. All the other structures were cobble platforms with or without well-defined retaining walls.

A third architectural measure of complexity is the number of rebuilding episodes in a given structure. Residents of Maya structures frequently refurbished and expanded them through time. Such episodes are

Table 5.8. Construction Episodes Among Excavated Residential Structures

Number of Episodes	Bajo Hill Site (N, 16)	La Caldera (N, 7)	Other (N, 6)
One	5		5
Two	4	1	1
More than two	5	6	
Unknown	2		

NOTE: N is the number of structures tested in each settlement.

evidence not only of long-standing occupation but also of increasing household size and prosperity, which enabled the residential unit to expand and improve its domicile (Table 5.8). Fifty-six percent of the structures tested at the Bajo Hill site were refurbished, usually in a conversion from a platform with masonry retaining walls and a perishable superstructure to a partially stone-walled structure with an interior room and a perishable roof. All of the structures tested at La Caldera were built in at least two phases and most underwent several renovations, which included such elaborations as construction of benches, replastering of floors, or conversion of walled structures into tall masonry platforms. In contrast, only one of the six structures tested elsewhere in the Far West Bajo study area was built in two phases, the unique Str. 5-B-1. All others are single phase platforms.

These measures of architectural complexity indicate that residents of Bajo Hill, La Caldera, and Thompson's Group built complex residences and maintained ancillary structures such as shrines and kitchens in their residential complexes. They constructed houses with masonry walls, benches, and plaster floors, decorated them with buttresses and painted walls, and renovated and expanded their residences with frequency. All of the evidence points to a substantial degree of prosperity and longevity throughout the residential zones. But there is also important variation among the groups in each zone. Most notably, each of the three settlements contains a composite group that is substantially larger than the others in that community (Fig. 5.23). As illustrated in Table 5.9, each of these "principal groups" is roughly three to six times larger than the average group size in each residential zone. Thompson's Group expresses a variant of this pattern. Group 6 is smaller in overall area than Group 10, but the individual structures are larger, taller, and more imposing. Robichaux interprets Group 10 as the resi-

Table 5.9. Average Group Size and Principal Group Size in Residential Zones

Residential Zone	Average Group Size (square m)	Principal Group Size (square m)	Difference Factor
Bajo Hill Site	167	1,058	6.34
La Caldera	144	855	5.93
Thompson's Group	223	820	3.68

dential center of the settlement and Group 6 as the administrative/ritual center. I therefore consider Group 6 to be the principal group at the site.

Each of the three principal groups integrated between five and eight structures. All three featured a pyramidal temple on the east side of the plaza, and at least two of the groups (Group A at La Caldera and Group 6 at Thompson's Group) contained vaulted buildings. Based on the size and complexity of these architectural groups, there is evidence for important internal differentiation within each of the three settlements.

That these large composite groups were also the earliest residences established is evident from the ceramic data. All three bajo communities yielded ceramic evidence indicating that settlement began by the Late Preclassic or Early Classic and continued into the Late/Terminal Classic. Occupational histories differed, however, in different parts of each settlement. At both Bajo Hill and La Caldera, Late Preclassic construction is documented only in the principal groups (Table 5.10). The Early Classic is represented only in

Table 5.10. Construction Episodes in Excavated Residential Groups by Time Period

Time Period	Bajo Hill Site (N, 10)	La Caldera (N, 6)	Thompson's Group (N, 6)	Other (N, 5)
Late Preclassic	1	1		1
Early Classic	3	2	3	
Early Late Classic	3	2	2	1
Late/Term. Classic	10	6	5	3

NOTE: N is the number of structures with datable construction episodes in each settlement. No direct evidence is available for Thompson's Group, because Robichaux did not excavate in structures; his data pertain to excavations in plazas and front platforms. Early Late Classic construction episodes are inferred from Robichaux's notes, where he reported ceramics ranged from the Early Classic to the Late Classic.

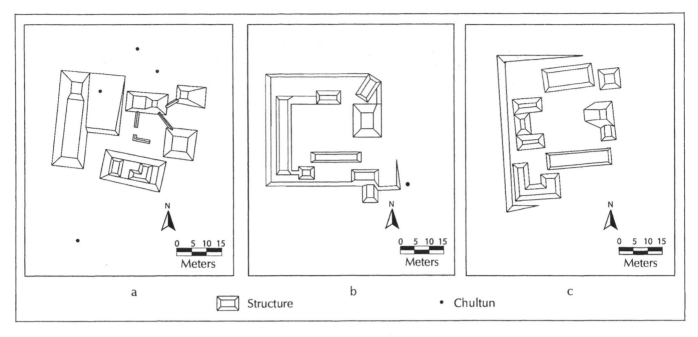

Figure 5.23. Principal architectural groups: *a*, Bajo Hill site; *b*, La Caldera; *c*, Thompson's Group. (Drafted by Ron Redsteer and Nicole Kilburn. Thompson's Group reproduced with permission of Hubert R. Robichaux; digital file provided by Francisco Estrada Belli, courtesy of the La Milpa Archaeological Project.)

these groups and one or two additional groups in each settlement. All other groups at Bajo Hill and La Caldera dated to the early Late Classic or Late/Terminal Classic. These data indicate that the largest groups were also the earliest to be occupied. Thompson's Group is not easily assessed because Robichaux did not excavate in structures, only plaza spaces and front platforms. He did report Early Classic ceramics in Group 6 and in two other groups, only one of which also yielded later material. Group 6 excavations contained ceramics dating from the Early Classic through the Late/Terminal Classic.

RESIDENTIAL ZONES IN RETROSPECT

The excavation and survey data from the Far West Bajo indicate that the residents of the settlements studied were neither urban elites nor poor rural dwellers. All of the Far West Bajo survey blocks were located between 1.5 km and 3.8 km (1–2.4 miles) from the main plaza at La Milpa. Tourtellot (Tourtellot and others 1997) suggests that the drop-off in settlement density he encountered at approximately 5 km (3.1 miles) along the LaMAP transects emanating from La

Milpa center marks the shift from suburban to rural settlement zones. If so, then all of the Far West Bajo study area should be considered part of La Milpa's suburbs and not the rural hinterland. Hence, the residential structures and agricultural features studied here should be comparable to those investigated elsewhere in the La Milpa sustaining area by Gair Tourtellot and his colleagues (1994, 1997, 1999) and John Rose (2000), among others (for example, Everson 2003). The patterns I document among Far West Bajo communities and the bajo agricultural zones are generally similar to those throughout the area surrounding La Milpa center, but there are some notable differences. For example, Tourtellot and others (1994) report a general pattern in their transects and survey blocks in which terraces and berms are situated on low slopes and often share space with small, informal mounds that appear to be of the same cobble construction as the agricultural features. More formal architectural groups occurred almost exclusively on hilltops, similar to the use zones I documented in this and earlier chapters. However, the LaMAP researchers also documented a pattern in which a single hill features both formal architecture on the hilltop and terraces and berms on the hillslope. In contrast, I observed a more dramatic spatial separation between residential and agricultural zones. Neither the Bajo Hill site, La Caldera, nor Thompson's Group is situated on a hill or ridge that also features substantial terracing or berms. Similarly, the ridgetops located above two of the agricultural zones, in Survey Blocks 2 and 5, contained at most a patio group or single large mound but did not feature large nodes of architecture.

Rose (2000) reports that excavations throughout his survey blocks in the 3–km (1.9–mile) radius immediately surrounding La Milpa yielded evidence for almost entirely Late Classic occupation. In his analysis, ceramics were divided into early and late categories around the A.D. 600 mark. In 50 excavations only 20.9 percent of deposits consisted of both early and late ceramic material. All of the excavations that produced datable sherds yielded late material, but none featured only early ceramics, a stark contrast to my findings in which 72 percent and 83 percent of structure excavations produced Late Preclassic and Early Classic ceramic material, respectively. Moreover, Rose reports that most of the structures he tested were single component, whereas many of my excavations revealed evidence for multiple rebuilding episodes. Clearly, the organization of agricultural zones and the occupational histories of the bajo communities I investigated differ substantially from others in the area immediately around La Milpa.

Guijarral is a rural agricultural site 8 km (5 miles) from La Milpa that is similar in many ways to the bajo communities I studied (Hughbanks 1998; Kunen and Hughbanks 2003). It, too, is located in an area of topographic and vegetative heterogeneity adjacent to a bajo and was the center of an area replete with agricultural terraces and berms indicative of intensive agricultural production. Guijarral features a principal architectural group that is larger and more formal than the other residential groups at the site, but here the similarities to the Far West Bajo communities end. For at Guijarral, most of the visible architecture is Late or Terminal Classic, with little ceramic evidence for buried Preclassic or Early Classic occupation levels. Moreover, Hughbanks (1998) reports that most of the residential structures he investigated consisted only of cobble-faced platforms with no stone superstructures and with little evidence of the plaster floors, masonry walls, and cut-stone facings that characterize the residential zones of the Far West Bajo communities.

Only those structures with evidence for occupation prior to the Late Classic reveal more formal construction. While this architectural pattern does support my argument for the greater wealth and resources of community founders, it also suggests a decline in the overall prosperity of Guijarral residents over time. It appears that Guijarral farmers faced more difficult circumstances than residents of the Far West Bajo communities and were unable to produce the agricultural surpluses necessary to invest in continued architectural improvement and embellishment of their homes.

A final source of comparative data comes from the research of Jon Lohse and Jon Hageman in the sustaining area (2.5–km or 1.6–mile radius) around Dos Hombres, a site in the RBCMA comparable in size and complexity to La Milpa. In their studies in the Dos Hombres suburbs, Hageman and Lohse (2003) identified four Plaza Plan 2 groups. These Tier 1 groups, as they are called, were comparable to the three principal groups I identified in that (a) they were the largest, most formal architecture in their settlements; (b) each featured a shrine on the east side of the plaza; and (c) each formed an architectural node around which smaller residential groups clustered. Hageman and Lohse identified these groups as important loci of political and economic power and postulated that they were the centers of corporate groups. More specifically, the corporate group leaders who would have resided in these Tier 1 groups played critical roles in agricultural management. This assessment is similar to the one I make for community founders in the next chapter, but there are important differences that I outline here. First, the Tier 1 group Hageman and Lohse discussed in greatest detail, the Barba Group, measured 398 square meters in area, whereas the principal groups in the Far West Bajo measured 1,058 square meters, 855 square meters, and 820 square meters. Considering that the three bajo groups were all more than double the size of the Dos Hombres example, they may represent the residences not just of corporate group or lineage heads, as the Dos Hombres researchers surmise, but of leaders of a larger social unit, such as a community. Second, Hageman and Lohse attributed some of the Tier 1 groups' role in agricultural management to their physical proximity to agricultural features, especially at the Barba Group and at another example, Las Terrazas. The Barba Group is associated with sets of footslope and cross-channel terraces and a box terrace is at Las Terrazas (Beach and others 2002). Because the principal groups in the Far West Bajo were remote from the agricultural zones, I propose that the pivotal role of community founders in resource management suggests economic control over a larger area and a broader social group than at Dos Hombres. Finally, the Dos Hombres data suggest that the four Tier 1 groups were occupied only during the Late Classic. Indeed, Hageman and Lohse argued that the corporate group settlement pattern arose in response to regional environmental changes and resource stress during this time. In contrast, the three principal groups in the Far West Bajo had much longer histories, histories that were distinct from the smaller residential groups that sprang up around them in later periods. This longevity suggests to me that the community founders established their preferential control over resources early, then transformed this control into positions of leadership and high social status, as displayed in the architecture of the principal groups. I next discuss the role that community founders played in controlling the productivity of the agricultural landscape and converting that production into strong civic and economic roles and elevated social status.

CHAPTER SIX

Spatial and Social Organization of the Far West Bajo Landscape

How was the landscape of the Far West Bajo organized and utilized by residents of the bajo communities? How did the reciprocal relationship between environmental change and human activity affect the organization of agriculture and settlement? Because the paleoenvironmental history of the bajo is intimately entwined with the changing resource management strategies employed by bajo residents, a pair of models helps us answer these questions and captures the spatial and social structure of the ancient agricultural landscape documented here. A variation on the garden-infield-outfield model of agriculture best describes the spatial organization of the Far West Bajo landscape during the Late Classic, after environmental degradation prompted residents to conserve depleted soil and water resources through an intensive program of terracing and berm construction. Variation in residential architecture and occupational history in the bajo communities is explained by a model of preferential access to critical natural resources by community founders.

ZONES OF USE: THE TRIPARTITE DIVISION OF THE LANDSCAPE

The environment of the Far West Bajo is ecotonal, consisting of upland hills and ridges, gentle slopes, and the (now) seasonally wet bajo. This heterogeneity provided ample possibilities for landscape modifications facilitating human activity. Residents of bajo communities divided the landscape into discrete zones, each with a distinct use pattern. Settlements were located on Bajo Hill or on ridgetops surrounding the bajo. Here, groups of structures and isolated platforms clustered together on high, flat terrain. In contrast to the residential zones, agricultural zones were located in gently sloping areas

of transitional or upland forest that surrounded the bajo. These areas were marked by dense concentrations of land and water management features, including terraces, berms, and circular rockpiles. Finally, the bajo itself served as a reservoir for basic resources and raw materials such as water, chert, clay, and organic soil. In summary, the bajo and its surroundings were divided into three distinct zones of human activity that corresponded to the three principal divisions of the natural landscape: residential zones in uplands and hilly areas, agricultural zones on the sloping bajo margins, and extraction zones in the bajo interior. The different use zones are each characterized by a particular distribution and configuration of cultural features. Beginning on the ridgetops and descending into the bajo, each activity zone corresponded to a decreasing level of intensity of use.

The division of the landscape into different use zones is best described by the garden-infield-outfield model of agricultural production documented in tropical regions throughout the world (Netting 1977; Stone 1996). The infield-outfield model is based on Johann Heinrich von Thünen's location model, which sought to explain agricultural land-use patterns and the distribution of rural settlements (described in Chisholm 1979). According to von Thünen, in an isolated state with a single urban center surrounded by a wilderness of uniform fertility, production will be distributed in a series of concentric rings around the city. The intensity of land use in each ring will increase with proximity to the city, since higher production costs associated with intensive production are offset by reduced transport costs (Chisholm 1979: 18). Generally, then, the most labor-intensive productive activities will be located nearer the city and the more spatially extensive activities will be located farther away. Von Thünen applied this idealized model to farm organization in order to understand where certain types of farms should be located in relation to a central market.

Von Thünen's model may be applied not only to multiple farms producing for a single market center, but also to individual farms within which are located diverse production activities. Thus, on a single farm "the intensity with which each crop is grown will decline as the distance from the farmstead increases: the farming system will vary from one part of the farm to another" (Chisholm 1979: 23). This variation of von Thünen's model applies in ethnographically documented situations of increasing population density. Among the Kofyar of Nigeria, Stone (1996) noted that as population density rose, cultivation of fields closest to residences increased in intensity, and extensive farming of more distant outfields diminished. Eventually, continued increases in population density led to denucleation of the village. Homesteads dispersed, and the resulting pattern was one of individual farms situated in the midst of intensively farmed infields. Thus, increased pressure on production led to fragmentation of the center and its breakup into constituent parts. Individual farmers scattered to be nearer to their infields to minimize both travel time and transport costs.

The combination of intensive cultivation of plots near residences and less intensive (extensive) use of hinterland fields has become known as the infield-outfield system of agriculture (Sanders 1981; Wolf 1966). Often, the system involves three complementary components (Netting 1977). Small plots of land immediately adjacent to the domicile may be used for kitchen gardening. This practice involves such labor-intensive and frequent practices as manuring, irrigation, and weeding, which are most easily done in close proximity to the house. Infields surrounding residences are cultivated intensively, often requiring investment in substantial landscape modifications such as terraces or irrigation canals. More distant fields, which require more travel time to reach, are usually cultivated in shifting fashion to maintain field fertility without investment in expensive land improvements. Diversification of field location and farming technique is a strategy to minimize risk in the event of crop failure. Furthermore, a system combining infields and outfields farmed with different cultivation practices spreads out labor, facilitating scheduling. Because farmers whenever possible will settle on the best available agricultural land, the most intensively used plots will also be those of the highest quality, allowing more marginal lands to be used less intensively.

Infield-outfield systems have been documented throughout the tropical world, and Mesoamerica is no exception. Netting (1977) used ethnographic analogy with the infield-outfield system of the Ibo of Nigeria to describe ancient Maya agriculture. In the Ibo case, use of outer farmlands, shortened fallow on fields closer in, and small kitchen plots where manuring and composting were practiced yielded a successful mixed cropping regime. This regime was characterized by a dispersed settlement pattern, in which each household compound was located in the middle of its own kitchen garden plots (Netting 1977: 311). Netting believed that a similarly varied system of agriculture might have characterized the Classic Maya. He suggested that a combination of multiple-cropped milpa, drained fields in swampy areas, terraces on slopes, and fixed-plot kitchen garden-orchards, tailored to local conditions, could have supported the dense populations that existed throughout the Maya lowlands during the Classic period. Netting cited the pattern of continuous but dispersed residence documented by archaeologists in the sustaining areas of major sites as evidence of a system marked by reliance on fixed-plot kitchen gardens (Netting 1977: 332; see also Turner and Sanders 1992).

Killion's (1990) ethnoarchaeological work in the Tuxtla mountains of Veracruz documented a contemporary infield-outfield system of agriculture that included house-lot gardens and orchards as a critical component. His study sought to link the organization of agriculture with the use of residential space, with the goal of providing insights into site structure that would benefit archaeologists. The idealized scheme of Tuxteco agriculture presented by Killion featured a central settlement zone consisting of individual house lots, each with space for a house-lot garden. Gardens were distinguished from nearby infields in that they produced a supplemental mix of economically useful and ornamental plants. Surrounding the settlement zone were infield agricultural holdings. Killion observed that the infields were located in a concentric zone within a 40-minute walk of the settlement zone. Beyond the infields was a ring of outfield agricultural holdings, located within a 3-to-5-hour walk from the settlement zone. Generally, Tuxteco farmers maintained a house-lot garden, one infield parcel, and one or more outfield parcels.

Like Killion, McAnany (1995) stressed the relationship between settlement configuration and the organization of production. Emphasizing the multicomponent nature of tropical farming systems, she postulated a system similar to that documented in the Tuxtlas for the ancient lowland Maya. The most intensive components of this system were permanently cultivated gardens and orchards surrounding residences. The presence of orchards at Maya sites has long been speculated on and has been reported at Coba (Folan and others 1979), where fruit trees and other economically useful species grew with elevated frequency within the settlement center. Beyond the orchards were "near-residential plots," or infields, which McAnany suggested were continuously cropped. Included in the infields were reclaimed marginal lands, such as slopes that required terracing and wetlands that required draining, all located within half a kilometer (0.3 mile) of residences. Variable-fallow plots, or outfields, were the most remote from residences. McAnany emphasized the variability inherent in this system, which included a range of land-use intensity arrayed in generally decreasing fashion from residences.

To summarize the garden-infield-outfield model, farming households invested decreasing amounts of labor in cultivation as the distance from house to agricultural field increased. In the immediate vicinity of the residence, kitchen gardens and orchards provided carefully tended spaces for fruits, vegetables, herbs, and medicinal plants. Surrounding the residences were intensively cultivated infields, where staple crops were grown with shortened fallow cycles and with such labor-intensive practices as irrigation and terracing. More distant fields may have been planted in staple crops as well, but often cultivation was shifting, with plots recovering their fertility through long fallow periods. Use of outfields generally did not involve labor or material investment in land modifications such as terraces or irrigation canals. The resulting pattern was one of houses within concentric zones of land, defined by decreasing intensity of use.

Looked at archaeologically, this arrangement of dispersed house mounds surrounded by large, "empty" tracts of lands is strikingly similar to the settlement pattern recorded for much of the Maya lowlands

(Drennan 1988). The garden-infield-outfield model seems to capture the variability inherent in Maya agriculture at the same time that it suggests a viable agricultural foundation for the dramatic increases in population density that characterized the lowlands during the Classic period.

McAnany (1995) suggested that during the Classic period, population was so dense as to create continuous rural settlements, with little space separating the sustaining area of one center from that of its neighbors. In consequence, reliance on various forms of intensive cultivation increased, the infields of one polity overlapping those of the neighboring polity. No vacant terrain remained for extensively cultivated outfields, and long-fallow shifting cultivation dropped out of the subsistence repertoire (Killion 1992; McAnany 1995). Killion (1992) noted, however, that outlying areas may have been used not only for extensive cultivation but also for hunting, gathering, or other raw material and resource procurement. I suggest that certain lands, such as the Far West Bajo, were conducive neither to residence nor to the demands of intensive agriculture and thus continued to be used as Killion suggested, as reservoirs of other essential resources.

Von Thünen's model sought to explain the organization of agricultural production in a homogenous landscape, which the Maya lowlands clearly is not. This raises an important point, which is that the concentric circles of the infield-outfield model are idealized. What may be abstracted from the scheme, therefore, is that an agricultural system tailored to local conditions will emphasize intensive agriculture in lands most conducive to heavy use and less intensive production on more marginal lands, as long as transportation costs do not limit this practice. In my reconstruction for the Far West Bajo, infields are defined as intensively cultivated fields and outfields as extensively used areas that may have been used for agriculture or for resource extraction. Although proximity to residences is an important consideration, the spatial distribution of infields and outfields does not always result in a system of neatly concentric rings around residences.

Most scholars working with contemporary examples of the infield-outfield model note that individual farmsteads stand at the center of the land-use rings (Netting 1977; Stone 1996). In contrast, I found that it was not the individual house but multiple houses clustered together in residential zones around which agricultural fields were arrayed. Each individual residential group was separated from its neighbors by small amounts of vacant terrain and residential zones were spatially distinct from the terraced fields, located in a separate zone. Sanders (1981: 363) made a similar observation, noting that Maya settlement illustrated the infield-outfield pattern "writ large." Such a settlement pattern supports my interpretation that the unit of intensive agricultural production was the residential community, not the individual farmstead.

The modified version of the garden-infield-outfield model of agriculture best explains the Late Classic land use pattern I documented in the Far West Bajo. Rather than the traditional concentric pattern of land use produced by such a system, there was a vertical arrangement of land use zones in which residences, infields, and outfields were distributed along a gradient of decreasing elevation (Fig. 6.1). This linearity is to some extent a result of the sampling design I used, which centered on the bajo interior and not on the surrounding ridges. As the LaMAP surveys have demonstrated, it is likely that if the uplands were taken as the center point, surrounding slopes and lowlands might indeed form concentric rings of use around them. More importantly, the locations of the bajo communities indicate that they were situated so as to take advantage of the resources offered by a heterogeneous environment. Residential areas were clustered on top of hills and ridges, where upland forest thrives. A cooling breeze, good visibility over agricultural lands below, relatively level ground, and timber and limestone for house construction were advantages provided by these locales for residence. Structures were dispersed enough to allow room for garden plots between buildings. In residential zones, no land was devoted to forms of agriculture that required significant landscape modification. Instead, distinct agricultural zones were positioned on the gentle slopes around the bajo margins. Consisting of dense concentrations of terraces, berms, and rockpiles, these areas were clearly dedicated to intensive farming. The terraces and berms not only served as components of an integrated agricultural system but may have had the added importance of delimiting and facilitating access to particular plots of agricultural land as such resources became scarce or degraded. The rockpiles and larger cobble platforms in these areas

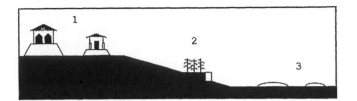

Figure 6.1. Schematic organization of a bajo community. (Drafted by Mary J. Galindo.)

served as foundations for perishable fieldhouses, small planting platforms, and corn cribs. In her analysis of infields at Pulltrouser Swamp, McAnany (1992: 200) relied on ethnographic studies that demonstrated that infields were generally located within a 40-minute walk or 2 km to 3 km (under 2 miles) from residences. In the Far West Bajo, agricultural zones were on average 1.5 km from residential zones, well within this radius.

A third zone of use is suggested by the presence of cultural features in different portions of the bajo itself. During the Preclassic and Early Classic periods, when the bajo was a permanent wetland, the crucial resource it provided was water. After the bajo's transformation into a seasonal swamp, it continued to provide critical raw materials as well as water for agriculture. The location of berms in areas of corozo bajo, particularly those features positioned strategically in relation to intermittent streams, means that water management designed to facilitate cultivation and prevent flooding occurred in certain parts of the bajo (Fig. 6.2). Rockpiles in areas of scrub bajo likely represent loci of chert collection, lithic tool manufacture, organic soil mining for terrace fertilization, or clay collecting (Chapter 3). They may also have served the same functions as the rockpiles in agricultural zones and represent fieldhouses, planting platforms, or corn cribs. Undoubtedly multiple activities took place in the bajo interior, at different times and in different locations. In essence, the bajo functioned as a repository for basic natural resources for residents of the surrounding bajo communities. As an outfield, it was useful either for raw material extraction, extensive agriculture, or both.

BAJO COMMUNITY ORGANIZATION

To answer the question of how the use of natural resources in the Far West Bajo affected the organiza-

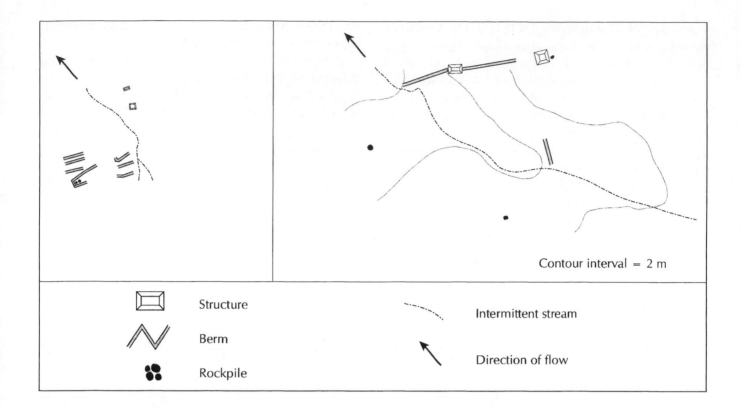

Figure 6.2. Relationship of berms to intermittent stream channels in the Far West Bajo.

tion of the residential zones, I examine variation in the architecture and occupational history of residential groups within each of the three residential zones and explore Levi's (1993, 1994, 1996) model of access to multiple production strategies. Evidence from other studies throughout the Maya lowlands indicates that community founders gained preferential access to critical resources. Aspects of residential variability, most notably length of occupation, size and complexity of house compounds, and extent of architectural elaboration, can be linked to access to productive resources by demonstrating that the residences of community founders, those with evidence for the longest occupation, were also the largest, most complex, and most elaborate in each community.

Uniqueness of Principal Groups

Results from test excavations in all three of the bajo communities demonstrate the community founder pattern. At the Bajo Hill site, several groups contained small amounts of Late Preclassic material in construction fill, including Groups A, B, C, H, I, K, L, N, and P. Of these, only Group A had a construction level that was purely Preclassic. This level was the lowest stratum in a test pit (Op. V29) placed in the Group A plaza. The excavation was located within the low stone walls that enclose part of the plaza in front of the eastern shrine. In all other groups, Late Preclassic sherds were mixed with material as late as the Late/Terminal Classic.

The Bajo Hill settlement expanded after the Late Preclassic, but Group A continued to be the focus of settlement. One new construction episode dating to this period was in the Group A shrine, where ceramics from the looters' trench and one test pit revealed an Early Classic floor. Several plaza test pits in and around Group A also yielded Early Classic ceramics. Other examples of new construction were found in Group B, just downslope from Group A, and in Group N. Early Classic material also appeared in new structures in Groups C and H, and in all the structures with Late Preclassic material.

All groups tested at the Bajo Hill site contained material dating to the early Late Classic and Late/Terminal Classic periods. Groups A, C, and I featured construction episodes that date to the early Late Classic, and Groups A, B, C, H, I, K, L, O, and P had Late/Terminal Classic construction episodes. Although not all groups were tested, a pattern seems clear. The large composite Group A was the earliest founded and continued to be the focus of settlement and, importantly, ritual practice, throughout the history of the Bajo Hill settlement. It was the only group tested with definitive construction in both the Late Preclassic and Early Classic periods. From the time of their founding, occupation was continuous at all groups, with new construction most common in the Early Classic and Late/Terminal Classic periods.

A similar pattern is documented at La Caldera. All groups tested, including A, E, F, I, X, and the Group B patio contained some Late Preclassic ceramics, but only Group A featured a construction level dating to that period. During the Early Classic, occupation continued in those groups and began in Group B structures and in Group I. Early Classic material was mixed with later ceramics except in Group I, where a small masonry-faced platform and the accompanying residential terrace were constructed during this period. Test pits in the Group A plaza, Group B patio, and both patios in Group F also yielded Early Classic sherds, indicating that at least some settlers were located in these groups during this time.

Group A yielded early Late Classic material; the one structure tested had construction dating to this period. In Group F, the lowest level of Patio 2 contained no sherds later than the early Late Classic. All other groups, including B, E, I, and X, also contained early Late Classic ceramics, but mixed with those of other periods. All groups except Group I featured structures built in the Late/Terminal Classic, and all groups were occupied at this time.

As at the Bajo Hill site, the earliest construction at La Caldera occurred in the principal Group A, which was founded in the Late Preclassic and continued to be occupied into the Late/Terminal Classic. During the Early Classic, a small platform was established near Group A. The other composite groups at La Caldera, which are smaller and do not feature eastern temples as large as the Group A temple, may have been founded in the Late Preclassic or Early Classic, but they demon-

strate unequivocal Late/Terminal Classic construction. No later material was recovered.

It is clear that the principal group of each bajo community I investigated was constructed in the earliest phase in which the settlement was occupied. Each of the principal groups demonstrated continuous occupation throughout the life of the community into the Late/Terminal Classic, when the area was abandoned. Both Group A at the Bajo Hill site and Group A at La Caldera provided evidence of multiple construction phases in which structures were enlarged, refurbished, and elaborated.

It is difficult to make a comparative case for Thompson's Group, because Robichaux did not excavate structures and tested only a few groups in limited places. Robichaux did not recover any Late Preclassic material but he did document Early Classic ceramics in Groups 1, 6, and 9. Group 6 was the principal group, a composite group with a temple on the east. Groups 1 and 9 were patio-focused groups and the excavation in Group 1 yielded no ceramics later than the Early Classic. Group 10, which was another large composite group but did not feature an eastern shrine, appeared to date to the Late/Terminal Classic, as did Group 19, a patio-focused group. Based on this scanty evidence, little can be said other than that the principal Group 6 was early and contained material indicative of continuous occupation into the Late Classic.

There is more to the pattern characterizing the principal group in each bajo community than simply early occupation. Each was also the most complex residential unit in terms of the configuration of its constituent structures and the most elaborate in terms of the architectural style of its buildings. All three of the principal groups were large composite groups, consisting of five, eight, and seven structures. At the Bajo Hill site, Group A was the only composite group and was one of only two to contain eastern temples. At La Caldera, there were four composite groups, but Group A was the largest, at 855 square meters. It was also the most regular in configuration, featured the largest plaza area, and had the largest temple. Finally, in Thompson's Group, Group 6 was not the largest residential unit, at 820 square meters, but it had the largest structures, the most complex configuration, and was the only group with an eastern shrine. All three principal groups thus consisted of residential structures, temples, and smaller square or rectilinear buildings.

The spatial configuration of the principal groups suggests two things. First, the households occupying them were larger than those occupying neighboring groups. The smaller buildings in each principal group may have been ancillary structures such as kitchens (Fry 1969; Haviland 1985) or they may have housed junior or dependent members of the household. Second, the presence of large plazas and shrines suggests that these residential groups played administrative or ritual roles in their respective communities. Fry has noted that at Tikal, family heads or those with higher social status were identified with large, complex residential groups, which often contained special-function structures indicative of clan leadership (Fry 1969; see also Becker 1971).

In addition to their configuration, the architectural style of the buildings also suggests that residents of the principal groups had elevated social status. Haviland (1981) cited several architectural measures of high social status at Tikal, including vaulting, masonry construction, presence of eastern shrines, elaborate burials within those shrines, and outbuildings as part of the residential complex.

Many of these elaborations were present in the three principal groups of the Far West Bajo communities. All three groups featured construction of dressed limestone masonry instead of cobble or rubble construction. Two of the three groups had vaulted structures, and all three had eastern shrines. In the one shrine in which a looters' trench was examined (in Group A at the Bajo Hill site), human bone in the backdirt indicated that at least two individuals had been buried in the temple (Appendix G). In addition, Group A at La Caldera had a large, partially looted cache containing human skeletal remains in front of the east temple. At Thompson's Group, a large cache vessel containing exotic materials such as coral, pyrite, and mother of pearl was discovered in front of the eastern temple in Group 6. As indicated by Table 6.1, the principal groups were extremely well-constructed; the presence of internal features such as benches are further indicators of elaboration.

All the evidence for early occupation; complex layout; rebuilding and refurbishing; presence of shrines, caches, and burials; and architectural elaboration indicates that residents of the three principal groups were set apart from other residents of these communities. They arrived first, pioneering the settlement of

Table 6.1. Architectural Elaboration of Principal Residential Groups

Feature	Bajo Hill	La Caldera	Thompson's Group
Masonry Platform	Yes	Yes	Yes
Partial Walls	Yes	No	No
Full Walls	No	Yes	Yes
Vaulting	No	Yes	Yes
Plastering	Yes	Yes	Yes
Benches	*	Yes	*
Burials, Caches	Yes	Yes	Yes

* Unknown

these communities. They remained, expanded, and rebuilt with frequency. They appear to have had higher social status than other community members, as indicated by the larger architecture of their compounds. They had greater economic resources, judging from the style and quality of their house construction. The presence of shrines in these groups suggests that residents of the principal groups may have served as ritual leaders of their communities. The large plaza spaces associated with their compounds also indicate an administrative or other public role. In short, the principal groups seem to have been the residences of community founders and leaders.

SETTLEMENT ECOLOGY, DOMESTIC ECONOMY, AND THE PRINCIPLE OF FIRST OCCUPANCY

I argued above that the stratification of the landscape into house lot, agricultural, and extraction zones explains the character of the bajo communities, in which residential settlements constitute discrete areas that are nucleated, yet dispersed enough to allow for garden plots. How might I explain the preferential position of the occupants of the principal groups within the settlements? Levi's (1993, 1994, 1996) work at San Estevan, Belize, provides some insight to this question. In her study of inter- and intracommunity residential variability, she focused on the interrelationship between settlement ecology and domestic economy. Examining the household level of settlement, Levi sought an explanation for differences in the configuration of house mound groups within the residential zone. Ideally, she reasoned, individual households will build their economic strategies so as to utilize micro-environmental variability. By doing so, household members increase productive opportunities while simultaneously minimizing risk. Thus, the range of options available, and the differential ability of households to make use of them, will affect the configuration of residential groups.

Using proximity to multiple ecological zones within the community as a proxy measure for access to diverse systems of agricultural production, Levi discerned a correlation between residential patterning and production options (Levi 1996: 104–105). The difference was reflected in the respective size and configuration of household residences. Paired platform groups were more common in low-diversity parts of San Estevan, whereas patio-focused and composite groups were more frequent in areas with high ecological diversity. Levi surmised that access to labor was the principle variable affecting household ability to utilize varied resources. Smaller households appeared to have been organized around fewer productive options, whereas larger households had the advantage of multiple production strategies.

Levi's reasoning provides a partial answer to the question, but the ability to marshal labor to take advantage of environmental resources is not the only variable distinguishing one household's economic potential from that of another. Are large households successful because they can utilize multiple ecological zones, or are successful households large because their success enables them to expand and support a larger family? Access to resources is not simply a matter of physical proximity. In the Far West Bajo there is no meaningful difference in the distance between any residential group and a particular resource in one bajo community and that of any other group in the same community. The relationship between settlement variability and natural resources must be governed by additional factors. For instance, at K'axob in northern Belize, McAnany (1995) demonstrated a close connection between land tenure and the organization of settlements based on the concept of lineage. Lineages, as McAnany views them, are primarily resource-holding groups linked to particular tracts of land and patches of resources. Continued residence in a defined location cements claims to those resources and solidifies the right of inheritance through the generations. The connection between residential groups and particular resources encourages both resi-

dential stability and proprietary use rights. This connection is especially important in systems of intensive agriculture, where improvements to land require investment of time, labor, and materials. Such systems are likely to develop only in situations where claims to the improved land, what Dunning and his colleagues (1999: 657) refer to as "intensifying investment in localized space," can be sustained.

Based on perceivable differences in architecture and composition of residential units within bajo communities, I hypothesize that differences in household access to resources existed in the Far West Bajo. How were claims to particular resources established, and how were they legitimized? How did inequality in resource claims develop? Levi (1993) has speculated that it was the size of the operative labor pool that governed use of productive resources. McAnany (1995) suggested that it was the first occupants of a region, the community founders, who gained access to prime lands. Socioeconomic advantages granted to founders who laid claims to these resources, backed up by continuous residence on or near the lands in question, led to the entrenchment of inequality in resource access between the founding group and later residents of the settlement. These later residents may have been noninheriting descendants of the original group or newcomers who joined the settlement. In either case they gained access to fewer or poorer quality resources. If their lands were marginal in quality, they may have been required to expend more effort to bring them into production. As a result, their economic standing was weakened.

McAnany (1995) referred to this phenomenon as the principle of first occupancy. She reported that at K'axob the largest and most elaborate platforms were those with Preclassic cores. Moreover, the more complex clusters of structures, which McAnany called alpha residences, featured shrines that were associated with ancestor veneration. These complexes were often surrounded by smaller residences, sometimes lacking shrines. The practice of ancestor veneration in the older, more complex residential groups may mean that their residents recognized and respected the role of the lineage in creating prosperity. In summary, McAnany traced the Preclassic presence at K'axob to the establishment of resource rights and cited differences in architectural units as suggesting varying statuses, community roles, and access to resources. Thus, residential architecture can serve as an indicator of patterns of resource inequality established at a settlement's founding.

The principle of first occupancy has been documented at many other sites. Ringle and Andrews (1988) determined that the principle was in operation during the Preclassic period at sites in Yucatan, including Komchen and Dzibilchaltun. They thought that a right to land, rather than other economic systems such as trade, was the basis for incipient differences in the size of residential platforms. Ringle and Andrews associated large residential platforms with land-owning descent groups. In contrast, smaller platforms were associated with families with more restricted access to land. In their view, residential stability served to establish ownership over surrounding fields, which through time contributed to elevated social and economic position. As population grew, access to lands became increasingly limited, and socioeconomic differences became more marked. Ringle and Andrews suggested a correspondence between large households and higher community status, with residents of large residential platforms playing civic roles such as conflict resolution and allocation of land to newer community members. In contrast, residents of the smaller platforms would have been families of less importance.

Tourtellot (1988) made a slightly different argument at Seibal, focusing not on the largest residential groups, but on the largest structures within residential groups as the potential homes of founders. He attributed the architectural prominence of these structures either to the founding family's early start in the area or to its greater access to resources. It is likely that the two reinforced each other. Tourtellot cited ceramic data, among other evidence identifying the residences of family heads, that showed that the largest structures were also the earliest structures in each residential group. Similarly, Haviland (1988) attributed to the family head the architecturally more complex structure in a residential group at Tikal whose history he examined in depth.

Through her research at Sayil, Carmean (1991) provided me a means to synthesize Levi's arguments for multiple production strategies and the principle of first occupancy expressed by McAnany, Tourtellot, and others. The mechanism is her suggestion that control of agricultural resources was connected to control of architectural labor. Wealthy households, which maintained preferential control over agricultural resources,

were able to produce a surplus that, Carmean argued, was used to feed construction labor. Economic wealth, in the form of agricultural production, was thus convertible into architectural labor and was expressed as investment in public displays of social status, namely, elaborate residences. Architectural embellishments such as vaulting, therefore, may be viewed as conspicuous consumption of agricultural resources. Differences in investment in architecture among residential groups demonstrate differences in access to and control of economic resources, primarily agricultural lands.

To explain how these economic differences developed, Carmean also turned to the principle of first occupancy. Families with the longest residence in an area were generally those granted prime agricultural lands and may also have been those closest to the village. Poorer families, then, farmed land that was inferior (less productive) as well as farther away, and they expended more effort and time in agricultural production and transportation. If, as Carmean has suggested, founding families at Sayil had first access to productive resources, that access would have served to perpetuate wealth differences between themselves and subsequent members of the community.

By linking agricultural production to architectural differences, it is possible to explain the variation that existed in the residential zones of the three Far West Bajo communities studied. This research ties the aspects of residential variability discussed above to access to critical resources through an argument for the primacy of community founders. I maintain that the high socioeconomic status of community founders, expressed most visibly in the architecture of the residence, was based on access to the greatest number and highest quality of productive resources. Founding families at each community established themselves first, building residential compounds and gaining access to prime agricultural lands. These compounds grew in size and elaboration as family size and economic prosperity increased. As population rose, either from multiple descendants of the original families or from the arrival of newcomers, new residential groups were established. These families made use of fewer or lower quality resources and thus had fewer resources to invest in domestic architecture. As production intensified in the face of environmental degradation, risk management favored diversification. Those families with access to multiple ecological zones were better positioned to develop multiple production strategies. Moreover, as soil erosion increased and water sources became scarcer, those same families could marshal the labor resources necessary to build the soil and water control mechanisms needed to ensure the continuing productivity of agricultural lands. Perhaps because early success increased their size, or perhaps because their original claims included terrain in various zones, founding families were most able to craft a diverse domestic economy. Their continued success over generations allowed them to invest agricultural surplus in architecture. The result was the larger, more complex, and more elaborate residential compounds that mark their homes.

RESOURCE SPECIALIZATION

Throughout this volume, I have explored the ways in which settlement pattern data offer insight into the relationship between the organization of subsistence production and social structure. In investigating how the bajo was utilized by residents of surrounding communities, it became clear that a garden-infield-outfield model best describes the partitioning of the landscape into residential, agricultural, and extractive zones. To understand how the productive strategies pursued by bajo community residents affected the social structure of those communities, I argued for the preferential role of community founders. I now look briefly at the implications of the linkage between agricultural production and settlement patterns for current models of Maya subsistence and social organization by focusing in particular on resource specialization in bajo communities.

In response to recent calls for fine-grained studies of local responses to the distribution of critical natural resources, I have documented the particular set of subsistence strategies adopted by one group of communities in the La Milpa sustaining area, in part as a response to anthropogenic environmental change. The combination of gardening, intensive terrace agriculture, bajo recessional cultivation, and extraction of raw materials from the bajo was a response to the specific suite of environmental resources available to these ancient Maya. Residents of bajo communities made use of this natural variability in crafting a highly diversified subsistence strategy. Such a practice lends support to the mosaic model of Maya subsistence that has now gained recognition among scholars.

Many scholars (Fedick 1996a; Lucero 1999; McAnany 1993) have noted that the dispersed pattern of Maya settlement is related to the inability of centers to control and manage critical resources in such a patchy environment as the Maya lowlands. Settlement location was less affected by the presence of nearby centers than it was by proximity to important resources. Reliance on exploitation of a varied landscape and, concomitantly, a suite of subsistence practices means that the densest non-urban settlements were located near the greatest number of production opportunities. Levi (1996) discerned such a correlation between residential patterning and production options at the household level, and I find a similar correlation at the community level. Bajo communities are ideal examples of settlements with access to multiple production and extraction opportunities. Looking out from the Far West Bajo, it is clear that the concentric model of a Maya community in which a ceremonial center is surrounded by elite residences and zones of ever smaller and poorer households with diminishing socioeconomic opportunities, does not apply.

The results here parallel those that other scholars claim for the organization of craft production in the Maya lowlands (Potter and King 1995; Rice 1987). Economic specialization was "tuned" to the distribution of resources and not to major centers. With the inception of terrace agriculture and the careful management of water through the construction of berms, residents of bajo communities established a specialty in intensive agricultural production. Already localized resources were made more localized through labor inputs that served to modify the landscape to increase the intensity of production. Although agricultural land as a general category cannot be considered a patchy resource, it appears that bajo margin lands, amenable to intensive agricultural production methods through substantial landscape modifications, were indeed limited and highly prized. Communities that were located near important resources developed a specialization in production or extraction based on those resources. Bajo communities are an excellent example of these "resource specialized communities" (Scarborough 1999).

CHAPTER SEVEN

Life in a Bajo Community

In the early dawn of a day in late May, two men entered the stone enclosure in front of the pyramid and bent to kneel on its steps. Behind them in the open plaza stood some 60 villagers, women, men, and children, watching solemnly. One man, bare-chested save for a polished shell disk hanging on a cord around his neck, set a small ball of copal incense to burn in an orange bowl. The second man, older than the first and with a distinctively shaped skull framed by hematite earflares, removed two chert knives from a deerskin bag hanging at his waist and placed them carefully on the steps of the temple. One knife was a flat ovoid made of a translucent pink stone. The other, black, had a long stem and a tapering point. Both had been crafted from stone specially imported from a town near the sea. The village's master flintknapper, who stood at the front of the crowd behind, had spent several weeks shaping and chipping the stone, then working the edges to a smooth sharpness. Now, they were being offered to the ancestors, whose bones resided inside the pyramid, with entreaties for the onset of rain and a successful harvest from the newly terraced fields.

After prayers in the small shrine atop the temple's high platform, and a sprinkling of copal on the knives, the two men slowly retreated. Then, leading a procession of villagers, they walked down off the hill, across a narrow stretch of land facilitating passage between gardens, and up a slight incline to the new fields. Here, all the village could see new terrace walls positioned to capture the precious soil that would begin to slip downslope with the onset of the heavy rains. Nearby, a long low wall stood poised to impound water from a channel, yet dry, that all present fervently hoped would soon run fast and full. As the sun rose over the ridge beyond the fields, a woman handed a small ceramic jar to one of the two men, who poured water from it into the stream channel. Finally, the villagers turned to face a large platform faced in white limestone blocks, atop which sat three neat pole and thatch structures. Here, the farmers would rest during the arduous months of planting, weeding, and harvesting and take meals, and here they might remain as the crops ripened, alert eyes watching to ward off hungry animal visitors. With luck, one such visitor might yield enough meat to share among several families. Farm implements, wooden benches, and several sleeping mats would be stored in one of the other structures. A group of women approached and mounted the platform, standing before the entrance of one of the huts. Crouching down, they placed inside the door a large unslipped ceramic water jar decorated with incising about the neck, a smaller red jar, two ring-based brown bowls, a large red plate with a thick, everted rim, and several fluted black cups. One woman withdrew a small pouch from her clothing and took from it several seeds of corn, placing a few in each of the bowls and on the plate. With these offerings of water and of corn, the villagers again asked the ancestors to intercede with the gods and bring rain, so that the fields might be planted and the crops flourish, bringing nourishment to all.

Although we can never know if such a ceremony actually occurred in front of Structure 2 in Plaza A of the Bajo Hill site and in the fields of Agricultural Zone 3, imagining the activities that were responsible for the archaeological deposits we study brings the landscape to life. Two bifaces, exquisitely crafted and never used, their edges still sharply defined, were placed on the steps of a ritual structure by somebody, for a specific purpose. Pieces of pottery, brown, black, cream, orange, and red, were found in the jumbled rock fill of terraces, berms, and rockpiles. Ultimately, what an archaeological study allows us to see are not broken pots, discarded tools, and abandoned houses lying in ruin, but traces of the behaviors, both mundane and extraordinary, that ancient peoples engaged in, that filled their lives, structured their relationships to relatives, neighbors, and more distant authorities, and defined their place in a world filled with natural and supernatural elements with which they were in close physical and spiritual contact. Archaeological research provides the raw data (sherds, chert flakes, limestone blocks, and human remains) and the spatial and temporal relationships among them to open a small window onto the lives of residents of the Far West Bajo: how they located and collected all the materials they needed to survive, built their houses, managed their farms, obtained and processed their food, adorned themselves, shared in ceremonies, and sent their dead to join the ancestors.

To recreate a vivid picture of what life might have been like for Far West Bajo residents throughout their centuries of occupation of this unique environment, I return again to the concept of the differentiation of zones of use based on the resources available in each. Beginning in the bajo interior, continuing onto the slopes of the bajo margin, and ending on the hilltops and ridges overlooking the bajo, I review all the evidence presented here concerning artifact and feature distributions, architectural developments, and chronology of residential and agricultural feature construction to describe the lifeways of bajo residents in as rich detail as possible.

THE BAJO INTERIOR

During the earliest years of life in the Far West Bajo, the wetland itself was more like a lake than a seasonal swamp, with stretches of open water ringed with cattails and other herbaceous vegetation such as sedges. Residents of small settlements on the surrounding ridges traveled down to the enclosed depression to gather water in large unslipped ceramic jars for transport back up the hill to their homes for various domestic uses. Based on skeletal evidence from nine burials and fragmentary bone recovered from looters' trenches (see Appendix G), the individuals responsible for water collection might have been women as well as men, for bones from both sexes exhibit the large muscle attachments and robust build characteristic of lives full of strenuous activity.

Another important activity in the bajo during these years may have been recessional agriculture, practiced on the edges of the inundated portions of the bajo. In such a practice, farmers waited until water levels receded slightly at the end of the rainy season in early winter before planting seeds, probably with digging

sticks, in the fertile, well-watered soils. Such recessional cropping provided a supplemental crop to the principal crop typically planted upland at the beginning of the rainy season in late spring or early summer. Unfortunately, we have no direct evidence of what crops may have been planted in the bajo because pollen recovered from Backhoe Trench 9 did not yield cultigens and no other soil samples were analyzed; most likely crops would have been much as they are today, corn and beans, supplemented with squash, chili, and other vegetables.

Paleoecological research indicates rapid silting in the Far West Bajo after a few hundred years and generations of occupation. Thus transformed, the bajo became a seasonal swamp with a dense clay floor, much greater surface runoff, and a new mix of woody and herbaceous vegetation. In response to these changes, bajo residents pursued an altered suite of activities to exploit the resources of the new environment. With water increasingly scarce, management of intermittent streams became a crucial component of agriculture. To cope, Far West Bajo farmers built rubble berms to divert water out of streams onto cultivated plots of land. Two streams for which we have evidence of this practice are in Agricultural Zone 3, in an area of upland forest slightly upslope from the bajo edge, and in the corozo bajo of Agricultural Zone 4 (see Fig. 6.2). Recessional farming may have continued in the ever-drier bajo interior, as shown by the small cobble piles constructed from naturally occurring chert nodules scattered in the bajo clay. These rockpiles may be the remnant foundations of fieldhouses with wooden walls and thatched roofs used by farmers when visiting their fields to store tools, eat meals, or to sleep during times when watching over the fields was necessary. They may also have served as elevated cribs for the storage of harvested crops before their transport to the villages. It is also possible that some of the rockpiles were constructed in areas that were still permanently inundated, as they tend to be located in the lowest parts of the bajo. If so, then the features would have elevated the roots of crops planted atop them out of the standing water.

After the transition from a perennial to a seasonal wetland was complete, sometime in the first few centuries A.D., the bajo continued to provide crucial resources for residents of the surrounding villages. The thick layer of clay now lining the bajo floor was a valuable resource for ceramic production. We can envision villagers walking downslope to the bajo to dig up clay for transport in baskets or other containers to outdoor work spaces under the eaves of their houses. This scenario is feasible, but is difficult to demonstrate archaeologically. We have more direct evidence of use of another resource: the chert nodules in the bajo clays. Many of the chert cobbles that had been mounded together to form rockpiles had flake scars, indicating that someone had begun to knap them, probably to assess the quality of the material for tool production. In fact, some of the rockpiles may represent the deliberate collection of nodules from the surrounding soil for systematic testing and selection of good stone. None of the chert I found in the Far West Bajo could be called high-quality, but there is clear evidence that bajo residents were producing tools at the location of the rockpiles. Excavation recovered primary, secondary, and tertiary flakes, illustrating the sequence of tool manufacture, at all four of the rockpiles tested in the bajo interior. Three of the four features also yielded formal bifacial tools as well as cores or informal flake or core tools. Subsequent transport of either viable nodules or finished tools to the villages upslope or the surrounding agricultural fields would have involved toting heavy loads of stone, a task that may help explain some of the activity-related changes seen in the skeletal remains recovered in excavation, such as those in Burials 5 and 6 (see Appendix G).

In addition to water, clay, and chert, an additional bajo resource was the peaty soil that formed in the bajo during its inundation and was later buried by colluviation. Evidence from excavation of one group of terraces (Op. V26) indicates that farmers mined this highly organic soil for fertilizer. Although this is the sole documented example, it hints at an important intensive agricultural practice around the bajo. As terracing became a major component of agricultural technology, maintenance of soil fertility was a critical concern. Deforestation had denuded the high slopes of their natural tree cover, and the soils collecting behind terrace walls were already thin. After multiple seasons of cultivation they were not high in nutrients, so bajo mucks rich in organic material could have served as beneficial fertilizer on the terraced fields. Transport of large quantities of peaty soil out of the bajo and onto the surrounding slopes must have been a highly labor-intensive practice, especially since the Maya had no beasts of burden. We can imagine farmers carrying heavy loads of soil in sacks on their backs, supported by a tumpline, along narrow trails through the forest.

As a final resource, we can assume that hunters forayed into the bajo forests for game. Today, scrub bajo is a welcoming habitat to herds of peccary and smaller creatures such as agouti, and corozo forest is home to certain large game birds like the curassow. Even if practiced opportunistically while engaged in any of the activities described above, hunting would have added important sources of protein to a largely vegetarian diet. Unfortunately, there is little evidence of hunting techniques, and neither projectile points, nor snares or traps, are known from the Far West Bajo.

BAJO MARGINS

Much of the daily life of Far West Bajo residents centered on farming, and thus much of the focus of activity was on the sloping bajo margins where the agricultural fields were located. During the Late Preclassic and Early Classic periods, when small to moderate numbers of villagers dispersed on high ridges around the bajo were practicing slash and burn farming, these lands were heavily altered by human activity. Tree clearing with hefty stone bifaces is indicated by the remains of tools found in excavations.

Other activities that farmers would have undertaken include seasonal burning of plots to clear vegetation prior to planting; sowing of crops such as corn, beans, and squash by placement of seeds into holes made by digging sticks; guarding crops against pests; weeding of invasive and unwanted plants; and harvesting the mature plants. Sharp chert flakes would have facilitated some of these tasks. Even though such a form of extensive agriculture leaves no direct archaeological trace, we believe that large scale land clearance, most likely for agriculture, was the primary impetus for the erosion that helped transform the bajo from a permanent to a seasonal wetland. As soils on the slopes lost their fertility and eroded downslope, Far West Bajo farmers invested increasingly large amounts of time, physical effort, and construction material in maintaining their fields so that food could be grown to support the villages. At the same time, it appears that ever-larger populations in La Milpa center placed added demand on suburban farmers to produce food for those members of the polity not directly engaged in agriculture.

What would the fields have looked like after intensification? Some farms would be delineated by rubble berms or field walls demarcating their boundaries. Considering the physical separation between village and farm and the increased labor and material investments made in fields, we can imagine that individual farmers wished to ensure that their lands, whether granted by usufruct, corporate group membership, or other land tenure system, were not encroached upon by others. Circumscription by walls would have been one way to protect them. Other fields might have been accessed by similar rubble alignments serving as walkways to facilitate travel between houses and fields, much like the one observed in Agricultural Zone 2.

Farmers invested in the construction and maintenance of terraces to create planting surfaces along the slopes. These features required the effort of initial construction from unshaped limestone boulders placed on bedrock scraped clean of overlying soil. Maintenance tasks included repair of the walls in order to retain the soil that built up behind them. Most terraces in their abandoned state today stand not more than two courses high, suggesting that upkeep of the walls was vital to the fields' success. Other activities apparently included replenishment of the planting surfaces with rich soils dug up from the bajo. How the labor for these tasks was divided and shared is not known, but we can envision groups of farm families cooperating to ensure that disrepair of facilities upslope was not permitted to adversely affect downslope fields.

In addition to the terraces, farmers built rubble berms in great number. Berms appear to have needed less careful construction than terraces, but they did require more construction material in the form of the limestone and chert fill of the features, which can be up to 2 m in diameter. Berms today are simply rubble alignments, but we may imagine, as Fedick (and others 2000) did for the Yalahau region of Yucatan, that they were originally larger earthen-covered features. Because many of the berms are thought to have channeled water toward or away from fields, their placement required careful planning, especially when they were built to adjoin terraces. Maintenance of these features would have required regular checking of the alignments to ensure that no holes or clogged areas prevented water from flowing as desired.

As in the bajo interior, the presence of rockpiles in the agricultural zones can be interpreted as indicating a number of different activities. Their use as elevated planting platforms is certainly possible. Farmers may have desired to increase the amount of moisture available to plants when deforestation and increased erosion meant that more water ran off the slope rather than soaking into the soil. In this case, the cobble fill of the features would have served as mulch, retaining moisture for plant roots to access in the soil below. Some people also manufactured stone tools in the vicinity, because the fill of most rockpiles contained small numbers of flakes and cores as well as tools such as bifaces and blades. Bifaces would have been useful for tilling the soil, and blades could have been used to cut weeds or crops or help shape wooden farm implements. Construction of the rockpiles themselves is not likely to have required large amounts of labor, planning, or cooperation. Most were haphazard collections of pebbles and cobbles, although some contained footing or anchor stones placed on bedrock scraped clean of overlying soil.

Although the agricultural zones were close enough to the villages for daily foot travel to attend to farming tasks, the presence of cobble platforms interspersed among the other features may mean that there were times when farmers stayed overnight in their fields. They also would have provided welcome shelter from the rain, since many farming tasks, including sowing, weeding, and harvesting, took place during the wet season. The platforms, usually measuring about 20 to 30 square meters, most likely supported pole and thatch superstructures that would have accommodated the farmer, any helpers, and necessary tools and equipment. The presence of a few ceramics in almost all of the cobble platforms tested may indicate that preparation and consumption of meals also took place there, at least occasionally. The large number and close spacing of these house remains should not confuse us, however, because it is likely that their flimsy construction made it necessary to rebuild them frequently, perhaps every few seasons, on a new stone foundation.

UPLAND VILLAGES

Most of the information I collected regarding nonagricultural activities comes from the residential zones in the uplands, especially from the Bajo Hill site and La Caldera. Although such activities were not the primary focus of my research, they help create a more complete picture of the lives of Far West Bajo residents. The Bajo Hill site and La Caldera were not merely farming villages; rather, they contained intriguing evidence for mundane domestic activities, craft production, long-distance trade, and ritual practices. This evidence hints at the wider web of relationships in which bajo dwellers were engaged, for surely they had contact with the urban environment of La Milpa center as well as with more distant Maya groups.

Houses occupied by residents of the Bajo Hill community were less elaborate than those at La Caldera but were solidly built and occupied through several stages of renovation. Some houses were probably pole and thatch structures atop stone platforms; today, only the platforms remain. Even these, however, were often faced with shaped limestone blocks carefully fitted together to form a veneer holding the rubble fill that elevated the house off the ground surface. Usually, the platform was topped with a lime plaster floor instead of the more expeditious packed earth surface often associated with such unassuming structures. Quarrying and shaping the stone, collecting wood, and burning the lime for the plaster were labor- and material-intensive tasks. Also, those houses built near the foot of the hillslope had thick clay layers between bedrock and the lowest construction level, presumably to keep the floors dry as the ground became saturated with rain.

Many of the houses at Bajo Hill were at some point renovated into partially stone-walled homes with limestone core-and-veneer walls rising perhaps waist-high, usually defining a single room. The remainder of the walls were likely constructed of wood or wattle-and-daub and topped with a thatch roof. Occupation of such houses must have been fairly long term, as excavation showed that residents refinished the plaster floors one to several times throughout the houses' duration. Inside, plastered masonry benches built against the interior of the walls provided sitting and sleeping spaces in some of the structures. Such benches were a common type of furniture among the Maya and it is not unusual to find burials inside them. Two individuals were buried inside such a bench in one of the partially walled houses we tested at the Bajo Hill site (Burials 1 and 2; see Appendix G).

Other features that were added to houses include plastered terraces or patios providing outdoor work space and rubble patio walls enclosing exterior spaces around the houses. We may imagine a number of activities taking place in these extramural areas, such as shaping ceramic pots, crafting stone bifaces and blades, corn grinding, cooking, and sewing. Broken pots, plates and bowls, polishing stones, fragmentary stone tools, manos, metates, and spindle whorls were all common finds in construction fill, and diverse trash deposits were mixed into the rubble alignments defining the edges of patios.

The houses at La Caldera were generally larger and more elaborate than those at Bajo Hill and featured more complex building histories. Several of the ones excavated had full-height masonry walls and doorways leading into multiple rooms. Many also contained evidence for floor replasterings as well as front terraces or patios. Curiously, many of the houses at La Caldera underwent a final renovation in which room spaces were filled with clean, compact marl to form tall stone-faced platforms, which presumably had at least plaster floors on top if not perishable superstructures. A number of architectural elaborations and special deposits were encountered in La Caldera's houses. In one instance, a wide plastered bench at the back of a room in a long, multiroomed structure on Plaza A was constructed above a cist burial containing the remains of an adult male (Burial 4, see Appendix G). In another, a large decorative marl buttress adorned the façade of a masonry-walled building that was later filled in to form a tall platform. A third example is the pyramidal temple defining the east side of Plaza A. Unfortunately, this tall structure is so badly looted that one can see straight through the building from front to back. The trenches did reveal, however, that two vaulted rooms once stood side by side, in front of which was placed an elaborate cache offering, discussed below. These impressive architectural elaborations suggest that certain structures at La Caldera, especially those around Plaza A, were shrines, meeting rooms, or receiving halls serving public or administrative functions. But this does not mean that residents of La Caldera did not also engage in more typical domestic tasks. Builders of a fourth structure on the east side of the settlement embedded the neck of a discarded ceramic jar into one of the walls to form a holder for a curtain to subdivide the interior space. Another building, a small square structure in Group F, may have been used as a kitchen. During excavation a large number of grinding stones of all shapes and sizes were recovered, suggesting that cooks might have undertaken their meal preparations here, away from the sleeping quarters.

Investigation into one of La Caldera's extramural spaces, the large terrace defined by a stacked boulder wall in Group E, provided evidence of craft specialization by community residents. Thousands of biface thinning flakes were recovered from among the wall stones and within the terrace fill. This density of uniform lithic debitage hints at the localized production of a specific kind of tool. Bifaces were ubiquitous at the site, and more than 60 whole or partial examples were recovered in excavations at La Caldera. They were also common in the agricultural and resource extraction zones throughout the Far West Bajo, with 25 examples from these locations. Apparently La Caldera residents manufactured utilitarian bifaces in the Group E patio and then swept the sharp debris against the wall for disposal. The low quality of the stone and the excessive thickness and extensive edge wear of the tools, including step and hinge fractures (Eguchi 2000), support my interpretation of these bifaces as primarily agricultural and land-clearing tools.

Teruyo Eguchi (2000), in an analysis of 50 of the bifaces from the Bajo Hill site and La Caldera, found a one-to-one ratio between proximal (N = 16) and distal (N = 16) fragments discarded in residential contexts. Following McAnany (1992), she interprets this finding as indicating an emphasis on near-residential cultivation or house gardening. According to McAnany, when a bifacial agricultural tool breaks in a field, the distal end is often discarded on site, but the proximal end is brought back to the house so that the haft can be refitted with a new blade. As cultivation intensifies and more farming activities take place closer to home, more tools break closer to home as well, with the result that distal ends are more likely to be discarded in residential middens. Today in the Maya area it is common for families to grow fruit trees, herbs, ornamentals, and medicinal plants as well as small plots of corn in kitchen gardens adjacent to their houses. Cultivation of open areas around residential groups is one of the components of the garden-infield-outfield model of land use. The dispersed arrangement of residential groups at all three bajo communities would have provided open space for gardening; however no botanical or soil phosphate data were collected to confirm this interpretation. Thus, Eguchi's discovery of equal numbers of distal and proximal biface fragments discarded in construction fill and midden around houses is the primary evidence for gardening at the Bajo Hill site and La Caldera.

Aside from the specialized biface production in Group E, the constant presence of lithic debitage in almost every excavation context points to the widespread manufacture and use of stone tools in everyday life. Perusing the artifact appendixes, the reader can see that sequences of primary, secondary, and tertiary flakes occurred in the fill of almost every structure and agricultural feature in the Far West Bajo. Formal tools like bifaces and informal tools involving utilized flakes and cores were common, indicating that the villagers were proficient in supplying their own stone tools for agricultural and domestic use. It is less certain whether the thinner fine-edged specimens, made from imported chert and found in some cache contexts, were also crafted on site.

Much less can be said about ceramic manufacture, since there was no direct evidence of pottery production in any of the excavations despite the abundance of the finished product: no firing areas; no stored clay, temper, or pigment; and no wasters or malformed pots. The only hint of manufacturing consisted of several small polishing stones like those used elsewhere to smooth the surfaces of ceramic vessels prior to firing. It is likely that at least some members of the villages produced pottery for use in cooking, food serving, and water storage, but evidence of this eludes us. What is not difficult to see, however, is the abundance of shapes and colors, pots both plain and fancy, at every house investigated. Most sherds were mixed into the construction fill of the buildings, and thus they do not represent a direct inventory of what was used by each individual household. In this same vein, the only whole vessels recovered were in caches at La Caldera and Thompson's Group. Traditionally, however, Maya archaeologists assume that artifacts incorporated into construction fill originated, if not from the structure in question, then from the same architectural group. With this caveat in mind, we can see that the most common vessel forms at both Bajo Hill and at La Caldera were bowls, plates, and jars, with vases, cups, and basins much less frequent. Bowls were black, brown, red, or orange, with bolstered rims, everted rims, and beveled lips. Some were polychrome. They were incurving, outcurving, or straight-sided. Most common was an orange-brown bowl with thick bolstered rim. Plates during early periods of occupation included some basal-flanged black and orange dishes, and fewer orange and cream polychrome plates. Later dishes were monochrome black, red, or brown, mottled orange-brown, and orange polychrome. Jars were especially common; most were large, unslipped vessels suited for water storage, with striated or appliquéd necks. Smaller jars were orange, red, black, brown, and later slate, some with everted or bolstered rims. Vases were uncommon, but typically orange or cream polychrome, monochrome black grooved, or red incised cylinders. Basins were orange or unslipped and striated. Unusual finds included sherds with stucco, hematite wash, and graffiti, along with several unslipped incensario fragments with appliquéd faces, and a few figurine fragments. Kosakowsky and Sagebiel (1999: 134) summarized La Milpa's local ceramic tradition as heavily focused on mottled slips in orange, brown, and cream tones, bolstered rim bowls, and local versions of Peten (Saxche and Palmar) polychromes. These observations extend to the ceramics of the Far West Bajo.

It is reasonable to assume that Maya kitchens were furnished with large bowls for cooking, jars for water and food storage, smaller bowls and plates for serving, and cups and vases for drinking. Plainer monochrome vessels were "everyday" dishes, with fancier painted plates and bowls akin to our "good china." Each household appeared to have had more of the former than the latter. The presence of jar, basin, and bowl fragments in many agricultural contexts probably means that at least beverages, if not complete meals, were taken into the fields. Kerry Sagebiel proposed another interpretation, that these sherds were deposited through erosion (sheet wash) or application of household waste as fertilizer.

Despite the ample ceramic evidence of food preparation and consumption, we have scant information regarding specific food preparations or even food remains. Aside from one possible kitchen structure containing multiple grinding stones, no other food preparation locations could be identified, although I assume that many meal-related tasks took place in outdoor work areas. The 20 manos and metates (whole or fragments) recovered from excavation contexts are thought to have been used by villagers, probably women, to grind corn. Botanical analyses were not conducted on any of the soil samples collected during the project, with the exception of the pollen count from Op. BH9. The decision not to pursue this avenue was partly a financial one and partly a pragmatic one, because previous attempts at macrobotanical analysis by one of my colleagues on samples from similar contexts yielded such poor results. Unfortunately, Belize's semitropical climate is not conducive to good preservation of organic material. Traditionally the Maya are thought to have subsisted primarily on corn and beans, along with squashes, chilies, tomatoes, avocados, and a variety of fruits and herbs. Protein in the diet came from eating corn and beans together and from supplemental animal protein. Hunting probably contributed deer, peccary, small rodents, birds, and other meat to the cooking pot, but in the Far West Bajo faunal remains were exceedingly rare and poorly preserved. Only one context yielded a significant quantity of animal bones (Op. V66A), mostly small pieces worked into beads, awls, or needles. These artifacts do demonstrate that animal bone was available and used for both utilitarian tools and decorative objects. One artifact from this context, a columnar bone piece decorated with carving, is almost identical to a bone ear flare identified at the northern Belize site of Cuello (Hammond 1991: 182, Fig. 8.30). No faunal analysis was conducted on either the worked or unworked bone.

Most Maya scholars think that the majority of foodstuffs were produced locally and that staple foods were rarely imported from other regions. But other objects were certainly traded, and the Far West Bajo clearly shows evidence of engagement in a long-distance trade network, even if on a small scale. Chert for the finely crafted bifaces found in some cache contexts appears to have been imported from the chert-bearing zone of coastal Belize. The fine-grained cream, rose, and yellowish brown cherts likely came from the area around Colha, and the grainier white and grey cherts used for the utilitarian bifaces were probably local to La Milpa. Another stone raw material that was imported is obsidian from the Maya highlands. This grayish volcanic glass makes extremely sharp, fine cutting implements and was highly valued for slicing tasks. In the Far West Bajo, obsidian appeared only in residential contexts, where 147 whole or broken blades or other small fragments were recovered. It is not surprising that the agricultural features yielded no obsidian, for the fragile blades were not suited to heavy chopping tasks. The vast majority of the blades or blade fragments were very small and showed obvious signs of having been whittled down with use and reworked until they broke or it was necessary to discard them because of their small size. A pair of whole blades was in the cache vessel in front of La Caldera's main pyramid, and they are longer, wider, and thicker than all other examples. A second set of three blades came from under the lowest plaster floor in Structure 3–A–3 at La Caldera. Production of obsidian blades required highly skilled artisans, and often the blades are thought to have been manufactured near their source and traded as finished products or on preshaped cores ready to be detached. One obsidian core was in La Caldera's Group F kitchen structure, suggesting the latter method of transport. A few small flakes indicated that retouch of the blades after initial use also occurred.

Another type of imported or exotic material found in the Far West Bajo communities was marine shell, especially conch (*Strombus gigas*). Most of the shell objects in excavations were finished decorative objects like pendants. The lack of shell fragments in these contexts indicates that the objects were likely imported in their finished state, probably from the Belizean coast some 80 km (50 miles) to the east. One example is a star-shaped pendant with a large central cut-out and a small perforation on each side to allow it to hang from a cord. The pendant, which is not flat but curved along the shell's natural shape, was carved from a large piece of conch. It was found during excavation of a patio wall on Bajo Hill. A second example is a rectangular rasp, approximately 12 cm long, also carved from a piece of conch (see Fig. 5.20). The thick rasp has a series of vertical indentations along one face, along with two horizontal incisions on the left side of the same face. This object was collected from a small isolated structure above the agricultural features in Survey Block 2. A third shell object is a small (4 cm) rectangular shell pendant with carved edges from La Caldera (see Fig. 5.15). It has incised decoration on the front and a small hole to facilitate hanging. All three of these objects were discarded (or lost) while still whole.

Most of the remaining shell objects were recovered in ritual contexts. Three large fragments of scallop shell were part of the cache in front of La Caldera's pyramid. Marine shell and coral were included in the cache in front of the temple in Group 6 at Thompson's Group. Several smaller pieces of shell, including one anvil-shaped piece and a piece of iridescent shell carved into the shape of a caiman head were in the

bedrock pit under Structure 3–F–10 at La Caldera. A few large spiral conch pieces and smaller mussel shell fragments that may have been unfinished raw material were recovered in the construction fill of houses at La Caldera and the Bajo Hill site.

The final type of exotic material that Far West Bajo residents were able to obtain was greenstone. Commonly called jade, greenstone features varied chemical signatures and comes from the Motagua river valley in Guatemala. It is a highly symbolic material in the Maya world view, associated with the watery underworld (because of its color) and therefore with the deities who are thought to reside there. In the best known Maya sites such as Tikal, jade beads, mosaics, and jewelry are often found in royal burials. Greenstone is also a frequent component of cache offerings throughout the Maya area. Usually considered a "prestige" good, it is not uncommon to find a few pieces in less exalted contexts. Only four pieces of greenstone were recovered from the Far West Bajo area, all but one in cache contexts. The exception, an exquisite greenstone celt with ground edges, was near the surface of Structure 1–P–2 near the base of Bajo Hill in a location that also contained several unusual objects grouped together, including a stone ball and three whole bifaces. The other greenstone artifacts were from La Caldera's pyramid, including a round, light green bead found in the backdirt of the looters' trenches and two pieces (one light green, polished, and uncarved and one a dark green broken bead) from inside the large cache vessel in front of the temple. Considering these fragmentary finds and the badly looted state of La Caldera's pyramid, it is highly likely that more greenstone items were originally included in the cache offering and perhaps inside the temple itself. Sadly, the full contents of the cache, which could have told us much about the ideology of the people who placed it ceremoniously at the base of the pyramid, will never be known.

Fortunately, we have information derived elsewhere that sheds light on the ritual activities of Far West Bajo residents. Studies of mortuary treatment, religious architecture, and cache assemblages in both elite and ordinary residential groups have led archaeologists to identify a suite of Maya religious beliefs, such as ancestor veneration and the association of death with passage into the underworld that demonstrate a shared world view regardless of social status (Kunen and others 2002). One of the most prevalent activities affiliated with this world view was caching, or the placement of votive offerings. Such offerings could be formal, enclosed in ceramic vessels and located at specific places within or under a building or stela, or less structured, consisting of a group of unusual objects in a context that was in some way marked as special. As with caches, many Maya burials were neither intricate nor located in special religious structures, but placed under the floors of ordinary houses. Such subfloor burials created permanent and physical links to deceased members of the household. Grave goods also varied from complete absence to elaborate deposits of ceramic vessels, jade earflares, shell pendants, obsidian eccentrics, and accompanying remains of animals or other humans. The caches and burials in the Far West Bajo provide us with the clearest picture we can hope to obtain of the ideological beliefs and religious practices of the Bajo Maya.

Of the seven deposits identified as caches, only two were formal offerings placed inside a ceramic vessel at the base of a religious structure. We cannot ascertain the complete contents or arrangement of the looted cache in front of La Caldera's main pyramid, but we do know that minimally it included jade beads, obsidian blades, chert bifaces, marine shells, and two 12-cm long pieces of human femoral bone. These objects were placed in or under a large gray jar, capped with a brown plate lid of a different ceramic type, and plastered into place on a floor in front of the temple. An orange vessel, also with a lid, whose contents (if any) were looted, was placed a few feet away. Such an assemblage is commonly referred to as a dedicatory offering, with the implication that it marked a significant event such as the erection or renovation of the temple or the burial of an important person within it. A second formal cache was excavated by Robichaux in front of a the Group 6 temple at Thompson's Group. He reported finding a large ceramic vessel placed in a hollow carved out of bedrock at the base of the structure; it contained pieces of marine shell, pyrite, obsidian, mother of pearl, coral, and quartz (Robichaux 1995: 390–395).

Two other caches included chert bifaces deposited on or beneath the now-eroded steps of small pyramids at Bajo Hill. The first of these deposits is the one depicted in the vignette at the opening of this chapter. During excavation of the small pyramid in Group A at the Bajo Hill settlement, we encountered two Colha chert bifaces at the interface between a layer of collapsed construction material and the building's fill, just where the front steps would be if they had survived intact. The exquisite craftsmanship of the knives and their impeccable condition mark them as an offering, an interpretation supported by other aspects of the pyramid such as its early date relative to the rest of the village's buildings, its enclosure within a set of stone walls, and the presence of bone fragments in the backdirt from the looters' trench that destroyed much of the building. The second example is slightly less clear, but involves a brown stemmed biface and three pieces of obsidian grouped on top of the floor that underlies what I interpret to be a pyramidal structure in Group O at the Bajo Hill settlement. The biface is similar to the stemmed knife in the cache just described. The tentative identification of a set of stairs on the front of the structure strengthens its interpretation as a temple, where people would be likely to place an offering. A third cache of two bifaces was located beneath the steps of Structure 3–F–10 at La Caldera, a residential structure that also contained an unusual ritual deposit, described below.

Two other deposits defy easy categorization. Both feature an unusual concentration of either unbroken or "exotic" objects, the kinds not likely to be thrown away in an ordinary trash pit. The first was in the same structure that yielded a greenstone celt and a large piece of conch from Bajo Hill's Group P. Excavation also uncovered a limestone ball on, and three bifaces just below, the lower of two plaster floors defining a room within the structure.

The second example is the bedrock pit beneath Structure 3–F–10 at La Caldera. The pit, carved with two steps on the north and a niche on the east, was filled with a collection of unusually large sherds, many of them polychrome; numerous bifaces; several hammerstones; and assorted carved shell and bone artifacts. The pit was capped by a series of plaster floors, one of which had been broken into multiple times for the burial of three individuals. Elsewhere (Kunen and others 2002) I have argued that the pit, its contents, and the associated burials consecrated a column of sacred space that was revisited by occupants of the overarching structure through several generations. Such an interpretation for this and all of the cache offerings discussed here is supported by our understanding of the ancient Maya's active relationship with the ancestors buried within temples and beneath house floors. This relationship involved performing religious or ceremonial acts in the special structures we refer to as temples, and the offering of special objects in places with symbolic meaning that were often tied physically to those same ancestors through their presence as burials.

That the deceased were incorporated into the lives of their descendants in the Far West Bajo communities is evident from the inclusion of burials in several of the houses at both Bajo Hill and La Caldera. Two primary kinds of information came from the burial assemblages. The first, focusing on the location of the burials and their furnishings, including formal grave preparation and grave goods, shows us what the Far West Bajo Maya considered to be appropriate treatment of the dead and what symbolic statements they made through the inclusion and positioning of the skeleton and associated offerings. The second, involving the antemortem condition of the bodies themselves, tells us not only about their age and sex but also something about the kinds of lives led by the deceased, including any diseases, nutritional deficiencies, skeletal abnormalities, or injuries they suffered and the types of activities they pursued.

Of the nine burials we excavated, only three were placed in specially prepared repositories. Two individuals (Burials 1 and 2) were enclosed, one above the other, within a plastered masonry bench inside the room of a house (Str. 1–B–2) in Group B at Bajo Hill. The lower of the two, a young adult male, was positioned inside a hole cut through the room floor so that the body rested on bedrock. The upper individual, a young adult female, rested on the floor. Both bodies were in a flexed (fetal) position and the heads of both were marked by vertical slab headstones. The female was not accompanied by any other grave goods but the male was buried with a broken obsidian blade, a miniature black pot that may be Early Classic (Balanza type), and three hematite ear flares (see Fig. 5.7).

A third burial (Burial 4), this one at La Caldera, was given a more elaborate treatment. It was enclosed in a limestone slab cist that was covered by a capstone and later overlain by several floors and a plastered masonry bench in Structure 3–A–3 in La Caldera's main plaza. The body of a middle-aged adult male, tightly flexed, rested on bedrock within the small cist. Unfortunately, the bones were extremely fragmentary. No grave goods accompanied this individual, which seems unusual considering the maturity of the man and that his presumably high status warranted burial

in a special chamber in a building so close to the main temple. Based on the stratigraphy of this unit, the body may have been interred sometime during the Late Preclassic; all other recorded burials are Late Classic.

The remaining burials were all subfloor interments, located under floors and within the construction fill of buildings, with no special grave preparation. Burials 3 and 9 were children, the former 3 to 5 years old and the latter 1 to 2 years old. The older child was in a flexed position below a lens of dense household trash in La Caldera's Group B, just behind the main temple. The cranium reveals the common Maya trait of cranial shaping that was thought to have been aesthetically pleasing. A single obsidian blade fragment accompanied the child's bones. The younger child was identified only by the presence of deciduous teeth mixed in with the skeletal material of an older individual (Burial 8). It is not clear if the child's remains represent a badly decayed primary burial or an offering accompanying the adult. Burial 8 was a young adult male in a flexed position in the subfloor fill of Structure 3–X–1 at La Caldera. The bones were fragmentary and were not accompanied by any grave goods.

The last three burials were all situated above the bedrock pit in La Caldera's Structure 3–F–10. Burials 5, 6, and 7 were placed in the cobble fill of the structure through holes cut into the plaster floor of a room above them. These holes were subsequently patched and the room continued to be used. There are only two holes and it appears that the latest burial, Burial 5, was inserted through one of the existing holes at a later time, for it intrudes upon the earlier Burial 6. The young adult male of Burial 5 was accompanied by a single human tooth offering, carved in a Romero B5 style, which may have had a cord wrapped around its root for hanging. This individual also demonstrates a tabular erect style of cranial shaping, in which the frontal cranial bone was artificially flattened. Interestingly, the individuals in Burials 5 and 7 may have been related, for they both demonstrate a skeletal anomaly in which the hamate (a bone in the hand) has no hamulus (hook). The individual in Burial 7 had one upper right incisor filed in Romero B2 style. Tooth filing, like cranial shaping, was considered by the Maya to be beautifying. No grave goods were with either Burial 6 or 7.

The skeletal material itself provides information about the lives led by these individuals (see also Appendix G). Dominant themes are strenuous physical activity, episodes of childhood nutritional stress, and numerous injuries. It is clear that at least these Far West Bajo residents lived difficult and at times dangerous lives, especially as portrayed in the adult burials from La Caldera. The two individuals in burials at the Bajo Hill site, although demonstrating strong muscle attachments, some nutritional stress, and activity-related tooth wear, appear to have been healthier. At La Caldera, the male identified in Burial 5 suffered from bone spurs and lipping caused by walking or running over rough terrain; a healed broken hand, perhaps from a fall; an episode of childhood nutritional stress evident in the teeth as linear enamel hypoplasia; and gum disease that led to antemortem tooth loss. Uneven wear on the molars as well as on the lingual side of the upper teeth reveals some sort of activity-related attrition.

The male of Burial 6 sustained a crushing fracture of one hand bone, a simple fracture of a second hand bone, and three fractures in the right foot and ankle, all of which might have resulted from the same fall. Enlargements on both the right and left femora suggest extreme activity involving the legs. The adult of Burial 7 had a fractured rib from a fall or blow to the chest, a deep healed incision in the skull, and bone spurs and enlarged muscle attachments indicative of an active life. In terms of dentition, this individual underwent two episodes of malnutrition or illness and suffered extreme periodontal disease causing numerous cavities, loss of molar teeth, and tooth abscesses. The one upper tooth recovered demonstrates extreme lingual side attrition.

The individual in Burial 8, although fragmentary, suffered numerous cavities, a prolonged period of childhood malnutrition or illness, and a long-term draining injury on the right ankle. Two additional individuals were identified from bone retrieved and catalogued from a looters' trench in La Caldera's Group B. One, a young, probably female adult suffered tooth loss, a healed parry fracture to the right ulna, and a healed blunt force injury to the front of the skull that may have resulted in the loss of the right eye. This individual also demonstrated marked cranial shaping of the tabular oblique type and possibly tooth filing in Romero B2 or B4 style. The second individual's bones, as well as those in Burials 3, 4, 9, and the looters' trench in Bajo Hill Group A were too fragmentary for meaningful study.

IN THE BAJO, LOOKING OUT

In many ways, the communities I have just described do not differ dramatically from other Maya villages of the lowlands. At nearly every site investigated, the behaviors and customs discussed here, including patterns of house construction, arrangement of domestic space, production and consumption of basic tools and utensils, engagement in trade, and display of a coherent set of religious or ideological beliefs form part of the culture or world view shared by members of ancient Maya society. The villages appear to have been founded and began their existence just as did many other Late Preclassic farming villages, with small groups of inhabitants dispersed across the landscape, engaging in swidden agriculture. The uniqueness of the bajo communities lies instead in the solution residents found to their predicament when the environmental foundations of their traditional way of life changed dramatically. After several centuries this way of life had, in effect, destroyed the ecosystem on which it depended. Resource specialization, involving intensified use of improved bajo margin lands as well as continued exploitation of the raw materials and resources of the bajo interior, can thus be seen as the innovative response of bajo residents to the unique environmental history of the Far West Bajo.

Why did I choose to study a small, self-contained upland bajo with no overt archaeological attractions such as imposing monuments or even patterns of raised fields? So many Maya studies are site-based, emphasizing the large architecture and royal histories of the better known monumental centers, while suburban and rural investigations are almost always incorporated into these larger projects as components of research on the center's sustaining area. In contrast, I wanted to study the settlements of ordinary Maya and to understand those settlements in their own right, not as subsidiary areas interesting only in terms of their relation to the center. By framing my study around the bajo communities, I acknowledged their identity as Maya villages with unique histories, not mere appendages of the larger polity. I also avoided privileging the remains of the settlements themselves (houses, temples, plazas) merely because they were the most visible features on the landscape.

Site-centered research has a natural tendency to emphasize the remains and, consequently, the activities, that occurred within settlements and to undervalue those features (and the actions that produced them) that are located elsewhere on the landscape. Few researchers take as their explicit subject the unprepossessing agricultural features that were so central to my study. Yet it was the careful mapping and excavation of these features that were key to understanding my "field site," unconventionally defined as it was. In a very real sense, then, the focus of my research was the bajo itself, the central element of the landscape I studied. This framing strategy represents an important aspect of landscape analysis, one that attempts to place in the foreground those aspects of the landscape that were most critical in structuring resource use and settlement.

I hope this volume demonstrates the value of landscape analysis in contextualizing ancient human adaptation. Without placing the settlement and agricultural histories of the Far West Bajo in their proper *reflexive* relationship with the environmental history of the bajo, it is impossible to see the innovation and resilience of bajo residents. Nor is it possible to understand the attraction that bajos held for the Maya, an attraction that has long puzzled modern schol-

ars. Some might argue that the intensification that characterized Classic period use of the Far West Bajo created what Tourtellot and his colleagues consider a "landscape of desperation" (see their discussion in Tourtellot and others 1995), and the evidence presented here for the health and nutritional status of bajo residents late in the occupation sequence would support this view. But it is also true that this specialized economy produced thriving villages within which dwelled a subset of high status local elite with deep ties to the community, ample access to land and labor resources, trading relationships with distant groups, and important religious and ritual responsibilities. The bajo communities weathered the Preclassic to Classic period transition successfully, remaining in and around the Far West Bajo for six hundred more years. The broader significance for anthropology of this local history is that intensive agricultural adaptations in prehistory should not be viewed only as examples of increasingly desperate attempts by ancient peoples to mitigate environmental damage but rather as successful systems of indigenous resource management.

Ceramics from Excavations in the Far West Bajo

Ceramics from excavations in the Far West Bajo were initially analyzed by Kerry Sagebiel, ceramicist for the Ancient Maya Land and Water Management Project. The sherd counts in this Appendix represent the results of her analysis in 2001. Sagebiel is reanalyzing all ceramics from the land and water management project and from the La Milpa Archaeological Project for her doctoral dissertation at the University of Arizona (Sagebiel 2003). She has indicated to me that the primary improvement in the new analysis is her ability to distinguish late Early Classic ceramics (Tzakol 2/3) from early Late Classic ceramics (Tepeu 1), resulting in a more refined chronological sequence.

Whereas the 2001 analysis I used distinguished four ceramic periods (Late Preclassic, Early Classic, early Late Classic, and Late/Terminal Classic), Sagebiel now recognizes eight periods that overlap slightly: Late Preclassic, early Early Classic, Early Classic, late Early Classic, Classic, early Late Classic, Late Classic, and Late/Terminal Classic. Additionally, many Far West Bajo sherds that were previously placed in the Unknown or eroded category are now grouped in the Classic period, a generic category that spans the Early and Late Classic periods. Overall, the number of unknown sherds has decreased substantially as a result.

Sagebiel's reanalysis has only minor implications for the interpretations I offer in this volume, affecting only seven excavation contexts. Accordingly, I altered my language slightly in text descriptions of these contexts to reflect Sagebiel's new understanding of their occupational history. I summarize the changes here.

Op. V42B: Subfloor fill, under the floor defined in Lot 11, now dates to the Early Classic, not the early Late Classic.

Op. V42C: The first of two construction phases (Lots 3 and 7) are now dated to the Early-Late Classic transition rather than the early Late Classic, indicating that ceramics date from the latest stages of the Early Classic and the earliest stages of the Late Classic.

Op. V51C: Both phases of construction are assigned to the Early Classic, not the early Late Classic.

Op. V52B: The first phase of construction dates to the Early-Late Classic transition, not the early Late Classic.

Op. V62A: A middle phase of construction dates to the Early-Late Classic transition, not the early Late Classic.

Op. V65B: The first phase of construction is assigned to the Early-Late Classic transition, whereas in 2001 this phase could not be dated securely.

Op. V67B: Construction of the residential terrace is assigned to the Early Classic, whereas in 2001 this assignment was tentative.

It is reassuring to note that Sagebiel's reassessment further strengthens the interpretation that the settlement and agricultural features associated with the Far West Bajo have surprisingly early dates. The substantial populations present by the Late Preclassic and Early Classic periods implemented an intensive agricultural system by the end of the Early Classic or the beginning of the Late Classic period.

Ceramics from Excavations in the Far West Bajo (Analysis by Kerry Sagebiel, 2001)

Block	Zone	Group	Op.	Subop.	Lot	Late Preclassic No.	%	Early Classic No.	%	Early Late Classic No.	%	Late Terminal Classic No.	%	Unknown (eroded) No.	%	Total
5	Agri-3		V26	A	1											
			V26	A	2									1	100.00	1
			V26	A	3											
			V26	A	4									3	100.00	3
			V26	A	5									1	100.00	1
1	Res.	A	V27	A	1									75	100.00	75
			V28	A	1			2	0.94	3	1.41	18	8.45	190	89.20	213
			V28	A	2			1	0.58	8	4.65	15	8.72	148	86.05	172
			V28	A	3			1	1.41	11	15.49	8	11.27	51	71.83	71
			V29	A	1							17	6.88	230	93.12	247
			V29	A	2	3	2.59			1	0.86	8	6.90	104	89.66	116
			V29	A	3	1	9.09							10	90.91	11
			V29	A	4	2	5.41	1	2.70					34	91.89	37
			V29	A	5	39	38.24			4	3.92			59	57.84	102
			V29	A	6	124	43.51							161	56.49	285
1	Res.	No.	V31	A	1									9	100.00	9
			V31	A	2					1	3.70	2	7.41	24	88.89	27
			V31	A	3							1	25.00	3	75.00	4
1	Res.	O	V32	A	1					2	7.41			25	92.59	27
			V32	A	2							1	0.74	134	99.26	135
			V32	A	3											
1	Res.	I	V34	A	1	2	1.71			3	2.56	1	0.85	111	94.87	117
			V34	A	2			1	1.56			1	1.56	62	96.88	64
			V34	A	3							1	2.17	45	97.83	46
1	Res.	No.	V35	A	1							1	0.11	8	0.89	9
			V35	A	2							13	30.95	29	69.05	42
			V35	B	1							1	20.00	4	80.00	5
			V35	B	2									6	100.00	6
			V35	B	3							1	6.25	15	93.75	16
1	Res.	I	V37	A	1					3	0.89	24	7.10	311	92.01	338
			V37	A	2					3	1.05	8	2.81	274	96.14	285
			V37	A	3					1	0.34	14	4.71	282	94.95	297
	Bajo		V38	A	1											
			V38	A	2			1	14.29	3	42.86			3	42.86	7
			V38	A	3											
			V38	B	1							1	50.00	1	50.00	2
			V38	B	2					2	1.60	3	2.40	120	96.00	125
			V38	B	3											
1	Res.	A	V39	A	1							1	14.29	6	85.71	7
			V39	A	2			2	2.67			19	25.33	54	72.00	75
			V39	A	3					1	1.15	30	34.48	56	64.37	87
			V39	A	4											
			V39	B	1					2	1.90	11	10.48	92	87.62	105
			V39	B	2	1	1.47	1	1.47	1	1.47	13	19.12	52	76.47	68
			V39	B	3	2	1.94	44	42.72					57	55.34	103
			V39	B	4									13	100.00	13
			V39	B	5									12	100.00	12
			V39	C	1	26	6.33	28	6.81	24	5.84	15	3.65	318	77.37	411
			V39	C	2	8	33.33	6	25.00					10	41.67	24
			V39	C	3									6	100.00	6
			V39	C	4									1	100.00	1
			V39	D	1					1	50.00			1	50.00	2

Ceramics from Excavations in the Far West Bajo (Analysis by Kerry Sagebiel, 2001), *continued*

Block	Zone	Group	Op.	Subop.	Lot	Late Preclassic No.	%	Early Classic No.	%	Early Late Classic No.	%	Late Terminal Classic No.	%	Unknown (eroded) No.	%	Total
1	Res.	A	V39	D	2			1	0.90	2	1.80	31	27.93	77	69.37	111
			V39	D	3					1	0.36	63	22.74	213	76.90	277
			V39	D	4							21	28.00	54	72.00	75
			V39	D	5							5	38.46	8	61.54	13
			V39	D	6			2	0.68	1	0.34	83	28.33	207	70.65	293
			V39	D	7									2	100.00	2
			V39	D	8	3	2.26	15	11.28	2	1.50			113	84.96	133
			V39	E	1	2	2.33	1	1.16	1	1.16	22	25.58	60	69.77	86
			V39	E	2					2	2.44	30	36.59	50	60.98	82
			V39	F	1					3	0.71	6	1.43	411	97.86	420
			V39	F	2			1	0.37			3	1.12	263	98.50	267
1	Res.	H	V40	A	1					3	1.47	15	7.35	186	91.18	204
			V40	A	2			1	0.19	9	1.68	11	2.05	515	96.08	536
			V40	A	3					2	20.00			8	80.00	10
			V40	B	1	1	0.34			1	0.34	11	3.73	282	95.59	295
			V40	B	2					1	0.52	13	6.81	177	92.67	191
			V40	C	1							1	3.85	25	96.15	26
			V40	C	2									19	100.00	19
			V40	D	1							4	13.33	26	86.67	30
			V40	D	2							2	4.88	39	95.12	41
1	Res.	B	V42	A	1									8	100.00	8
			V42	A	2							3	4.76	60	95.24	63
			V42	A	3							1	6.25	15	93.75	16
			V42	A	4					1	0.66	8	5.26	143	94.08	152
			V42	A	5			2	0.80	2	0.80	21	8.40	225	90.00	250
			V42	A	6	2	2.20			5	5.49	12	13.19	72	79.12	91
			V42	B	1							1	5.88	16	94.12	17
			V42	B	2							3	11.11	24	88.89	27
			V42	B	3	1	0.67	2	1.34	13	8.72	35	23.49	98	65.77	149
			V42	B	4									4	100.00	4
			V42	B	5											
			V42	B	6											
			V42	B	7							2	7.41	25	92.59	27
			V42	B	8									17	100.00	17
			V42	B	9							38	90.48	4	9.52	42
			V42	B	10											
			V42	B	11			18	13.85	13	10.00			99	76.15	130
			V42	B	12							1	10.00	9	90.00	10
			V42	B	13											
1	Res.	C	V42	C	1									7	100.00	7
			V42	C	2					1	0.54	7	3.80	176	95.65	184
			V42	C	3			46	3.72	59	4.77			1132	91.51	1237
			V42	C	4									2	100.00	2
			V42	C	5							2	22.22	7	77.78	9
			V42	C	6					1	5.56			17	94.44	18
			V42	C	7			16	18.18	3	3.41			69	78.41	88
			V42	D	1			1	1.52	1	1.52	2	3.03	62	93.94	66
			V42	D	2	3	0.92	6	1.85	3	0.92	10	3.08	303	93.23	325
1	Res.	P	V51	A	1									31	100.00	31
			V51	A	2			3	1.60	4	2.13	10	5.32	171	90.96	188
			V51	A	3	2	0.09	11	0.50	30	1.37	274	12.49	1876	85.54	2193
			V51	A	4			2	1.64	11	9.02	12	9.84	97	79.51	122
			V51	A	5					11	7.19			142	92.81	153
			V51	A	6			23	4.13	90	16.16	14	2.51	430	77.20	557
1	Res.	O	V51	B	1							8	7.08	105	92.92	113
			V51	B	2					3	1.05	31	10.88	251	88.07	285
			V51	B	3					2	0.90	37	16.59	184	82.51	223

Ceramics from Excavations in the Far West Bajo (Analysis by Kerry Sagebiel, 2001), *continued*

Block	Zone	Group	Op.	Subop.	Lot	Late Preclassic No.	%	Early Classic No.	%	Early Late Classic No.	%	Late Terminal Classic No.	%	Unknown (eroded) No.	%	Total
1	Res.	O	V51	B	4					4	1.09	34	9.24	330	89.67	368
			V51	B	5											
			V51	B	6							1	3.45	28	96.55	29
1	Res.	No.	V51	C	1					1	4.76			20	95.24	21
			V51	C	2							14	5.53	239	94.47	253
			V51	C	3			1	1.45	3	4.35			65	94.20	69
			V51	C	4	2	1.85	4	3.70	2	1.85			100	92.59	108
			V51	C	5									1	100.00	1
			V51	C	6									20	100.00	20
1	Res.	K	V52	A	1							21	4.18	481	95.82	502
			V52	A	2									68	100.00	68
			V52	A	3					2	1.92	8	7.69	94	90.38	104
			V52	A	4	1	0.32	1	0.32	2	0.63	11	3.49	300	95.24	315
1	Res.	I	V52	B	1					2	0.98	9	4.41	193	94.61	204
			V52	B	2	1	0.34	1	0.34	2	0.68	6	2.03	286	96.62	296
			V52	B	3	8	14.04	4	7.02	2	3.51	1	1.75	42	73.68	57
			V52	B	4							1	2.27	43	97.73	44
			V52	B	5	2	0.95	2	0.95	9	4.27	15	7.11	183	86.73	211
			V52	B	6							9	8.82	93	91.18	102
			V52	B	7			1	1.33	2	2.67	2	2.67	70	93.33	75
			V52	B	8	1	2.86			3	8.57			31	88.57	35
			V52	B	9	7	25.93			1	3.70			19	70.37	27
			V52	B	10									17	100.00	17
1	Res.	L	V53	A	1	2	1.77					14	12.39	97	85.84	113
			V53	A	2									3	100.00	3
			V53	A	3	6	5.56	1	0.93	1	0.93	5	4.63	95	87.96	108
			V53	A	4			1	1.89			2	3.77	50	94.34	53
2	Agri-1		V58	A	1									1	100.00	1
			V58	A	2											
			V58	A	3											
			V58	A	4											
			V58	A	5											
			V58	A	6									1	100.00	1
			V58	B	1									8	100.00	8
			V58	B	2	1	0.93			3	2.80			103	96.26	107
			V58	B	3											
			V58	C	1											
			V58	C	2	2	25.00							6	75.00	8
			V58	C	3											
			V59	A	1									9	100.00	9
			V59	A	2					3	5.56	1	1.85	50	92.59	54
			V59	A	3			1	1.72					57	98.28	58
			V59	A	4			2	7.69					24	92.31	26
			V59	A	5									3	100.00	3
			V59	B	1									6	100.00	6
			V59	B	2			3	7.14			1	2.38	38	90.48	42
			V59	B	3											
			V60	A	1									19	100.00	19
			V60	A	2					1	2.38	2	4.76	39	92.86	42
			V60	A	3	1	6.67							14	93.33	15
			V60	A	4											
			V60	A	5					3	15.79			16	84.21	19
			V60	A	6											
			V60	A	7									9	100.00	9
2	Res.	B	V60	B	1			3	1.27	6	2.53	10	4.22	218	91.98	237
			V60	B	2	24	15.48			2	1.29	6	3.87	123	79.35	155
			V60	B	3	1	50.00							1	50.00	2

Ceramics from Excavations in the Far West Bajo (Analysis by Kerry Sagebiel, 2001), *continued*

Block	Zone	Group	Op.	Subop.	Lot	Late Preclassic No.	%	Early Classic No.	%	Early Late Classic No.	%	Late Terminal Classic No.	%	Unknown (eroded) No.	%	Total
2	Res.	B	V60	B	4							1	50.00	1	50.00	2
			V60	B	5											
2	Res.	A	V61	A	1	12	26.09							34	73.91	46
			V61	A	2	14	66.67							7	33.33	21
			V61	A	3	5	41.67							7	58.33	12
			V61	A	4											
			V61	A	5											
3	Res.	A	V62	A	1											
			V62	A	2					1	1.69			58	98.31	59
			V62	A	3					3	3.95	4	5.26	69	90.79	76
			V62	A	4							2	3.92	49	96.08	51
			V62	A	5									7	100.00	7
			V62	A	6									12	100.00	12
			V62	A	7	2	1.87	1	0.93	1	0.93	16	14.95	87	81.31	107
			V62	A	8									10	100.00	10
			V62	A	9							1	11.11	8	88.89	9
			V62	A	10	9	56.25							7	43.75	16
			V62	A	11	1	100.00							0	0.00	1
			V62	A	12											
			V62	A	13					2	20.00			8	80.00	10
			V62	A	14									1	100.00	1
			V62	A	15							1	7.14	13	92.86	14
			V62	A	16					1	1.22	12	14.63	69	84.15	82
			V62	A	17							13	52.00	12	48.00	25
			V62	A	18	3	8.33					2	5.56	31	86.11	36
			V62	A	19							2	16.67	10	83.33	12
			V62	A	20			2	2.63			2	2.63	72	94.74	76
			V62	A	21			2	4.00	1	2.00			47	94.00	50
			V62	A	22					1	4.17			23	95.83	24
			V62	A	23	4	12.12	2	6.06					27	81.82	33
			V62	A	24	1	4.35					5	21.74	17	73.91	23
			V62	A	25											
			V62	A	26									3	100.00	3
			V62	A	27									1	100.00	1
			V62	B	1			2	1.09	4	2.17	4	2.17	174	94.57	184
			V62	B	2			2	0.82	9	3.69	5	2.05	228	93.44	244
			V62	C	1							1	5.56	17	94.44	18
			V62	C	2											
			V62	C	3					3	5.17	16	27.59	39	67.24	58
3	Res.	B	V63	A	1			2	1.55	2	1.55	10	7.75	115	89.15	129
			V63	A	2							4	13.33	26	86.67	30
			V63	A	3					2	3.23	14	22.58	46	74.19	62
			V63	A	4			3	1.51	18	9.05	21	10.55	157	78.89	199
			V63	A	5					57	7.43	127	16.56	583	76.01	767
			V63	A	6							3	7.50	37	92.50	40
			V63	A	7							16	21.62	58	78.38	74
			V63	A	8					8	4.37	28	15.30	147	80.33	183
			V63	A	9			13	4.36	3	1.01	18	6.04	264	88.59	298
			V63	A	10			6	3.85	4	2.56	9	5.77	137	87.82	156
			V63	B	1			3	2.31	2	1.54	12	9.23	113	86.92	130
			V63	B	2			1	0.56	2	1.12	10	5.62	165	92.70	178
			V63	B	3			1	0.75			9	6.72	124	92.54	134
			V63	B	4									2	100.00	2
			V63	B	5			1	3.13	2	6.25			29	90.63	32
			V63	B	6			1	2.44	2	4.88	2	4.88	36	87.80	41
			V63	B	7	1	1.47	3	4.41	6	8.82	7	10.29	51	75.00	68
3	Res.	E	V65	A	1							1	8.33	11	91.67	12

Ceramics from Excavations in the Far West Bajo (Analysis by Kerry Sagebiel, 2001), *continued*

Block	Zone	Group	Op.	Subop.	Lot	Late Preclassic No.	%	Early Classic No.	%	Early Late Classic No.	%	Late Terminal Classic No.	%	Unknown (eroded) No.	%	Total
3	Res.	E	V65	A	2									56	100.00	56
			V65	A	3									78	100.00	78
			V65	A	4							1	33.33	2	66.67	3
			V65	A	5							1	6.25	15	93.75	16
			V65	A	6					1	6.67			14	93.33	15
			V65	A	7							2	5.13	37	94.87	39
			V65	A	8											
			V65	A	9							1	8.33	11	91.67	12
			V65	A	10							1	50.00	1	50.00	2
			V65	A	11									3	100.00	3
			V65	A	12	1	14.29	1	14.29					5	71.43	7
			V65	A	13									5	100.00	5
			V65	B	1									19	100.00	19
			V65	B	2					2	8.33	3	12.50	19	79.17	24
			V65	B	3									5	100.00	5
			V65	B	4					1	1.41	2	2.82	68	95.77	71
			V65	B	5					2	1.38	30	20.69	113	77.93	145
			V65	B	6	1	0.82			4	3.28	2	1.64	115	94.26	122
			V65	B	7							8	15.38	44	84.62	52
			V65	B	8	4	4.71	3	3.53	6	7.06			72	84.71	85
3	Res.	F	V66	A	1											
			V66	A	2			1	14.29					6	85.71	7
			V66	A	3							11	18.03	50	81.97	61
			V66	A	4							14	15.38	77	84.62	91
			V66	A	5							3	60.00	2	40.00	5
			V66	A	6							2	14.29	12	85.71	14
			V66	A	7	1	0.86	17	14.66	2	1.72	4	3.45	92	79.31	116
			V66	A	8											
			V66	A	9							71	84.52	13	15.48	84
			V66	A	10					10	10.75	48	51.61	35	37.63	93
			V66	A	11			2	2.04	5	5.10	7	7.14	84	85.71	98
			V66	A	12							10	47.62	11	52.38	21
			V66	A	13			2	1.40	11	7.69	30	20.98	100	69.93	143
			V66	A	14			2	0.91	16	7.31	81	36.99	120	54.79	219
			V66	A	15			1	0.46	20	9.17	100	45.87	97	44.50	218
			V66	A	16			2	0.20	93	9.12	284	27.84	641	62.84	1020
			V66	A	17			1	1.20	1	1.20	32	38.55	49	59.04	83
			V66	A	18					11	2.35	158	33.76	299	63.89	468
			V66	A	19											
			V66	A	20					7	1.21	163	28.25	407	70.54	577
			V66	A	21			1	0.57	2	1.14	46	26.29	126	72.00	175
			V66	A	22			3	0.48	9	1.44	154	24.56	461	73.52	627
			V66	A	23			3	0.78	1	0.26	74	19.32	305	79.63	383
			V66	A	24					10	4.33	80	34.63	141	61.04	231
			V66	A	25					1	0.74	34	25.19	100	74.07	135
			V66	A	26					2	1.68	39	32.77	78	65.55	119
			V66	A	27			2	0.59	9	2.64	119	34.90	211	61.88	341
			V66	A	28			1	0.17	6	0.99	168	27.77	430	71.07	605
			V66	A	29			1	0.15	13	1.95	166	24.89	487	73.01	667
			V66	A	30			2	0.44	15	3.33	119	26.39	315	69.84	451
			V66	A	31			1	0.25	3	0.74	110	26.96	294	72.06	408
			V66	B	1			4	1.42	1	0.36	2	0.71	274	97.51	281
			V66	B	2											
			V66	B	3			6	46.15	1	7.69			6	46.15	13
			V66	B	4			1	3.13	4	12.50			27	84.38	32
			V66	B	5											
			V66	B	6					1	3.57	2	7.14	25	89.29	28

Ceramics from Excavations in the Far West Bajo (Analysis by Kerry Sagebiel, 2001), *continued*

Block	Zone	Group	Op.	Subop.	Lot	Late Preclassic No.	%	Early Classic No.	%	Early Late Classic No.	%	Late Terminal Classic No.	%	Unknown (eroded) No.	%	Total
3	Res.	F	V66	C	1							9	3.03	288	96.97	297
			V66	C	2			1	0.52	1	0.52	9	4.71	180	94.24	191
			V66	C	3					2	1.14	2	1.14	171	97.71	175
			V66	C	4			6	1.37	10	2.28	9	2.05	413	94.29	438
			V66	D	1											
			V66	D	2							9	13.85	56	86.15	65
			V66	D	3							13	5.80	211	94.20	224
			V66	D	4							18	22.78	61	77.22	79
			V66	D	5							5	10.42	43	89.58	48
			V66	D	6			5	0.48	10	0.95	53	5.05	982	93.52	1050
			V66	D	7					1	5.56			17	94.44	18
			V66	D	8					1	1.05	6	6.32	88	92.63	95
			V66	D	9							14	8.75	146	91.25	160
			V66	D	10							5	23.81	16	76.19	21
			V66	D	11					3	1.46	17	8.25	186	90.29	206
			V66	D	12					1	0.47	29	13.55	184	85.98	214
			V66	D	13					1	3.57	4	14.29	23	82.14	28
3	Res.	I	V67	A	1	6	5.66	10	9.43	1	0.94	2	1.89	88	82.24	107
			V67	A	2	10	1.64	19	3.13	9	1.48	17	2.80	553	90.95	608
			V67	A	3	1	0.89	6	5.36	2	1.79	3	2.68	100	89.29	112
			V67	A	4			1	3.03					32	96.97	33
			V67	A	5			6	10.91					49	89.09	55
			V67	A	6	1	2.13	2	4.26	2	4.26			42	89.36	47
			V67	A	7			9	6.12					138	93.88	147
			V67	A	8			5	6.94					67	93.06	72
			V67	A	9			28	17.18					135	82.82	163
			V67	A	10	1	2.00	4	8.00	1	2.00			44	88.00	50
			V67	A	11			2	2.47					79	97.53	81
			V67	A	12			2	9.52					19	90.48	21
			V67	B	1	1	0.13	10	1.34	6	0.80	22	2.95	708	94.78	747
			V67	B	2			32	9.76	5	1.52	2	0.61	289	88.11	328
			V67	B	3									1	100.00	1
			V67	B	4	3	0.94	62	19.38	1	0.31			254	79.38	320
3	Res.	X	V68	A	1							4	100.00	0	0.00	4
			V68	A	2					1	1.64	9	14.75	51	83.61	61
			V68	A	3							8	34.78	15	65.22	23
			V68	A	4							2	100.00	0	0.00	2
			V68	A	5							3	12.50	21	87.50	24
			V68	A	6											
			V68	A	7											
			V68	A	8											
			V68	A	9					1	2.33	8	18.60	34	79.07	43
			V68	A	10									3	100.00	3
			V68	A	11									2	100.00	2
			V68	A	12	2	2.67	1	1.33	8	10.67	6	8.00	58	77.33	75
			V68	A	13									5	100.00	5
			V68	A	14											
			V68	B	1									40	100.00	40
			V68	B	2									77	100.00	77
			V68	C	1					1	0.53	20	10.70	166	88.77	187
			V68	C	2			3	0.33	38	4.13	119	12.95	759	82.59	919
			V68	C	3							8	9.88	73	90.12	81
			V68	C	4	1	0.19	4	0.77	12	2.31	72	13.85	431	82.88	520
4	Agri-2		V69	A	1									2	100.00	2
			V69	A	2											
			V69	A	3											
			V69	A	4											

Ceramics from Excavations in the Far West Bajo (Analysis by Kerry Sagebiel, 2001), *continued*

Block	Zone	Group	Op.	Subop.	Lot	Late Preclassic No.	%	Early Classic No.	%	Early Late Classic No.	%	Late Terminal Classic No.	%	Unknown (eroded) No.	%	Total
4	Agri-2		V69	B	1											
			V69	B	2											
			V69	B	3											
			V69	B	4											
4	Res.	Z	V69	C	1											
			V69	C	2											
			V69	C	3											
			V69	C	4											
4	Agri-2		V70	A	1											
			V70	A	2											
			V70	A	3											
			V70	B	1					1	33.33			2	66.67	3
			V70	B	2									4	100.00	4
			V70	B	3											
			V70	A	1											
			V70	C	2									5	100.00	5
			V70	C	3									3	100.00	3
			V70	C	4									3	100.00	3
			V70	C	5											
			V70	C	6											
			V70	D	1											
			V70	D	2			21	16.41	4	3.13	1	0.78	102	79.69	128
			V70	D	3			1	50.00					1	50.00	2
			V70	D	4											
4	Res.	T	V71	A	1									2	100.00	2
			V71	A	2							1	33.33	2	66.67	3
			V71	A	3	1	10.00	1	10.00	1	10.00			7	70.00	10
			V71	A	4											
4	Agri-2		V71	B	1			2	8.70					21	91.30	23
			V71	B	2	2	6.67	3	10.00	2	6.67			23	76.67	30
			V71	B	3	2	7.69	2	7.69			3	11.54	19	73.08	26
			V71	C	1											
			V71	C	2			6	12.50					42	87.50	48
	Bajo		V72	A	1											
			V72	A	2											
			V72	B	1											
			V72	B	2											
			V72	B	3											
5	Agri-3		V73	A	1	3	42.86							4	57.14	7
			V73	A	2	1	6.25							15	93.75	16
			V73	A	3									18	100.00	18
			V73	A	4									4	100.00	4
			V73	A	5											
			V73	A	6											
			V73	B	1											
			V73	B	2											
			V73	B	3											
			V73	B	4	2	100.00							0	0.00	2
			V73	B	5											
5	Res.	B	V74	A	1											
			V74	A	2											
			V74	A	3											
			V74	B	1											
			V74	B	2					2	5.56	1	2.78	33	91.67	36
			V74	B	3	4	7.55	3	5.66	1	1.89	4	7.55	41	77.36	53
			V74	B	4									2	100.00	2
			V74	B	5	1	6.67	1	6.67			1	6.67	12	80.00	15

Ceramics from Excavations in the Far West Bajo (Analysis by Kerry Sagebiel, 2001), *continued*

Block	Zone	Group	Op.	Subop.	Lot	Late Preclassic No.	%	Early Classic No.	%	Early Late Classic No.	%	Late Terminal Classic No.	%	Unknown (eroded) No.	%	Total
5	Res.	B	V74	C	1							1	8.33	11	91.67	12
			V74	C	2									49	100.00	49
5	Res.	B	V74	C	3											
			V74	D	1											
			V74	D	2							3	30.00	7	70.00	10
			V74	D	3	2	4.65	2	4.65	2	4.65	7	16.28	30	69.77	43
			V74	E	1							1	33.33	2	66.67	3
			V74	E	2									2	100.00	2
			V74	E	3											
			V74	E	4									1	100.00	1
			V74	E	5									2	100.00	2
			V74	E	6											
			V74	E	7											
			V74	E	8									3	100.00	3
			V74	E	9									2	100.00	2
			V74	E	10											
			V74	E	11									5	100.00	5
			V74	E	12									1	100.00	1
			V74	E	13									1	100.00	1
			V74	E	14									2	100.00	2
			V74	E	15											
			V74	E	16									1	100.00	1
			V74	E	17									1	100.00	1
			V74	E	18									1	100.00	1
			V74	E	19									1	100.00	1
			V74	E	20							1	100.00	0	0.00	1
			V74	E	21											
			V74	E	22											
			V74	E	23											
			V74	E	24											
			V74	E	25											
			V74	E	26											
			V74	E	27									1	100.00	1
			V74	E	28											
			V74	E	29											
			V74	E	30											
			V74	E	31											
			V74	E	32									1	100.00	1
			V74	E	33									1	100.00	1
			V74	E	34									1	100.00	1
			V74	E	35									1	100.00	1
			V74	E	36											
			V74	E	37											
			V74	E	38									1	100.00	1
			V74	E	39									1	100.00	1
			V74	E	40											
			V74	F	1	4	8.33	7	14.58	2	4.17	4	8.33	31	64.58	48
5	Agri-3		V75	A	1											
			V75	A	2					1	25.00			3	75.00	4
			V75	A	3											
5	Res.	D	V75	B	1											
			V75	B	2											
			V75	B	3	1	3.23	1	3.23			1	3.23	28	90.32	31
			V75	B	4											
			V75	B	5											
	Total					*402*	*1.02*	*635*	*1.61*	*957*	*2.43*	*4364*	*11.09*	*33003*	*83.85*	*39,361*

Lithic Flakes from Excavations in the Far West Bajo

Block	Zone	Group	Op.	Subop.	Lot	Total No.	Total Weight (g)	Primary No.	Primary Weight (g)	Secondary No.	Secondary Weight (g)	Tertiary No.	Tertiary Weight (g)	Shatter No.	Shatter Weight (g)
5	Agri-3		V26	A	1	15	27.6					1	0.8	14	26.8
			V26	A	2	2	15.6					1	7.5	1	8.1
			V26	A	3	3	12.6	1	10.5					2	2.1
			V26	A	4										
			V26	A	5	2	5.5							2	5.5
1	Res.	A	V27	A	1	56	153.8	1	5.4	4	22.2	11	41.8	40	84.4
			V28	A	1	13	173.3	1	2.8			2	9.6	10	160.9
			V28	A	2	2	8.0			1	6.2	1	1.8		
			V28	A	3	44	346.1	3	26.1	6	53.0	6	23.5	29	243.5
			V29	A	1	51	401.4	1	2.0	3	99.5	9	58.1	38	241.8
			V29	A	2	65	1706.2	2	23.2	4	130.2	11	120.8	48	1432.0
			V29	A	3	12	213.9							12	213.9
			V29	A	4	45	321.8			1	1.8	8	52.6	36	267.4
			V29	A	5	18	365.0			1	4.8	1	7.6	16	352.6
			V29	A	6	16	77.1					5	16.0	11	61.1
1	Res.	N	V31	A	1	5	28.3			1	6.1			4	22.2
			V31	A	2	67	415.5	2	16.3	7	221.7	11	26.9	47	150.6
			V31	A	3	4	49.8			1	49.4			3	0.4
1	Res.	O	V32	A	1										
			V32	A	2	5	21.9					1	1.0	4	20.9
			V32	A	3										
1	Res.	I	V34	A	1	88	589.7	3	36.4	13	174.8	25	165.5	47	213.0
			V34	A	2	48	171.7	1	3.1	1	0.7	10	18.8	36	149.1
			V34	A	3	38	509.7			1	25.2	10	83.1	27	401.4
1	Res.	N	V35	A	1	1	3.4	1	3.4						
			V35	A	2	2	61.7			1	59.0			1	2.7
			V35	B	1	3	13.9							3	13.9
			V35	B	2	2	10.3					2	10.3		
			V35	B	3	2	14.7							2	14.7
1	Res.	I	V37	A	1	46	948.2	2	51.1	2	62.0	5	194.6	37	640.5
			V37	A	2	70	245.1	3	10.4	2	37.5	11	22.9	54	174.3
			V37	A	3	50	272.1			11	143.3	7	26.9	32	101.9
	Bajo		V38	A	1										
			V38	A	2	211	1927.0	31	819.0	66	600.0	100	414.5	14	93.5
			V38	A	3										
			V38	B	1										
			V38	B	2	75	1247.1	11	220.8	42	894.5	22	131.8		
			V38	B	3	13	197.1	2	39.6	3	84.0	6	63.0	2	10.5
1	Res.	A	V39	A	1	99	631.8	4	41.8	13	174.8	26	166.6	56	248.6
			V39	A	2	67	710.6	2	9.7	3	39.8	11	40.7	51	620.4
			V39	A	3	44	525.6			1	25.2	13	89.5	30	410.9
			V39	A	4										
			V39	B	1	29	323.6	1	7.4	1	6.8	12	117.0	15	192.4
			V39	B	2	29	276.1	3	38.6	7	112.6	15	107.5	4	17.4
			V39	B	3	30	411.2	1	17.2	1	2.8	5	73.5	23	317.7
			V39	B	4	18	151.6			1	37.1	7	74.9	10	39.6
			V39	B	5	3	114.4	2	85.2					1	29.2
			V39	C	1	107	1103.6	8	362.2	36	434.2	53	257.6	10	49.6
			V39	C	2	49	174.0			4	24.6	36	117.0	9	32.4
			V39	C	3	22	105.7	1	0.8	1	44.4	9	13.8	11	46.7
			V39	C	4										
			V39	D	1										

Lithic Flakes from Excavations in the Far West Bajo (continued)

Block	Zone	Group	Op.	Subop.	Lot	Total No.	Weight (g)	Primary No.	Weight (g)	Secondary No.	Weight (g)	Tertiary No.	Weight (g)	Shatter No.	Weight (g)
1	Res.	A	V39	D	2										
			V39	D	3	3	47.2					1	32.0	2	15.2
			V39	D	4										
			V39	D	5										
			V39	D	6	11	571.8	2	493.1	3	55.4	6	23.3		
			V39	D	7	1	1.7					1	1.7		
			V39	D	8	4	42.4	1	18.0					3	24.4
			V39	E	1	6	316.6	1	70.3	5	246.3				
			V39	E	2	12	129.2	4	35.0	4	75.4	4	18.8		
			V39	F	1	62	254.4	1	2.2			9	31.7	52	220.5
			V39	F	2	101	352.6			3	47.0	6	16.1	92	289.5
1	Res.	H	V40	A	1	7	27.8					7	27.8		
			V40	A	2	44	346.7	2	94.0	7	103.0	31	103.8	4	45.9
			V40	A	3										
			V40	B	1	17	137.3			5	62.8	12	74.5		
			V40	B	2	11	173.9			2	143.3	6	24.2	3	6.4
			V40	C	1	2	12.4	1	3.3			1	9.1		
			V40	C	2										
			V40	D	1										
			V40	D	2										
1	Res.	B	V42	A	1										
			V42	A	2	15	228.4					2	77.8	13	150.6
			V42	A	3	4	22.0					1	2.5	3	19.5
			V42	A	4	26	93.8					4	34.9	22	58.9
			V42	A	5	36	629.6			4	189.8	6	54.5	26	385.3
			V42	A	6	7	216.2	2	125.2	3	78.1	2	12.9		
			V42	B	1	2	20.2			1	17.7	1	2.5		
			V42	B	2	2	38.6							2	38.6
			V42	B	3	1	2.7					1	2.7		
			V42	B	4										
			V42	B	5	3	5.4					3	5.4		
			V42	B	6										
			V42	B	7	14	44.8					5	10.2	9	34.6
			V42	B	8	2	9.5							2	9.5
			V42	B	9	7	106.0			3	84.8			4	21.2
			V42	B	10										
			V42	B	11	28	789.4	1	18.8	3	541.0	4	10.5	20	219.1
			V42	B	12										
			V42	B	13										
1	Res.	C	V42	C	1										
			V42	C	2										
			V42	C	3	121	900.2	8	109.8	12	79.9	31	266.3	70	444.2
			V42	C	4										
			V42	C	5	2	75.1	1	10.0					1	65.1
			V42	C	6	8	99.8	1	49.4	1	12.8	3	15.0	3	22.6
			V42	C	7	4	13.9			1	4.0	2	8.4	1	1.5
			V42	D	1	5	24.3							5	24.3
			V42	D	2	13	78.9	1	1.2			7	11.1	5	66.6
1	Res.	O	V51	A	1										
			V51	A	2	3	28.8					2	27.5	1	1.3
			V51	A	3	64	1646.1	4	246.0	18	641.5	33	614.4	9	144.2
			V51	A	4										
			V51	A	5	12	156.3			2	35.5	4	52.4	6	68.4
			V51	A	6	20	302.4	1	26.7	1	5.7	8	119.6	10	150.4
			V51	B	1	4	16.9	1	8.0	1	1.6	1	3.3	1	4.0
			V51	B	2	2	50.2							2	50.2
			V51	B	3	3	56.2							3	56.2

Lithic Flakes from Excavations in the Far West Bajo (*continued*)

Block	Zone	Group	Op.	Subop.	Lot	Total No.	Total Weight (g)	Primary No.	Primary Weight (g)	Secondary No.	Secondary Weight (g)	Tertiary No.	Tertiary Weight (g)	Shatter No.	Shatter Weight (g)
1	Res.	O	V51	B	4	1	53.2							1	53.2
			V51	B	5										
			V51	B	6	2	26.4	1	9.9			1	16.5		
1	Res.	N	V51	C	1	1	8.3							1	8.3
			V51	C	2	7	44.6	1	28.6			2	6.4	4	9.6
			V51	C	3	21	624.4	2	187.5			6	79.0	13	357.9
			V51	C	4	51	817.8			5	120.0	9	78.8	37	619.0
			V51	C	5	2	20.2					1	4.1	1	16.1
			V51	C	6										
1	Res.	K	V52	A	1	66	200.0	1	1.3	14	58.0	36	116.3	15	24.4
			V52	A	2	8	35.1	1	10.0			4	11.7	3	13.4
			V52	A	3	13	30.0	1	1.3	1	2.6	4	6.1	7	20.0
			V52	A	4	40	131.0			1	7.5	14	21.0	25	102.5
1	Res.	I	V52	B	1	11	232.5	3	78.5	3	11.0	4	41.0	1	102.0
			V52	B	2	40	427.1	2	54.7	5	86.4	26	208.0	7	78.0
			V52	B	3	4	70.9	1	40.4			3	30.5		
			V52	B	4	2	29.2							2	29.2
			V52	B	5	9	19.7					3	3.8	6	15.9
			V52	B	6	13	215.0			3	53.4	6	148.2	4	13.4
			V52	B	7	5	37.9			1	19.7	1	4.3	3	13.9
			V52	B	8	9	243.8	1	107.8	2	51.0	6	85.0		
			V52	B	9	6	703.8	2	81.3	1	15.8	1	1.6	2	605.1
			V52	B	10	8	209.5	2	134.1	3	46.3	3	29.1		
1	Res.	L	V53	A	1	7	52.3					7	52.3		
			V53	A	2										
			V53	A	3	6	41.0	2	19.9			2	17.2	2	3.9
			V53	A	4	5	41.0					3	30.1	2	10.9
2	Agri-1		V58	A	1	109	1037.1	15	105.3	13	122.0	26	29.8	55	780.0
			V58	A	2	68	736.0	8	145.2	6	34.8	6	47.0	48	509.0
			V58	A	3	37	86.5	6	38.8	6	19.5	21	21.9	4	6.3
			V58	A	4	57	277.6	4	119.3	20	95.1	25	25.2	8	38.0
			V58	A	5	13	385.2	1	178.0	2	157.1	4	35.3	6	14.8
			V58	A	6	15	151.1	1	20.8	11	126.5	3	3.8		
			V58	B	1	70	1131.4	14	229.5	20	234.9	19	71.8	17	595.2
			V58	B	2	44	1221.5	6	287.3	20	620.0	9	69.9	9	244.3
			V58	B	3	1	2.8							1	2.8
			V58	C	1	1	83.6	1	83.6						
			V58	C	2	3	370.3	1	4.9	1	328.5	1	36.9		
			V58	C	3	3	16.8	1	7.5			2	9.3		
			V59	A	1	22	244.1	1	11.8	9	32.9	8	27.7	4	171.7
			V59	A	2	21	*	3	*	9	*	6	*	3	*
			V59	A	3	6	161.3	1	21.4	3	88.0	1	10.2	1	41.7
			V59	A	4	4	280.7	2	216.7	2	64.0				
			V59	A	5										
			V59	B	1	7	277.1	1	127.3	3	103.6	1	2.7	2	43.5
			V59	B	2	26	610.0	8	396.3	6	99.0	8	105.6	4	9.1
			V59	B	3	2	8.8	1	6.9			1	1.9		
			V60	A	1	6	118.7	1	20.6	1	70.8			4	27.3
			V60	A	2	32	1053.6			4	34.7	7	100.0	21	918.9
			V60	A	3	7	110.2			1	70.8	2	12.1	4	27.3
			V60	A	4										
			V60	A	5	10	50.3	1	2.4	2	18.4	5	20.1	2	9.4
			V60	A	6										
			V60	A	7	4	20.0	1	9.3			3	10.7		
2	Res.	B	V60	B	1	27	338.9	1	50.4	1	34.5	16	227.4	9	26.6
			V60	B	2	89	1461.7	7	195.1	18	378.6	23	382.5	41	505.5
			V60	B	3	8	302.1			1	88.5	4	120.1	3	93.5

Lithic Flakes from Excavations in the Far West Bajo (continued)

Block	Zone	Group	Op.	Subop.	Lot	Total No.	Total Weight (g)	Primary No.	Primary Weight (g)	Secondary No.	Secondary Weight (g)	Tertiary No.	Tertiary Weight (g)	Shatter No.	Shatter Weight (g)
2	Res.	B	V60	B	4	12	81.3			1	20.1	3	20.6	8	40.6
			V60	B	5										
2	Res.	A	V61	A	1	65	546.9	1	15.8	1	12.0	11	148.5	52	370.6
			V61	A	2	49	181.8	2	27.0	15	37.9	15	37.9	17	79.0
			V61	A	3	4	7.1					4	7.1		
			V61	A	4										
			V61	A	5										
3	Res.	A	V62	A	1										
			V62	A	2	15	35.6	1	8.5			4	3.0	10	24.1
			V62	A	3	18	206.9			3	116.3	4	8.7	11	81.9
			V62	A	4	4	7.2					2	5.6	2	1.6
			V62	A	5	2	18.5							2	18.5
			V62	A	6	3	29.5			1	25.1	1	2.4	1	2.0
			V62	A	7										
			V62	A	8	4	5.9					1	0.9	3	5.0
			V62	A	9	1	25.6							1	25.6
			V62	A	10	28	327.1			4	161.1	12	58.5	12	107.5
			V62	A	11										
			V62	A	12										
			V62	A	13	2	4.8							2	4.8
			V62	A	14										
			V62	A	15	2	28.6					1	1.7	1	26.9
			V62	A	16	10	39.1			3	18.2	3	7.7	4	13.2
			V62	A	17	6	46.4			2	35.2	4	11.2		
			V62	A	18	16	69.9	2	7.7	2	12.6	12	49.6		
			V62	A	19										
			V62	A	20										
			V62	A	21										
			V62	A	22	28	228.8	1	16.6	3	18.1	3	9.0	21	185.1
			V62	A	23	13	26.3					2	4.9	11	21.4
			V62	A	24	7	13.9					1	0.4	6	13.5
			V62	A	25	3	144.8			1	132.6	1	6.8	1	5.4
			V62	A	26	7	17.2			1	7.3			6	9.9
			V62	A	27	1	10.5	1	10.5						
			V62	B	1	37	432.0	3	89.6	4	111.5	13	162.9	17	68.0
			V62	B	2	24	277.6	2	25.6	4	148.4	7	13.0	11	90.6
			V62	C	1	3	20.5			1	4.5			2	16.0
			V62	C	2										
			V62	C	3	14	161.9			1	5.8	2	19.1	11	137.0
3	Res.	B	V63	A	1	2	11.0					2	11.0		
			V63	A	2	9	245.5					1	56.5	8	189.0
			V63	A	3	10	195.0			1	10.8	5	70.8	4	113.4
			V63	A	4	35	672.4	19	326.8	6	231.3	4	82.4	6	31.9
			V63	A	5	38	622.2			2	5.1	16	296.3	20	320.8
			V63	A	6	20	144.4	1	40.6	1	6.4	7	31.4	11	66.0
			V63	A	7										
			V63	A	8	7	141.0	1	106.5			2	3.7	4	30.8
			V63	A	9	4	134.0			2	125.1			2	8.9
			V63	A	10	2	231.0	1	181.0					1	50.0
			V63	B	1	14	492.1	1	5.9	2	29.0	1	17.1	10	440.1
			V63	B	2										
			V63	B	3	12	132.0			2	21.2	8	80.2	2	30.6
			V63	B	4										
			V63	B	5	9	294.2			1	4.1	1	10.6	7	279.5
			V63	B	6	15	359.6			1	51.8	2	13.0	12	294.8
			V63	B	7	24	470.2			4	174.3	7	163.2	13	132.7
3	Res.	E	V65	A	1	2	7.7					1	1.5	1	6.2

Lithic Flakes from Excavations in the Far West Bajo (*continued*)

Block	Zone	Group	Op.	Subop.	Lot	Total No.	Weight (g)	Primary No.	Weight (g)	Secondary No.	Weight (g)	Tertiary No.	Weight (g)	Shatter No.	Weight (g)
	Res.	E	V65	A	2	20	184.2					6	32.3	14	151.9
			V65	A	3										
			V65	A	4										
			V65	A	5	4	17.6					2	12.2	2	5.4
			V65	A	6	4	9.6							4	9.6
			V65	A	7	8	123.4					1	1.3	7	122.1
			V65	A	8										
			V65	A	9										
			V65	A	10										
			V65	A	11	6	15.1					6	15.1		
			V65	A	12										
			V65	A	13										
			V65	B	1										
			V65	B	2	722	1179.7	15	75.3	54	174.1	277	433.5	376	496.8
			V65	B	3	166	295.4			18	88.9	88	133.0	60	73.5
			V65	B	4	1159	2102.2	14	38.1	159	480.8	287	714.2	699	869.1
			V65	B	5										
			V65	B	6	59	650.3			1	9.3	2	7.5	56	633.5
			V65	B	7	973	1740.6	13	49.6	425	1042.0	105	291.4	430	357.6
			V65	B	8	56	488.9	3	16.4	5	5.2	3	0.5	45	466.8
3	Res.	F	V66	A	1	1	1.1			1	1.1				
			V66	A	2	8	23.8							8	23.8
			V66	A	3	6	63.5			1	4.4			5	59.1
			V66	A	4	9	102.2	1	49.6			3	9.6	5	43.0
			V66	A	5	4	14.0					4	14.0		
			V66	A	6										
			V66	A	7										
			V66	A	8										
			V66	A	9										
			V66	A	10	15	196.0					7	75.5	8	120.5
			V66	A	11	4	16.8			1	6.1	2	7.3	1	3.4
			V66	A	12										
			V66	A	13	14	203.8	3	12.8	2	26.4	6	11.3	3	153.3
			V66	A	14	44	633.3	1	0.7	4	59.6	4	4.7	35	568.3
			V66	A	15	24	143.1			4	62.2	18	58.0	2	22.9
			V66	A	16	176	3945.0	21	787.4	43	1547.9	69	964.2	43	645.5
			V66	A	17	15	51.4	1	3.4	5	30.2	9	17.8		
			V66	A	18										
			V66	A	19										
			V66	A	20	62	429.6	3	37.2	6	60.8	31	197.1	22	134.5
			V66	A	21	31	627.1			17	580.4	10	45.1	4	1.6
			V66	A	22	87	1402.0	5	152.7	23	546.1	37	693.5	22	9.7
			V66	A	23	76	1127.8	3	13.7	22	924.6	31	179.7	20	9.8
			V66	A	24	39	780.1			6	115.6	9	97.3	24	567.2
			V66	A	25	28	92.0			3	54.5	8	22.0	17	15.5
			V66	A	26	26	27.7			2	5.5	1	6.7	23	15.5
			V66	A	27	18	1002.7			7	484.1	11	518.6		
			V66	A	28	120	2633.0	6	236.5	29	1064.0	55	1275.5	30	57.0
			V66	A	29	84	772.2	4	9.5	27	500.5	28	151.6	25	110.6
			V66	A	30	33	459.0			6	158.0	6	158.0	21	143.0
			V66	A	31	64	474.1			11	175.0	27	127.8	26	171.3
			V66	B	1	20	108.2			3	60.0	4	4.1	13	44.1
			V66	B	2										
			V66	B	3	1	36.0							1	36.0
			V66	B	4										
			V66	B	5	2	24.3					1	13.9	1	10.4
			V66	B	6	1	113.2			1	113.2				

Lithic Flakes from Excavations in the Far West Bajo (continued)

Block	Zone	Group	Op.	Subop.	Lot	Total No.	Total Weight (g)	Primary No.	Primary Weight (g)	Secondary No.	Secondary Weight (g)	Tertiary No.	Tertiary Weight (g)	Shatter No.	Shatter Weight (g)
3	Res.	F	V66	C	1	20	159.1	4	65.6	7	51.2	6	41.3	3	1.0
			V66	C	2	13	127.2	5	101.2	3	12.6	5	13.4		
			V66	C	3	17	55.1			2	11.2	6	12.1	9	31.8
			V66	C	4	41	231.6	5	40.9	6	48.9	3	12.0	27	129.8
			V66	D	1										
			V66	D	2	3	29.3			1	20.9	2	8.4		
			V66	D	3	16	206.6	2	143.4	5	30.8	6		3	32.4
			V66	D	4	13	63.7	1	3.1	4	28.3	6	31.5	2	0.8
			V66	D	5	8	90.3	3	54.1			3	15.2	2	21.0
			V66	D	6	139	957.6	12	187.4	31	314.4	47	304.2	49	151.6
			V66	D	7	1	4.9					1	4.9		
			V66	D	8	1	50.6					1	50.6		
			V66	D	9	21	268.7	2	69.2	2	114.4	7	75.5	10	9.6
			V66	D	10	4	18.5					3	15.9	1	2.6
			V66	D	11	31	1069.0	1	54.4	14	723.6	13	179.2	3	111.8
			V66	D	12	36	143.2			7	51.1	12	59.1	17	33.0
			V66	D	13	1	3.1			1	3.1				
3	Res.	I	V67	A	1	29	447.5	5	51.9	8	118.4	10	170.0	6	107.2
			V67	A	2	72	1758.8	10	801.3	7	139.0	28	699.1	27	119.4
			V67	A	3	37	467.5	1	8.8	21	280.7	12	175.2	3	2.8
			V67	A	4	5	13.2	1	4.6	2	3.8	2	4.8		
			V67	A	5	13	123.0			4	74.9	7	35.4	2	12.7
			V67	A	6	17	32.1	1	5.5	2	5.6	9	12.1	5	8.9
			V67	A	7	52	616.9	5	111.5	9	100.0	29	156.6	9	248.8
			V67	A	8	27	69.1	2	8.6			18	51.3	7	9.2
			V67	A	9	32	445.3	3	120.3	5	189.9	10	23.7	14	111.4
			V67	A	10										
			V67	A	11										
			V67	A	12	8	20.2					5	9.4	3	10.8
			V67	B	1	155	956.9	22	189.8	39	270.5	61	445.0	33	51.6
			V67	B	2	57	1602.2	3	85	13	318.3	16	173.5	25	1025.4
			V67	B	3	46	1060.5	12	315.2	10	244.1	11	272.2	13	229.0
			V67	B	4	35	575.4	3	75.5	5	31.4	21	463.6	6	4.9
3	Res.	X	V68	A	1										
			V68	A	2	63	565.4	8	127.3	6	106.0	7	21.2	42	310.9
			V68	A	3	11	41.7			1	1.0	3	5.7	7	35.0
			V68	A	4	61	1159.3	1	138.5			1	0.8	59	1020.0
			V68	A	5	6	11.4					2	0.8	4	10.6
			V68	A	6	84	999.4	2	10.1	1	52.8	9	41.5	72	895.0
			V68	A	7										
			V68	A	8	31	303.8	1	6.9			3	6.9	27	290.0
			V68	A	9	26	239.1			2	8.2	2	61.4	22	169.5
			V68	A	10										
			V68	A	11										
			V68	A	12	15	192.1			2	21.7	1	42.6	12	127.8
			V68	A	13	1	92.6							1	92.6
			V68	A	14	17	260.3							17	260.3
			V68	B	1	38	115.3	6	26.6	13	51.0	6	11.1	13	26.6
			V68	B	2	47	291.6	5	43.7	9	50.2	11	25.1	22	172.6
			V68	C	1	19	707.0	9	609.4	2	34.8	5	33.8	3	29.0
			V68	C	2	198	4307.7	29	833.6	91	1802.3	21	147.4	57	1524.4
			V68	C	3	19	404.9					2	56.5	17	348.4
			V68	C	4	312	5259.1	8	450.0	29	647.1	27	381.7	248	3780.3
4	Agri-2		V69	A	1	23	158.3			1	20.4	1	2.0	21	135.9
			V69	A	2										
			V69	A	3										
			V69	A	4										

Lithic Flakes from Excavations in the Far West Bajo (*continued*)

Block	Zone	Group	Op.	Subop.	Lot	Total No.	Weight (g)	Primary No.	Weight (g)	Secondary No.	Weight (g)	Tertiary No.	Weight (g)	Shatter No.	Weight (g)
4	Agri-2		V69	B	1										
			V69	B	2										
			V69	B	3	3	246.0					1	103.0	2	143.0
			V69	B	4										
4	Res.	Z	V69	C	1	35	410.7			4	20.0	4	97.3	27	293.4
			V69	C	2	137	1115.3	2	73.2	9	135.8	10	73.3	116	833.0
			V69	C	3	4	128.0							4	128.0
			V69	C	4										
4	Agri-2		V70	A	1	77	1207.3	2	3.0	3	140.9	1	9.5	71	1053.9
			V70	A	2	59	1513.3	2	126.9	4	344.0			53	1042.4
			V70	A	3	14	39.0			5	2.6	3	2.8	6	33.6
			V70	B	1	2	6.0					2	6.0		
			V70	B	2	35	1169.1			2	209.9	2	17.2	31	942.0
			V70	B	3	7	294.4					1	53.7	6	240.7
			V70	C	1	6	195.1							6	195.1
			V70	C	2	12	435.7	3	151.8	4	93.2	2	67.2	3	123.5
			V70	C	3	11	46.3			6	25.0	4	14.1	1	7.2
			V70	C	4	11	80.7	1	6.0	4	62.7	5	10.9	1	1.1
			V70	C	5										
			V70	C	6										
			V70	D	1	22	1023.4	2	64.8	15	929.6	5	29.0		
			V70	D	2	51	2201.9	13	593.7	21	1016.7	13	498.0	4	93.5
			V70	D	3	6	142.3			1	5.0	3	111.8	2	25.5
			V70	D	4										
4	Res.	T	V71	A	1										
			V71	A	2	6	68.1					2	29.0	4	39.1
			V71	A	3	92	934.9	14	303.0	7	154.6	19	175.1	52	302.2
			V71	A	4										
4	Agri-2		V71	B	1	56	495.0			9	142.0	2	2.5	45	350.5
			V71	B	2	130	1634.0	14	221.6	56	797.7	46	455.0	14	159.7
			V71	B	3	83	1272.9	7	160.5	38	695.4	28	306.2	10	110.8
			V71	C	1										
			V71	C	2	29	459.8	3	24.4	2	139.9	15	196.1	9	99.4
	Bajo		V72	A	1										
			V72	A	2	47	672.8	7	117.2	9	219.0	15	119.6	16	217.0
			V72	B	1	3	127.6			1	106.0			2	21.6
			V72	B	2	60	536.3	2	10.1	19	256.2	37	266.0	2	4.0
			V72	B	3	3	102.1					1	18.0	2	84.1
5	Agr-3		V73	A	1	14	291.9	6	251.5	2	17.0	6	23.4		
			V73	A	2	39	583.2	13	440.0	10	25.7	7	64.7	9	52.8
			V73	A	3										
			V73	A	4	6	120.3			3	5.8	3	114.5		
			V73	A	5										
			V73	A	6										
			V73	B	1										
			V73	B	2	5	238.7	2	157.8	2	69.1	1	11.8		
			V73	B	3										
			V73	B	4	6	78.7			5	74.2	1	4.5		
			V73	B	5										
5	Res.	B	V74	A	1										
			V74	A	2	4	28.5							4	28.5
			V74	A	3										
			V74	B	1										
			V74	B	2	7	48.0							7	48.0
			V74	B	3	39	951.8	1	7.2	7	177.0	14	297.7	17	469.9
			V74	B	4	1	9.6							1	9.6
			V74	B	5	36	982.7	2	125.1	9	217.0	5	87.4	20	553.2

Lithic Flakes from Excavations in the Far West Bajo *(continued)*

Block	Zone	Group	Op.	Subop.	Lot	Total No.	Total Weight (g)	Primary No.	Primary Weight (g)	Secondary No.	Secondary Weight (g)	Tertiary No.	Tertiary Weight (g)	Shatter No.	Shatter Weight (g)
5	Res.	B	V74	C	1	3	16.8			2	12.0	1	4.8		
			V74	C	2										
			V74	C	3										
			V74	D	1	29	78.1							29	78.1
			V74	D	2	21	190.7			1	1.0	4	13.5	16	176.2
			V74	D	3	42	1440.1	1	113.4	1	15.6			40	1311.1
			V74	E	1	24	72.1	5	21.7	3	17.4	9	29.9	7	3.1
			V74	E	2	10	35.4							10	35.4
			V74	E	3										
			V74	E	4	14	11.6					3	4.0	11	7.6
			V74	E	5	3	15.9							3	15.9
			V74	E	6	4	5.8	1	2.5					3	3.3
			V74	E	7										
			V74	E	8	8	55.1					1	6.6	7	48.5
			V74	E	9	13	67.8			1	4.4			12	63.4
			V74	E	10										
			V74	E	11	6	13.9					1	6.8	5	7.1
			V74	E	12	31	96.0			8	39.6	2	5.0	21	51.4
			V74	E	13	6	80.0							6	80.0
			V74	E	14	2	9.7							2	9.7
			V74	E	15										
			V74	E	16										
			V74	E	17	1	2.3							1	2.3
			V74	E	18										
			V74	E	19	3	7.4							3	7.4
			V74	E	20	4	20.6			1	9.6	2	9.1	1	1.9
			V74	E	21										
			V74	E	22										
			V74	E	23										
			V74	E	24										
			V74	E	25										
			V74	E	26										
			V74	E	27										
			V74	E	28	1	6.4							1	6.4
			V74	E	29										
			V74	E	30										
			V74	E	31	5	15.0							5	15.0
			V74	E	32										
			V74	E	33										
			V74	E	34	1	1.8							1	1.8
			V74	E	35	2	6.3							2	6.3
			V74	E	36	4	27.7					1	8.6	3	19.1
			V74	E	37										
			V74	E	38	8	14.7					1	0.1	7	14.6
			V74	E	39	5	8.7					1	4.3	4	4.4
			V74	E	40	1	2.4							1	2.4
			V74	F	1	61	2207.6	5	420.0	26	868.7	25	911.8	5	7.1
5	Agri-3		V75	A	1										
			V75	A	2	5	164.9					2	111.5	3	53.4
			V75	A	3	13	116.2					3	7.0	10	109.2
5	Res.	D	V75	B	1										
			V75	B	2	57	1046.2			1	84.8	3	13.2	53	948.2
			V75	B	3	7	48.3	1	15.6			3	7.5	3	25.2
			V75	B	4	8	62.7	1	7.2			6	50.7	1	4.8
			V75	B	5	2	17.6			1	7.5	1	10.1		
Total						11,542	120,096.4+	636	16,684.3+	2,138	32,329.2+	3,109	23,150.3+	5,659	47,932.6+

* Not recorded

Lithic Tools from Excavations in the Far West Bajo

Block	Zone	Group	Op.	Subop.	Lot	Blades No.	Weight (g)	Bifaces No.	Weight (g)	No. Prox.	No. Med.	No. Dist.	No. Whole	Un-known	Tools or Cores No.	Weight (g)
5	Agri-3		V26	A	1											
			V26	A	2											
			V26	A	3											
			V26	A	4											
			V26	A	5											
1	Res.	A	V27	A	1											
			V28	A	1											
			V28	A	2											
			V28	A	3			1	148.0					1	1	58.0
			V29	A	1										4	442.5
			V29	A	2	1	7.4	1	48.7					1	1	212.0
			V29	A	3											
			V29	A	4	1	6.1									
			V29	A	5											
			V29	A	6			1				1				
1	Res.	N	V31	A	1											
			V31	A	2										1	24.7
			V31	A	3											
1	Res.	O	V32	A	1											
			V32	A	2											
			V32	A	3											
1	Res.	I	V34	A	1	1	26.6								1	488.9
			V34	A	2											
			V34	A	3			2		2						
1	Res.	N	V35	A	1											
			V35	A	2											
			V35	B	1											
			V35	B	2										1	122.7
			V35	B	3											
1	Res.	I	V37	A	1										2	441.1
			V37	A	2											
			V37	A	3										1	134.7
	Bajo		V38	A	1											
			V38	A	2			2	237.0	1			1		19	3621.5
			V38	A	3											
			V38	B	1			1	94.0				1			
			V38	B	2										3	1058.1
			V38	B	3										2	260.0
1	Res.	A	V39	A	1	1	26.6								1	488.9
			V39	A	2			1	118.4			1				
			V39	A	3											
			V39	A	4											
			V39	B	1											
			V39	B	2			1	*		1					
			V39	B	3			3	126.4	1		1	1		1	109.4
			V39	B	4	2	8.7									
			V39	B	5											
			V39	C	1	4	17.2	9	1131.7					9	1	191.6
			V39	C	2										1	200.0
			V39	C	3	2	3.8									
			V39	C	4											
			V39	D	1											

Lithic Tools from Excavations in the Far West Bajo (continued)

Block	Zone	Group	Op.	Subop.	Lot	Blades No.	Weight (g)	Bifaces No.	Weight (g)	No. Prox.	No. Med.	No. Dist.	No. Whole	Un-known	Tools or Cores No.	Weight (g)
1	Res.	A	V39	D	2											
			V39	D	3			1	216.4	1					1	42.1
			V39	D	4											
			V39	D	5											
			V39	D	6										1	190.4
			V39	D	7											
			V39	D	8			1	34.8	1					3	710.0
			V39	E	1	1	1.7	3	814.6		2		1		3	416.4
			V39	E	2										2	1222.1
			V39	F	1	3	19.2									
			V39	F	2	2	4.5									
1	Res.	H	V40	A	1			2	561.6		1		1			
			V40	A	2			1	93.1		1				1	189.0
			V40	A	3											
			V40	B	1	2	6.8									
			V40	B	2											
			V40	C	1											
			V40	C	2											
			V40	D	1											
			V40	D	2											
1	Res.	B	V42	A	1											
			V42	A	2	1	3.8									
			V42	A	3											
			V42	A	4	2	5.6	1	21.9				1			
			V42	A	5											
			V42	A	6			3	299.9	3					1	259.9
			V42	B	1											
			V42	B	2											
			V42	B	3											
			V42	B	4											
			V42	B	5											
			V42	B	6											
			V42	B	7											
			V42	B	8											
			V42	B	9											
			V42	B	10											
			V42	B	11			2	588.2				2		2	125.3
			V42	B	12											
			V42	B	13											
1	Res.	C	V42	C	1											
			V42	C	2											
			V42	C	3			2	40.2	1	1				2	159.5
			V42	C	4											
			V42	C	5										1	204.6
			V42	C	6										1	156.4
			V42	C	7											
			V42	D	1	1	1.3									
			V42	D	2											
1	Res.	O	V51	A	1											
			V51	A	2	1	12.3	4	500.2	1	1	2				
			V51	A	3	2	67.8	7	1137.5	2		3	2		9	885.5
			V51	A	4										1	142.5
			V51	A	5			1	110.6			1				
			V51	A	6			1	14.2	1					1	161.0
			V51	B	1										1	61.7
			V51	B	2			2	113.4	1		1				
			V51	B	3											

Lithic Tools from Excavations in the Far West Bajo (*continued*)

Block	Zone	Group	Op.	Subop.	Lot	Blades No.	Weight (g)	Bifaces No.	Weight (g)	No. Prox.	No. Med.	No. ·Dist.	No. Whole	Un-known	Tools or Cores No.	Weight (g)
1	Res.	O	V51	B	4	1	17.6	3	*				1	2	1	*
			V51	B	5											
			V51	B	6											
1	Res.	N	V51	C	1											
			V51	C	2											
			V51	C	3			1	29.9	1						
			V51	C	4	1	44.8	1	230.4			1			3	766.7
			V51	C	5											
			V51	C	6											
1	Res.	K	V52	A	1	1	35.5									
			V52	A	2											
			V52	A	3			1	308.0				1			
			V52	A	4	2	4.3									
1	Res.	I	V52	B	1										1	414.0
			V52	B	2											
			V52	B	3			1	195.0	1						
			V52	B	4											
			V52	B	5			1	*					1		
			V52	B	6											
			V52	B	7											
			V52	B	8											
			V52	B	9										2	344.7
			V52	B	10										1	84.9
1	Res.	L	V53	A	1			1	383.7				1			
			V53	A	2											
			V53	A	3											
			V53	A	4										1	103.1
2	Agri-1		V58	A	1	1	1.9								1	57.3
			V58	A	2			1	165.7		1				7	3264.1
			V58	A	3										1	117.1
			V58	A	4	1	18.8	1	53.9				1			
			V58	A	5	3	79.5									
			V58	A	6											
			V58	B	1			1	206.3	1						
			V58	B	2	1	11.6	2	429.0	1		1			3	757.9
			V58	B	3											
			V58	C	1											
			V58	C	2			1			1					
			V58	C	3											
			V59	A	1										1	60.3
			V59	A	2			1						1	3	
			V59	A	3											
			V59	A	4											
			V59	A	5											
			V59	B	1											
			V59	B	2	2	5.6								2	426.2
			V59	B	3											
			V60	A	1											
			V60	A	2											
			V60	A	3										1	435.7
			V60	A	4											
			V60	A	5										1	19.8
			V60	A	6											
			V60	A	7			1	36.7			1				
2	Res.	B	V60	B	1			2	300.0	1		1			2	370.9
			V60	B	2	1	3.3	1	33.7	1					1	89.6
			V60	B	3											

Lithic Tools from Excavations in the Far West Bajo (continued)

Block	Zone	Group	Op.	Subop.	Lot	Blades No.	Blades Weight (g)	Bifaces No.	Bifaces Weight (g)	No. Prox.	No. Med.	No. Dist.	No. Whole	Un-known	Tools or Cores No.	Tools or Cores Weight (g)
2	Res.	B	V60	B	4			1	24.1	1						
			V60	B	5											
2	Res.	A	V61	A	1	4	15.5								4	464.4
			V61	A	2											
			V61	A	3	3	12.8									
			V61	A	4											
			V61	A	5											
3	Res.	A	V62	A	1											
			V62	A	2											
			V62	A	3			1	7.0		1					
			V62	A	4											
			V62	A	5											
			V62	A	6											
			V62	A	7											
			V62	A	8											
			V62	A	9											
			V62	A	10											
			V62	A	11											
			V62	A	12											
			V62	A	13											
			V62	A	14											
			V62	A	15											
			V62	A	16											
			V62	A	17											
			V62	A	18											
			V62	A	19											
			V62	A	20											
			V62	A	21											
			V62	A	22											
			V62	A	23											
			V62	A	24											
			V62	A	25											
			V62	A	26											
			V62	A	27											
			V62	B	1	2	19.6	2	28.7			2			1	316.9
			V62	B	2											
			V62	C	1			2	580.1				2			
			V62	C	2											
			V62	C	3			2	136.4	1		1			2	643.3
3	Res.	B	V63	A	1			1	170.5			1			1	291.0
			V63	A	2	1	1.5	1	170.4			1				
			V63	A	3										2	523.9
			V63	A	4			3	469.6	1	1		1		1	496.8
			V63	A	5	1	74.6	8	1062.7	2		4	2		1	285.7
			V63	A	6										1	129.5
			V63	A	7											
			V63	A	8			1	71.5				1			
			V63	A	9											
			V63	A	10	1	25.6									
			V63	B	1			1	27.0			1			1	764.6
			V63	B	2											
			V63	B	3			1				1				
			V63	B	4										1	21.5
			V63	B	5											
			V63	B	6										1	156.9
			V63	B	7										1	140.5
3	Res.	E	V65	A	1										1	421.5

Lithic Tools from Excavations in the Far West Bajo (*continued*)

Block	Zone	Group	Op.	Subop.	Lot	Blades No.	Weight (g)	Bifaces No.	Weight (g)	No. Prox.	No. Med.	No. Dist.	No. Whole	Un-known	Tools or Cores No.	Weight (g)
3	Res.	E	V65	A	2											
			V65	A	3											
			V65	A	4											
			V65	A	5											
			V65	A	6											
			V65	A	7										1	65.5
			V65	A	8 .											
			V65	A	9											
			V65	A	10											
			V65	A	11											
			V65	A	12											
			V65	A	13											
			V65	B	1											
			V65	B	2	6	8.3	1	11.2	1						
			V65	B	3	2	2.5									
			V65	B	4	5	45.1	1	16.8			1			2	127.9
			V65	B	5											
			V65	B	6											
			V65	B	7			1	13.3			1			1	129.0
			V65	B	8	3	105.6									
3	Res.	F	V66	A	1											
			V66	A	2											
			V66	A	3											
			V66	A	4	1	7.5									
			V66	A	5											
			V66	A	6											
			V66	A	7											
			V66	A	8											
			V66	A	9											
			V66	A	10											
			V66	A	11			2	345.0				2			
			V66	A	12											
			V66	A	13			1	11.5	1						
			V66	A	14											
			V66	A	15											
			V66	A	16	2	21.8	2	257.3				2		2	682.2
			V66	A	17			1	77.5				1			
			V66	A	18			6	1239.5				6			
			V66	A	19			1	62.1				1			
			V66	A	20			5	676.4				5		4	1597.0
			V66	A	21										1	364.5
			V66	A	22			1	275.0				1			
			V66	A	23										1	634.5
			V66	A	24			2	139.0				2		1	133.1
			V66	A	25											
			V66	A	26											
			V66	A	27											
			V66	A	28			1	168.0				1		1	243.5
			V66	A	29	4	3.6	2	500.3				1	1	6	1238.1
			V66	A	30			1	69.0				1			
			V66	A	31											
			V66	B	1										1	66.4
			v66	B	2											
			V66	B	3										1	59.5
			V66	B	4											
			V66	B	5											
			V66	B	6											

Lithic Tools from Excavations in the Far West Bajo *(continued)*

Block	Zone	Group	Op.	Subop.	Lot	Blades No.	Weight (g)	Bifaces No.	Weight (g)	No. Prox.	No. Med.	No. Dist.	No. Whole	Un-known	Tools or Cores No.	Weight (g)
3	Res.	F	V66	C	1										1	58.3
			V66	C	2			2	287.8	1			1			
			V66	C	3			2	277.2	1			1		7	1131.9
			V66	C	4	2	59.4								2	169.2
			V66	D	1											
			V66	D	2			1	522.9				1		3	694.9
			V66	D	3										1	82.7
			V66	D	4			1	*			1			2	*
			V66	D	5											
			V66	D	6	3	5.4	1	60.8			1			2	275.5
			V66	D	7											
			V66	D	8											
			V66	D	9			1	76.5		1					
			V66	D	10											
			V66	D	11										1	525.6
			V66	D	12			1	95.6		1					
			V66	D	13											
3	Res.	I	V67	A	1										2	572.7
			V67	A	2			1	117.5	1					1	247.6
			V67	A	3			1	121.6	1					3	865.8
			V67	A	4										1	29.3
			V67	A	5	1	13.7									
			V67	A	6										1	73.6
			V67	A	7										1	132.0
			V67	A	8	2	1.9									
			V67	A	9											
			V67	A	10											
			V67	A	11											
			V67	A	12										1	10.5
			V67	B	1			1	106.4		1				4	804.8
			V67	B	2											
			V67	B	3			1	182.2			1			3	234.8
			V67	B	4											
3	Res.	X	V68	A	1											
			V68	A	2	1	4.2								2	66.6
			V68	A	3											
			V68	A	4											
			V68	A	5											
			V68	A	6											
			V68	A	7			2	351.5			1		1		
			V68	A	8											
			V68	A	9											
			V68	A	10											
			V68	A	11											
			V68	A	12			1	140.2			1				
			V68	A	13											
			V68	A	14										1	303.0
			V68	B	1											
			V68	B	2											
			V68	C	1			1	144.0	1						
			V68	C	2			3	687.4		1	2			12	1957.2
			V68	C	3											
			V68	C	4			3	224.6		2			1	5	1618.6
4	Agri-2		V69	A	1											
			V69	A	2											
			V69	A	3											
			V69	A	4											

Lithic Tools from Excavations in the Far West Bajo (*continued*)

Block	Zone	Group	Op.	Subop.	Lot	Blades No.	Weight (g)	Bifaces No.	Weight (g)	No. Prox.	No. Med.	No. Dist.	No. Whole	Un-known	Tools or Cores No.	Weight (g)
4	Agri-2		V69	B	1											
			V69	B	2											
			V69	B	3											
			V69	B	4											
4	Res.	Z	V69	C	1											
			V69	C	2	1	2.8									
			V69	C	3											
			V69	C	4											
4	Agri-2		V70	A	1										1	260.8
			V70	A	2										2	846.0
			V70	A	3											
			V70	B	1											
			V70	B	2			1	335.2					1	2	1108.8
			V70	B	3											
			V70	C	1											
			V70	C	2			1	116.7			1			3	598.4
			V70	C	3										2	62.8
			V70	C	4											
			V70	C	5											
			V70	C	6											
			V70	D	1			1	73.6			1			1	216.3
			V70	D	2	1	24.8	1	147.2					1	14	3551.0
			V70	D	3											
			V70	D	4											
4	Res.	T	V71	A	1											
			V71	A	2										1	67.8
			V71	A	3											
			V71	A	4											
4	Agri-2		V71	B	1										1	59.9
			V71	B	2	2	2.8								3	318.2
			V71	B	3	1	4.6								1	185.2
			V71	C	1											
			V71	C	2											
	Bajo		V72	A	1											
			V72	A	2											
			V72	B	1											
			V72	B	2	1	1.7								1	55.9
			V72	B	3											
5	Agri-3		V73	A	1			1	257.4			1			2	394.4
			V73	A	2	1	4.0	2	428.0			1	1		3	692.0
			V73	A	3										1	387.5
			V73	A	4											
			V73	A	5											
			V73	A	6											
			V73	B	1											
			V73	B	2										1	127.4
			V73	B	3											
			V73	B	4										3	204.6
			V73	B	5											
5	Res.	B	V74	A	1											
			V74	A	2											
			V74	A	3											
			V74	B	1											
			V74	B	2											
			V74	B	3			1	60.9		1					
			V74	B	4											
			V74	B	5										3	717.0

Lithic Tools from Excavations in the Far West Bajo (*continued*)

Block	Zone	Group	Op.	Subop.	Lot	Blades No.	Weight (g)	Bifaces No.	Weight (g)	No. Prox.	No. Med.	No. Dist.	No. Whole	Un-known	Tools or Cores No.	Weight (g)
5	Res.	B	V74	C	1											
			V74	C	2											
			V74	C	3											
			V74	D	1											
			V74	D	2											
			V74	D	3			1	250.1					1		
			V74	E	1											
			V74	E	2											
			V74	E	3											
			V74	E	4											
			V74	E	5											
			V74	E	6											
			V74	E	7											
			V74	E	8											
			V74	E	9											
			V74	E	10											
			V74	E	11											
			V74	E	12											
			V74	E	13										1	102.5
			V74	E	14											
			V74	E	15											
			V74	E	16											
			V74	E	17											
			V74	E	18											
			V74	E	19											
			V74	E	20											
			V74	E	21											
			V74	E	22											
			V74	E	23											
			V74	E	24											
			V74	E	25											
			V74	E	26											
			V74	E	27											
			V74	E	28											
			V74	E	29											
			V74	E	30											
			V74	E	31											
			V74	E	32											
			V74	E	33											
			V74	E	34											
			V74	E	35											
			V74	E	36											
			V74	E	37											
			V74	E	38											
			V74	E	39											
			V74	E	40											
			V74	F	1			1	136.6					1		
5	Agri-3		V75	A	1											
			V75	A	2										2	264.2
			V75	A	3											
5	Res.	D	V75	B	1										1	501.2
			V75	B	2			1	175.4	1						
			V75	B	3											
			V75	B	4											
			V75	B	5											
	Total					92	*911.6*	159	*20,810.3+*	35	19	34	45	26	247	*50,667.0+*

* Not recorded

Groundstone from Excavations in the Far West Bajo

Block	Zone	Group	Op.	Subop.	Lot	No.	Total Weight (g)	Mano Whole	Mano Frag.	Metate Whole	Metate Frag.	Hammerstone or Polishing stone	Other Whole	Other Frag.	Green-stone
1	Res.	A	V39	A	2	1	784.0						1		
			V39	B	2	1	451.0				1				
			V39	C	1	1	409.1				1				
1	Res.	H	V40	B	2	1	83.1					1			
1	Res.	B	V42	A	1	1	*			1					
1	Res.	O	V51	A	1	1	75.9								1
			V51	A	2	1	138.4		1						
			V51	A	3	1	29.3							1	
			V51	A	6	2	2034.4		1				1		
			V51	B	1	1	871.4				1				
			V51	B	2	1	579.2		1						
			V51	B	6	1	232.7		1						
1	Res.	I	V52	B	1	1	189.0		1						
			V52	B	2	1	46.9				1				
			V52	B	9	1	1004.5				1				
3	Res.	A	V62	A	3	1	1589.0						1		
			V62	A	6	1	146.1							1	
			V62	C	1	1	0.3								1
			V62	C	2	2	3.7								2
3	Res.	B	V63	A	4	1	594.5						1		
3	Res.	E	V65	B	1	1	71.4						1		
3	Res.	F	V66	A	15	1	389.8					1			
			V66	A	18	1	115.8					1			
			V66	A	23	2	1287.2					2			
			V66	A	24	1	31.1					1			
			V66	A	28	2	243.2							2	
			V66	A	31	1	398.0				1				
			V66	B	1	1	499.3	1							
			V66	C	4	1	427.0	1							
			V66	D	2	1	200.3		1						
			V66	D	3	1	1031.6	1							
			V66	D	4	3	2066.7	2		1					
			V66	D	11	1	117.0	1							
3	Res.	I	V67	A	2	1	334.0						1		
3	Res.	X	V68	A	6	1	144.3					1			
Total						41	16,619.2+	6	6	2	6	7	8	2	4

* Not recorded

Obsidian from Excavations in the Far West Bajo

Block	Zone	Group	Op.	Subop.	Lot	No.	Total Weight (g)	Proximal	Medial	Distal	Fragment	Whole	Other
1	Res.	A	V29	A	2	2	*				2		
			V29	A	5	2	*				2		
1	Res.	N	V31	A	2	1	*				1		
1	Res.	O	V32	A	2	1	*				1		
1	Res.	I	V34	A	3	1	*				1		
1	Res.	I	V37	A	2	1	*				1		
1	Res.	A	V39	A	1	1	1.0		1				
			V39	A	3	1	1.0	1					
			V39	B	2	1	0.1		1				
			V39	D	4	1	1.0		1				
			V39	F	2	2	1.1	1	1				
1	Res.	H	V40	A	1	1	0.1		1				
			V40	A	2	1	0.8		1				
			V40	B	1	4	4.5	2	2				
			V40	B	2	1	1.3		1				
1	Res.	B	V42	A	1	1	0.8		1				
			V42	A	4	1	1.1	1					
			V42	B	12	1	1.4				1		
1	Res.	O	V51	B	1	1	1.0		1				
			V51	B	4	3	1.6	1	1				1
1	Res.	N	V51	C	1	1	2.0	1					
1	Res.	I	V52	B	1	1	0.7		1				
			V52	B	2	1	0.9	1					
			V52	B	8	1	0.3				1		
3	Res.	A	V62	A	1	1	0.5				1		
			V62	A	2	1	0.8		1				
			V62	A	3	1	0.7		1				
			V62	A	5	1	1.2					1	
			V62	A	9	1	0.2			1			
			V62	A	10	3	2.6					3	
			V62	A	11	1	0.3				1		
			V62	A	16	1	0.5		1				
			V62	B	2	1	0.6		1				
			V62	C	1	1	0.5					1	
			V62	C	2	5	8.5				3	2	
			V62	C	3	1	1.2					1	
3	Res.	B	V63	A	5	15	10.5		3	2	10		
			V63	A	7	1	0.4				1		
			V63	B	2	4	3.7				4		
			V63	B	5	1	1.4		1				
3	Res.	E	V65	A	11	1	1.3				1		
			V65	B	1	1	2.4						1
			V65	B	8	1	0.5		1				
3	Res.	F	V66	A	3	1	1.9	1					
			V66	A	4	1	0.5		1				
			V66	A	12	1	0.8		1				
			V66	A	16	3	3.3		3				
			V66	A	18	4	4.6		4				
			V66	A	19	1	1.1		1				
			V66	A	20	12	7.2		10	1	1		
			V66	A	21	3	0.4		3				
			V66	A	22	5	4.1		2	3			

Obsidian from Excavations in the Far West Bajo (*continued*)

Block	Zone	Group	Op.	Subop.	Lot	Total No.	Total Weight (g)	Number of Proximal	Medial	Distal	Fragment	Whole	Other
3	Res.	F	V66	A	23	6	1.8	1	1		4		
			V66	A	24	1	0.5		1				
			V66	A	25	2	0.6		1		1		
			V66	A	27	2	*				2		
			V66	A	29	7	6.7	2	5				
			V66	A	30	4	1.2		4				
			V66	C	2	3	1.1		3				
			V66	C	3	1	2.1	1					
			V66	D	3	2	1.8		2				
			V66	D	5	1	0.9		1				
			V66	D	6	2	1.2	2					
			V66	D	9	2	4.4	1					1
			V66	D	12	4	1.0		1		3		
3	Res.	I	V67	B	2	1	0.8	1					
3	Res.	X	V68	C	2	1	1.3				1		
5	Res.	B	V74	C	2	1	0.4		1				
			V74	D	1	2	1.8		2				
Total						147	109.9+	17	69	7	43	8	3

* Not recorded

Fauna and Shell from Excavations in the Far West Bajo

Block	Zone	Group	Op.	Subop.	Lot	Total No.	Weight (g)	Comments
Fauna								
3	Res.	E	V65	A	3	4	1.2	Unidentified animal bone
3	Res.	F	V66	A	11	1	*	Unidentified animal bone
			V66	A	14	1	*	Unidentified animal bone
			V66	A	16	3	2.5	1 linear bead; unidentified animal bone
			V66	A	18	2	0.5	1 polished bone, tapering to point; 1 polished bone fragment
			V66	A	20	2	0.5	1 piece modified animal bone; 1 unidentified animal bone
			V66	A	21	1	*	Unidentified animal bone
			V66	A	22	6	1.4	1 polished bone segment; 1 modified animal bone; 4 unidentified animal bone
			V66	A	23	6	0.1	1 bone awl fragment; 1 modified animal bone; 4 unidentified animal bone
			V66	A	24	2	0.6	1 polished bone with rounded tip; 1 unidentified animal bone
			V66	A	25	3	1.0	1 carved bone awl with serpent motif; 1 polished bone with tapered ends; 1 unidentified animal bone
			V66	A	26	1	*	Unidentified animal bone
			V66	A	27	2	*	Unidentified animal bone
			V66	A	28	8	7.9	1 circular bead; 2 carved bone segments; 1 polished bone awl; 1 burned bone fragment; 3 unidentified animal bone
			V66	A	29	5	2.2	Ribs with ends cut off and rounded
			V66	A	30	2	*	Unidentified animal bone
			V66	A	31	4	2.5	1 thin polished hollow bone; 1 polished bone segment with drilled holes; 2 unidentified animal bone
			V66	D	6	1	*	Unidentified animal bone
3	Res.	X	V68	C	4	1	14.4	Antler fragment
Total						55	34.8+	
Shell								
1	Res.	I	V37	A	1	1	*	Shell pendant
1	Res.	O	V51	A	3	1	66.9	*Strombus gigas* (conch) fragment (bottom column)
2	Res.	B	V60	B	4	1	99.4	Rectangular artifact (rasp?) with incising
3	Res.	A	V62	A	14	2	12.4	Marine shell fragments
			V62	A	19	1	1.9	Marine shell
			V62	C	1	3	46.1	Scalloped marine shells, one with drilled hole
3	Res.	B	V63	A	10	1	0.1	Marine shell
3	Res.	F	V66	A	19	1	65.0	Polished marine shell fragment
			V66	A	21	1	6.8	Conch fragment
			V66	A	22	1	0.1	Abalone-mother of pearl fragment
			V66	A	23	3	6.6	Marine shell fragments; 1 curved, 2 spiral
			V66	A	25	1	0.6	Marine shell fragment
			V66	A	29	1	*	Marine shell
			V66	A	30	2	1.4	1 anvil-shaped carved shell; 1 shell carved as caiman head
			V66	D	6	6	5.1	5 mussel shell fragments, 1 carved pendant with incising
3	Res.	X	V68	C	4	1	7.3	Triangular conch fragment
Total						27	319.7+	

* Not recorded

Prehistoric Burials in the Far West Bajo, Belize

Julie Mather Saul and Frank P. Saul

Burial 1 (Op. V42B–5)

Type. Primary burial, under bench, resting on floor. Vertical headstone placed just west of head.

Position. Flexed, head to west, pelvis to east, lying on back with knees slightly to the left side (north), both hands under flexed legs (one resting on chest closer to knees; the other on abdomen, closer to pelvis; could not determine which hand was which).

Condition. Very eroded and fragmentary.

Sex. Female; based on auricular area of pelvis (elevated), sharp upper orbit margin (left lateral), plus small size and gracility of bones.

Age. Young Adult (20–35 years); based on very slight dental attrition.

Dental findings. Two cervical caries observed (both mandibular) in the 25 teeth. No Linear Enamel Hypoplasia (LEH; indicates stress to child during tooth crown formation, could be due to illness or malnutrition). No calculus. Trace of periodontoclasia (indicates gum disease and resorption of bony tooth socket, which leads to antemortem tooth loss). Lingual Surface Attrition of Maxillary Anterior Teeth (LSAMAT) present on maxillary incisors.

Skeletal findings. No signs of treponema on tibiae. Strongly marked muscle attachments (small but strong woman): Humeri: very strongly marked deltoid tuberosities. Right ulna: very strongly marked supinator crest. Femora: strongly marked lineae aspera.

Dental decoration. None.

Cranial shaping. Unknown.

Teeth present: 25. Maxillary: all six molars, one right and one left premolar, one canine, right lateral and mesial incisors. Mandibular: all three left molars, 1st and 2nd right molars, all four premolars and both canines, right lateral and mesial incisors, left lateral incisor.

Bone present. All partial, fragmentary and eroded: both humeri, ulnae and radii; right and left hand metacarpals and phalanges; ribs; pelvis; right and left femora; right and left tibiae; fibulae; cranial (including left lateral orbit margin, right temporal); and mandible.

Burial 2 (Op. V42B–12)

Type. Primary burial under bench, in hole cut through floor; body resting on bedrock. Vertical headstone placed just south of head.

Position. Flexed, head to south, pelvis to north, probably on left side facing west. (Cranial fragments and teeth found at north end belong to skull found at headstone in south end, skull fragments can be joined together; result of bioturbation.)

Condition. Eroded, fragmentary and incomplete.

Sex. Probable Male; based on robusticity of occipital bone (the nuchal region in particular) and long bone robusticity.

Age. Young Adult (20–35 years); based on very slight dental attrition and persistence of mammelons on mesial incisor.

Dental findings. Linear Enamel Hypoplasia present on canines, late in crown formation (3–5 years). No caries in the 12 teeth. No LSAMAT. Slight calculus. Right lateral incisor is a peg incisor (genetic anomaly). Somewhat more wear on left mandibular incisors (right not recovered), left mandibular canine, and first premolar than on other teeth, possibly due to use wear of some sort, chipping, or both.

Dental decoration. Probably not, but not all teeth that were typically decorated were present.

Cranial shaping. Unknown.

Teeth present. 12. Maxillary: left mesial incisor, right lateral incisor, right canine, one premolar, one molar.

Mandibular: left mesial and lateral incisors, both canines, both left premolars, right first or second molar.

Bone present. Some eroded cranial fragments, mostly from occiput; very eroded shafts of right and left femora, tibiae, humeri, scapulae, possible radius or ulna.

Burial 3 (Op. V63A–5)

Type. Primary burial.

Position. Placed face down, head pointing approximately south, pelvis north. Flexed (knees to chest), arms bent at elbows, forearms crossed at chest (right arm closest to chest), head turned to right shoulder (facing west).

Condition. Eroded and fragmentary.

Age. 3–5 years; based on dental development.

Sex. Immaturity precluded sex determination.

Skeletal findings. No tibial signs of treponemal infection, no Spongy or Porotic Hyperostosis Cranii.

Dental findings. No caries in the 16 deciduous teeth present.

Cranial shaping. Tabular shaping of unknown variety; partial frontal bone is flattened with bulge just anterior to coronal suture, typical of tabular shaping. The shape of the partial left parietal also suggests cranial shaping.

Deciduous teeth present. Maxillary: 4 molars, 2 canines, 4 incisors. Mandibular: 1 molar, 2 canines, 3 incisors.

Permanent tooth crowns partially formed. Maxillary: first right molar, 1 premolar, 2 canines, right and left lateral incisors, left mesial incisor. Mandibular: right and left first molars, 2 premolars, 2 canines, all 4 incisors.

Bone present (all fragmentary). Skull, mandible, right and left clavicles, right and left radii and ulnae, femur shaft, right and left tibiae and fibulae, few other small scraps including rib, vertebrae.

Burial 4 (Op. V62–A–26)

Type. Primary burial in cist under bench, body resting on bedrock.

Position. Flexed, head to south, pelvis to north, on left side facing west; right upper arm parallel to vertebral column, arm bent at elbow, lower arm crossing east–west over left femur; left upper arm crossing east–west under head, elbow bent, lower arm running south–north along west wall.

Sex. Male; based on pelvic fragments (narrow greater sciatic notches) and cranial robusticity (blunt orbital rims, rugged inion region).

Age. Middle Adult (35–55 years); based on dental attrition and presence of minor arthritic lipping on vertebral body fragments.

Dental findings. 3 maxillary teeth only. Periodontoclasia and antemortem tooth loss evident from edentulous mandible fragment. Linear Enamel Hypoplasia present on canines, late in crown formation (3–5 years). Slight calculus present. Presence of caries unknown due to extreme postmortem erosion of crowns and roots. Presence or absence of LSAMAT unknown.

Skeletal findings. Most bone too eroded and incomplete for analysis. Fragments of cervical and other vertebral bodies bear slight arthritic lipping, probably age related. No signs of treponema on tibial shafts.

Dental decoration. Unknown.

Cranial shaping. Unknown.

Teeth present. 3 maxillary teeth: 2 canines and 1 premolar.

Bone present. Fragments of skull, mandible, right scapula, clavicle, talus, proximal ends of right radius and ulna, shafts of right radius and ulna, left radius or ulna shaft, vertebral fragments, right and left shafts of femora, tibiae, and fibulae, humeri, metacarpal and metatarsal shafts.

Burial 5 (Op. V66–A–15)

Type. Primary burial.

Position. Flexed, on left side, head south; hips north, facing west. Feet together at pelvis, hands at feet. This burial was inserted into the upper part of an earlier burial (Burial 6), thus disturbing it. Remains are fragmentary.

Sex. Male; based on narrow left sciatic notch and

depressed auricular surface, overall robusticity, including nuchal crest protrusion on occiput.

Age. 25–30 years; based on persistence of epiphyseal scars on distal femur, proximal tibia and proximal humerus, sternal rib end Iscan 4, recent fusion of annular epiphyses on vertebrae, 3rd molars erupted with slight attrition, overall slight dental attrition.

Dental decoration. None.

Possible grave goods: An accompanying tooth offering, an extra maxillary canine, is present that is too small and too eroded to belong to the earlier burial into which Burial 5 was inserted. This canine is decorated in Romero B-5 style and also has on its root what may be carving (crosshatched Pop design) or perhaps patterning that could result from a thin cord wrapped around it for hanging.

Cranial shaping. Tabular Erect + + (Frontal bone flattened and inclined with the occipital bone in a more or less perpendicular plane).

Activity related changes. Slight osteoarthritic lipping on vertebral bodies, with a small osteophyte on body of L4 or L5; lipping around edges of tarsal articular surfaces (sharp rims), especially talus and calcaneus. Large heel spur on right calcaneus where abductor hallux and flexor digitorum brevis originate; caused by walking or running, especially across rough terrain. All of the above may relate to walking or running or climbing across rough terrain carrying burdens.

Trauma. Healed fracture of 5th metacarpal (bone in palm proximal to fifth finger along edge of hand).

Other skeletal findings. Genetic or developmental anomaly? Left hamate of wrist with no hook and no sign of trauma (related to Burial 7?). Presence or absence of treponemal disease and Ossified Subperiosteal Hemorrhages could not be determined. Spongy or Porotic Hyperostosis not present.

Dental findings. LEH: 2 episodes, between the ages of 3 to 5 years. Caries: 9 of the 27 teeth present have caries cavities; most are cervical and interproximal; one (mandibular M1) is interproximal but higher on the crown. Periodontoclasia: moderate to severe. Left molars show more attrition than right molars, indicating a one-sided activity, either one-sided chewing or some sort of tool use of the left molars. LSAMAT moderate on all maxillary canines and incisors (activity or diet related attrition?). Calculus: moderate calculus present in general with severe calculus on mandibular incisors.

Burial 6 (Op. V-66-15)

This individual is larger and much more robust than Burial 5. There is a color difference in bone as well as much more postmortem erosion.

Type. Primary burial.

Position. Flexed (possibly on back), with hands and feet at pelvis, head to south and hips to north. This burial is slightly below and to the north and east of Burial 5, which was inserted into the upper part of this burial at a later date. Remains are fragmentary and incomplete.

Sex. Male; based on extreme muscularity and large size. Left femur maximum A–P diameter is 32.6 mm, left femur head diameter estimate (edge is missing) is 46.8mm, left radius head diameter is 25.6 mm.

Age. 20–30 years; sternal rib end Iscan Phase 3, lack of osteoarthritic lipping on all articular surfaces, persistence of epiphyseal line for distal femur.

Dental decoration. Not determined, no teeth found.

Cranial shaping. Not determined, only a few fragments recovered.

Trauma. A healed apparent crushing (from above) fracture of the proximal end of a hand phalanx (side not determined). Fracture of the proximal end of the left 4th metacarpal (bone of the palm proximal to the ring finger). Three fractures involving the right foot and ankle: compression fracture of talus; compression fracture of the 3rd cuneiform; fracture at proximal end of 2nd or 3rd metatarsal. (The navicular and 1st cuneiform are normal; the other tarsals are missing). A compression fracture of the talus can be the result of jumping or falling from a great height and landing so as to cause the foot to absorb the major impact. Only a fragment of the navicular and the 2nd cuneiform (both normal) were recovered for the left foot, which does not rule out damage to the left foot. The hand fractures could conceivably have resulted from the same fall.

Activity related changes. Large Poirer's facet on left femur measuring 6.4 cm along the edge of the femur head and extending 3.8 cm down the femoral neck at its farthest point (this portion is missing for right femur); may be a result of extreme extension, as when moving downhill. Enlarged fovea on heads of left and right femora; may be a function of extreme activity involving the legs.

Other skeletal findings: Presence or absence of treponemal disease, Spongy or Porotic Hyperostosis, and Ossified Subperiosteal Hemorrhages cannot be determined due to fragmentary, incomplete, and eroded nature of remains.

Burial 7 (Op. V66A-15)

Type. Primary burial.

Position. Flexed on back, head north and hips south, with knees to the left side (east), right hand on chest under chin, left hand unknown. The head extended into the north wall of the excavation. Excavators discovered the burial when pelvic and foot fragments appeared in the screen. Very fragmentary and incomplete.

Sex. Unknown. Mandible is small and somewhat bilobate, teeth are small, mastoid process is equivocal, metrics could be either male or female (right humeral head diameter estimate, edge missing, is 45 mm; right radial head diameter estimate, edge missing, is 20.1 mm).

Age: 25–40 years; based on degree of attrition, periodontoclasia and antemortem tooth loss, small fragment of sagittal suture present is fused internally, slight trace of persistence of distal femur epiphyseal scar.

Dental decoration. Romero B–2 type filing on lateral corner of maxillary right central incisor. No other anterior maxillary teeth are present.

Cranial shaping. Not determined.

Skeletal findings. Genetic or developmental anomaly? Right hamate of wrist with no hook (related to Burial 5?). Presence or absence of treponemal disease, Spongy or Porotic Hyperostosis, Ossified Subperiosteal Hemorrhages could not be determined.

Trauma. Inwardly displaced healed fracture of left rib (number unknown); could have been caused by blow to chest or fall onto chest. Healed sharp force injury, on parietal fragment of skull. Fine striations parallel a deeper groove with a V-shaped floor. Reactive bone surrounds the cut (particularly at one end) and the edges are raised.

Activity related changes. Pronounced muscle attachments on metacarpals and phalanges of right hand (no left hand present). Slight laminal spurring of thoracic vertebrae. Slight anterior compression of fragments of 2 thoracic or lumbar vertebral bodies, also osteophyte formation.

Dental findings. Anomalous 3-rooted mandibular 3rd molar. Linear Enamel Hypoplasia: 2 episodes present on maxillary incisor, one on mandibular canine. Nonspecific indicators of 2 periods of malnutrition, illness, or both. Caries cavities: 5 of the 10 teeth present are carious, some massive. Extreme to severe periodontoclasia and antemortem tooth loss. All teeth present are barely attached to the jaw. The right mandibular 2nd molar is missing antemortem and the 3rd molar has drifted forward at an angle. Abscesses: some present at the tips of the roots of the left mandibular canine and both left premolars. LSAMAT: extreme (++++) present on the right central incisor (no other maxillary anterior teeth present).

Burial 8 (Op. V68A-9)

Type. Primary burial.

Position. Flexed on left side or on back with knees west, head to the south (slightly west), and hips to the north (slightly east). Very fragmentary and incomplete.

Sex. Male; based on pelvic morphology: narrow greater sciatic notch, configuration of pubic bone, depressed auricular surface, size of superior articulation of sacrum relative to width of sacrum; also strongly everted gonial angle of mandible.

Age. 25–35 years. No persistence of epiphyseal scar on proximal femur, fusion of sacral elements 1 and 2, lack of lipping on vertebral body fragments, lack of lipping on odontoid process, moderate dental attrition, all tooth roots complete.

Dental decoration. Unknown.

Cranial shaping. Unknown.

Skeletal findings. Presence or absence of treponemal disease, Spongy or Porotic Hyperostosis and Ossified Subperiosteal Hemorrhages cannot be determined due to the fragmentary and incomplete nature of the remains.

Trauma. A long-term draining injury is present on the right calcaneus in the articulation for the talus. An opening with raised and rounded edges tapers down into the body of the calcaneous.

Dental findings. Periodontoclasia: moderate. Antemortem tooth loss: unknown. Caries cavities: cervical caries present on 6 of the 17 teeth present. Calculus: slight presence. Linear Enamel Hypoplasia: present; a wide band on maxillary canine and lateral incisor, indicating a prolonged period of malnutrition, illness, or both at around 4–6 years. LSAMAT: present (slight) on the maxillary incisors that are present (right central, left lateral).

Burial 9 (Op. V68A–9)

Position. Unknown. Individual is represented only by teeth that were found in the laboratory in a packet marked "misc. Op. V68A-9" and therefore were probably recovered in screening of dirt from Burial 8. Since this is a young child, any skeletal remains, if originally present, may not have survived. Impossible to tell if this child was a primary burial or secondary tooth cache or burial or offering.

Sex. Unknown.

Age. 18 months ± 6 months (1–2 years); based on erupted deciduous left maxillary central incisor with broken root plus half-formed crowns of permanent maxillary and mandibular 1st molars.

Cache (Op. V62C)

Human bone. Right femur mid-proximal portion of shaft about 12 cm long. Left (?) femur mid-portion shaft about 12.5 cm long (the posterior ⅓ of the shaft fragment is missing). Both femur shaft fragments are very eroded.

Sex. Could not be determined for either femur.

Age. Both femora probably adult; based on size and cortical density.

Bajo Hill Site Structure 1–A–2 Looters' Trench (Op. V39C-1)

Fragmented skeletal remains of at least two individuals found in the backdirt screened from the looters' trench on the rear of the east pyramidal structure of Group A. Left and right proximal femur fragments similar in size but of different contours in the subtrochanteric area.

Sex. At least one probable male, based on brow ridges and maximum femur anterior-posterior diameter (31; when >30, probably male).

Age. One probable middle adult (35–50 years); one probable young adult (20–35 years), based on dental attrition.

Skeletal findings. One individual was larger, based on large tibia; one individual was smaller, based on small radii.

La Caldera Group B Looters' Trench

Scattered and commingled skeletal remains of two individuals were recovered from the surface within and surrounding a looters' trench.

Individual A (smaller individual)

Sex. Either a female or an abnormally small male. Female characteristics: small size and gracility of all bone; small mandible with narrow ramus; long bone metrics. Male characteristics: somewhat marked brow ridges at glabella; nuchal region of occiput somewhat rugged; right orbit upper rim blunt; wide mandible; supramastoid crests and mastoid processes are equivocal.

Age. Young adult, 20–30 years; based on recent fusion of proximal tibial epiphysis, recent fusion of annular epiphyses on vertebral fragments, open coronal and lambdoid cranial sutures (sagittal is fused, but skull is shaped, which could impact on closure), and very slight dental attrition.

Dental decoration. Possible filing of lateral corner of mandibular left lateral incisor (Romero B–2 or B–4).

Cranial shaping. Marked tabular oblique shaping.

Dental findings. Cervical caries on both teeth present. No linear enamel hypoplasia present on single maxillary canine present, but this is not conclusive. Presence or absence of LSAMAT unknown. Mandible shows antemortem tooth loss.

Skeletal findings. No signs of treponema on left tibia (right missing). No Spongy or Porotic Hyperostosis.

Trauma: Healed parry fracture of distal right ulna (no apparent fracture of right radius). Healed blunt force injury to right frontal including orbit region, resulting in extensive remodelling (and probable atrophy due to possible lack of vision in the right eye).

Stature estimate: The maximum tibia length of 316 mm falls within the range of females at the site of Altar de Sacrificios (tibial maximum length of 308–337 mm). This is shorter than the Altar male tibial maximum length range, which is 363–380 mm. Using Genoves' formula, the stature estimate for Individual A is: if female, 147 cm ± 2 cm; if male, 153 cm ± 2 cm.

Teeth present. Maxillary right canine and mandibular left lateral incisor.

Bone present. Nearly complete skull and mandible (fragmentary but reconstructed), portion of distal right humerus, right radius shaft, left radius proximal shaft, right ulna (nearly complete), portions of right and possibly left hands (2 metacarpals, one right; 7 phalanges), right scapula fragment, left femur shaft with neck, separate partial femur head (side not determined), portions of distal femur condyle, right patella, nearly complete left tibia, fragment of proximal tibia condyle, portions of right and left feet (4 tarsals, one phalanx), fibula shaft fragment, sacral fragments, anterior vertebral body fragment, fragment of C1 vertebra, rib fragments and other various long bone fragments.

Individual B (larger individual)

Sex. Unknown (male, or a large robust female).

Age. Adult, but not an old adult (cranial fragment has open coronal and sagittal sutures).

Bone present. Femur fragment, left parietal fragment, fragment of lateral orbit.

NOTE: A two-inch femur shaft fragment from one of these individuals (uncertain which one) has what appears to be woven bone on the surface indicative of some sort of inflammatory-infectious process.

POPULATION OVERVIEW

The individuals described here range from primary burials, through contents of a cache, to bone salvaged from the back dirt of two looters' trenches. Some individuals are represented by only a few fragments or by teeth whereas others are more complete. This small population consists of 12 adults (with a female-to-male-to-undetermined ratio of 1:6:5) and two young children (yielding an adult-to-immature ratio of 12:2). Eight are young adults, two are middle adults, two can only be said to be "adults" and the children are 3–5 and 1–2 years of age. Although the total number of individuals (14) is too low for any population-wide conclusions to be drawn, some interesting information has been obtained.

Dentally, this small group of people suffered from the same problems observed in other Maya populations: caries cavities, abscesses, periodontoclasia (PDC), antemortem tooth loss (AMTL), calculus. Linear Enamel Hypoplasia (LEH), a horizontal defect in the enamel of the tooth crown representing a devel-

opmental arrest during the process of tooth crown formation, is a permanent record of a nonspecific systemic disturbance (malnutrition, infection, or other disease processes) that occurred during early childhood (Saul 1972; F. Saul and J. Saul 1989, 1991, 2000; J. Saul and F Saul 1997). Common among the ancient Maya, it is present in this group in all but one of the six evaluable adults (the female).

Spongy or Porotic Hyperostosis Cranii (S/PH), characterized by expansion of marrow tissue and reorientation of the diploe between the inner and outer tables of the skull, results in a sievelike pattern of porosities. This lesion is possibly associated with several varieties of anemia, especially iron deficiency anemia, perhaps in conjunction with protein deficiency. Underlying factors in the Maya area include iron deficient soil; the high-carbohydrate, low-protein, maize-dependent Maya diet; absorption problems resulting from the introduction of chelating agents into the gut from the grinding stones used in food preparation; the effects of intestinal parasites and chronic diarrhea (Saul 1972, 1977; F. Saul and J. Saul 1989, 1991, 2000; J. Saul and F. Saul 1997). This lesion was a common and often severe finding in both Preclassic and Classic peoples of Altar de Sacrificios and Seibal (Saul 1972, 1977). S/PH was not present in the two evaluable individuals here, and its incidence in the total population of this area cannot be inferred.

Treponemal disease, as indicated by "sabre shin tibiae," cranial lesions, or both, was also not present in the three assessable individuals. Skeletal lesions suggestive of treponemal disease have been observed on skeletal remains at several other Maya sites (Saul 1972, F. Saul and J. Saul 1991; J. Saul and F. Saul 1997). The lack of indications on these three individuals does not mean that it was absent in the larger population.

Intentional cranial shaping and dental decoration were practiced by the Maya throughout their history (F. Saul and J. Saul 2001). A commonly used cranial shaping technique involved a flat board or other such device placed across the forehead of an infant, producing a flattening and inclination of the frontal bone, referred to by Imbelloni and Dembo (Comas 1960) as "Tabular" shaping. This frontal flattening device was linked to another shaping device on the back of the head. Variations in the angle of this posterior compression resulted in two different "styles" of shaping the back portion of the skull. In the "Erect" style, the back of the head was pressed into a vertical plane; in the "Oblique" style, the back of the skull was manipulated into a backward tilt almost parallel to the frontal bone. Teeth were modified or decorated through actions like filing, engraving, and inserts. A catalogue of "styles" published by Romero (1970), based on locations, symmetry, and shape of filings as well as presence or absence of inserts, engraving, or both, is a convenient guide for describing decorated teeth within in a population.

Intentional cranial shaping occurred in all three individuals whose skulls could be properly assessed and dental decoration was observed in two of the five evaluable individuals. Tabular shaping of an unknown variety is evident on the skull of the three-to-five-year-old child. The skull of one male with undecorated teeth was shaped in Tabular Erect style. Individual A (sex unknown) from the La Caldera looters' trench back dirt had both decorated teeth (Romero type B–2 or B–4) and pronounced Tabular Oblique cranial shaping. The teeth of Burial 7 (sex unknown) were decorated in Romero B–2 fashion, but the skull could not be evaluated for shape.

Developmental anomalies appear in three individuals. One young male has a "peg" maxillary incisor. The hamates of two other individuals, one male and one of uncertain sex, developed with no hamulus or "hook," which may suggest a familial relationship. One of these last two individuals also has a mandibular 3rd molar with three roots, instead of the normal two roots.

Lingual Surface Attrition of the Maxillary Anterior Teeth (LSAMAT) without corresponding oblique attrition of the mandibular anterior teeth, caused either by use of these teeth as tools or through consumption of a particular food in a particular manner (as yet unknown), has been observed in several Maya groups. Turner and Machado (1983) recorded LSAMAT at an Archaic Brazilian site and Irish and Turner (1987) noted its presence in prehistoric Panama. We first documented LSAMAT in the Preclassic population of Cuello (F. Saul and J. Saul 1989, 1991, 2000; J. Saul and F. Saul 1997) and since have observed it in other Maya groups. It was present in five of the six evaluable individuals in the Far West Bajo.

Activity indicators such as healed trauma, enlarged muscle attachments, osteoarthritis, and sharply marked articular borders provide a glimpse into the lives of individuals. Healed trauma is present in five indi-

viduals, a rather high incidence. The following brief "thumbnail" sketches ("Osteobiographies") of a few of the individuals who once lived in this region are based on these activity indicators, plus other information gleaned from their bones and teeth.

Burial 5

A 25-30 year old male, robust and strong, was buried flexed on his left side, feet and hands at his pelvis with his head toward the south and hips to the north. He was inserted into, and hence disturbed, the upper part of Burial 6 (thorax, head). His skull is shaped in pronounced Tabular Erect style and he has no dental decoration. Changes on vertebrae and foot and ankle bones suggest an active life climbing, running, or walking across rough terrain carrying burdens. He has a healed fracture of the 5th metacarpal (the bone on the outside edge of the palm proximal to the little finger). Such a fracture could be the result of accidentally hitting the edge of the hand on a hard object, as in a fall, or could come from hitting someone or something with his hand. As a young child (3–5 years of age), he had two periods of time when he was ill, malnourished, or both severe enough to form the distinctive grooves of Linear Enamel Hypoplasia. He may have chewed more on the right side of his mouth, or possibly used his right back teeth as tools. Like most other Maya, he had a lot of caries cavities (9 of the 27 teeth present had them) and gum disease. He also showed LSAMAT. Lack of Spongy or Porotic Hyperostosis Cranii suggests that he did not suffer from iron deficiency anemia. There is no other apparent pathology or trauma, but many of the bones are very eroded and fragmentary. He is one of two individuals with a hamate (wrist bone) that lacks a "hook" (hamulus), which may suggest a genetic relationship to the individual in Burial 7. An unusual carved and decorated human canine tooth was found with his remains and may have been interred with him.

Burial 6

An individual larger and more muscular than the one in Burial 5, and about the same age (20–30), was buried in a flexed position, probably on his back, with his hands and feet at his pelvis and head to the south. He was positioned slightly below and to the north and east of Burial 5, who was inserted into the upper part of this burial (thorax, head) at a later date, disturbing it. He may have walked with a limp. Healed fractures of the right foot (compression fractures of the talus and 3rd cuneiform plus a proximal fracture of the 2nd or 3rd metatarsal) and left hand (crushing fracture of an unsided phalanx and a fracture of the left 4th metacarpal) point toward a fall resulting in a hard landing on the right foot and perhaps involving the left hand. (The left foot is too fragmentary to evaluate.) A Poirer's facet on the left femur neck (right not available) and enlarged fovea on both femoral heads also suggest an extremely active physical lifestyle, possibly involving extreme extension of the leg as in moving downhill. No other dental or skeletal information is available.

Burial 7

A 25–40 year old individual whose sex could not be determined was buried in a flexed position on the back with knees to the left, right hand on the chest under the chin, and left hand position unknown. The head of Burial 7 extended into the north wall of the excavation. This person had suffered both sharp and blunt force injury in the past, resulting in an inwardly displaced healed left rib fracture (a blow to the chest?) and a healed incised wound on the left side of the head (parietal). These injuries could be from combat. Laminal spurring of thoracic vertebrae and anterior compression of two vertebral bodies with osteophyte formation suggest vigorous activity that stressed the back, as in carrying heavy burdens. Marked muscle attachments for bones of the right hand and fingers indicate increased hand activity with strong gripping action (wielding a weapon?). We do not know if it was a one-handed activity, as the left hand is too fragmentary to assess. This individual may have had a familial relationship to Burial 5, as both have a hamate that lacks a "hook." Dentally, Burial 7 has an anomalous 3-rooted 3rd mandibular molar and suffered from severe dental problems, resulting in severe periodontoclasia and antemortem tooth loss as well as mandib-

ular dental abscesses. Two periods of illness, malnutrition, or both occurred in early childhood, as indicated by Linear Enamel Hypoplasia. Romero type B–2 dental decoration is present but cranial shaping could not be evaluated. LSAMAT is extreme on the only appropriate tooth present, the right central incisor.

Burial 8

This 25–35 year-old male probably moved with a pronounced painful limp. His right calcaneous bears a long-term draining wound located on the articulation for the talus. He suffered a prolonged period of illness, malnutrition, or both during early childhood, resulting in a particularly wide band of Linear Enamel Hypoplasia. He, too, had the typical Maya abundance of carious teeth. Although head shaping and dental decoration could not be evaluated, he did engage in whatever activity produces LSAMAT. He was buried in a flexed position either on his left side or on his back with the legs pushed over to his left. His head pointed slightly west of south and his hips slightly east of north.

La Caldera's Individual A

Located in the back dirt of a looter's trench, Individual A (sex unknown) shows classic signs of blunt force injury. The right ulna bears a healed "parry" fracture. This type of fracture comes from using the forearm as a shield to protect the head from a blow. Unfortunately, in this case, the "shield" did not protect the head; a healed fracture is present on the right forehead, involving the right orbit. Vision of the right eye probably was adversely affected. Whether this injury came from hand-to-hand combat in warfare or a beating is unknown. If this individual were female, she would have been approximately 147 cm ($\pm$ 2 cm) tall, and if male, he would have been approximately 153 cm ($\pm$ 2 cm) tall. The length of the tibia used in these calculations based on formulae of Genovés is within the range for females at Altar de Sacrifícios.

References

Comas, Juan
  1960 *Manual of physical anthropology*. Charles C. Thomas Press, Springfield, Illinois.

Genovés, Santiago
  1964 Introdución al estudio de la proporción entre los huesos largos y la reconstrución de la estatura en

restos mesoamericanos. *Anales de Antropología* 1: 47–62. Instituto de Investigaciones Históricas, Universidad Nacional Autónoma de México, México.

Irish, Joel D., and Christy G. Turner, II
1987   More Lingual Surface Attrition of the Maxillary Anterior Teeth in American Indians: Prehistoric Panamanians. *American Journal of Physical Anthropology* 73: 209–213.

Romero Molina, Javier
1970   Dental Mutilation, Trephination and Cranial Deformation. In *Handbook of Middle American Indians: Physical Anthropology*, edited by T. Dale Stewart. pp. 50–67. University of Texas Press, Austin.

Saul, Frank P.
1972   The Human Skeletal Remains of Altar de Sacrificios: An Osteobiographic Analysis. *Papers of the Peabody Museum of Archaeology and Ethnology* 63(2). Harvard University, Cambridge.

Saul, Frank P.
1977   The Paleopathology of Anemia in Mexico and Guatemala. In "Porotic Hyperostosis: An Enquiry," edited by Eve Cockburn, pp. 10–15, 18, cover. *Paleopathology Association Monograph 2.* Detroit.

Saul, Frank P., and Julie M. Saul
1989   Osteobiography: A Maya Example. *Reconstruction of Life from the Skeleton*, edited by Mehmet Y. Iscan and Kenneth A. R. Kennedy, pp. 287–302. Alan R. Liss, New York.

Saul, Frank P., and Julie M. Saul
1991   The Preclassic population of Cuello. *Cuello: An Early Maya Community in Belize*, edited by Norman Hammond, pp. 134–158. Cambridge University Press, Cambridge.

Saul, Frank P., and Julie M. Saul
2000   The People of Rio Azul. *Rio Azul Reports 5, The 1987 Season*, edited by R. E. W. Adams, pp. 240–254. Mesoamerican Archaeological Research Laboratory, University of Texas, San Antonio.

Saul, Frank P., and Julie M. Saul
2001   Cosmetic Alterations of the Face and Body. In *The Archaeology of Ancient Mexico and Central America: An Encyclopedia*, edited by Susan Toby Evans and David L. Webster, pp. 291–295. Garland Publishing, New York.

Saul, Julie M., and Frank P. Saul
1997   The Preclassic Skeletons from Cuello. *Bones of the Maya: Recent Studies of Ancient Skeletons*, edited by Stephen L. Whittington and David M. Reed, pp. 28–50. Smithsonian Press, Washington.

Turner II, Christy G., and Lilia M. Cheuiche Machado
1983   A New Dental Wear Pattern and Evidence for High Carbohydrate Consumption in a Brazilian Archaic Skeletal Population. *American Journal of Physical Anthropology* 61: 125–130.

References

Adams, Richard E. W.
1980   Swamps, Canals, and the Locations of Ancient Maya Cities. *Antiquity* 54(212): 206–214.

Adams, Richard E. W., and Woodruff D. Smith
1981   Feudal Models for Classic Maya Civilization. *Lowland Maya Settlement Patterns*, edited by Wendy Ashmore, pp. 335–349. University of New Mexico Press, Albuquerque.

Adams, Richard E. W., W. E. Brown Jr.,
and T. Patrick Culbert
1981   Radar Mapping, Archaeology, and Ancient Maya Land Use. *Science* 213(4515): 1457–1463.

Aldenderfer, Mark S., Larry R. Kimball,
and April Sievert
1989   Microwear Analysis in the Maya Lowlands: The Use of Functional Data in a Complex-Society Setting. *Journal of Field Archaeology* 16(1): 47–60.

Arnold, Jeanne E., and Anabel Ford
1980   A Statistical Examination of Settlement Patterns at Tikal, Guatemala. *American Antiquity* 45(4): 713–726.

Ashmore, Wendy
1991   Site-Planning Principles and Concepts of Directionality among the Ancient Maya. *Latin American Antiquity* 2(3): 199–226.

Baker, Jeffrey
1997   Prehispanic Wetland Agriculture in Northwestern Belize. Paper presented at the 62nd Annual Meeting of the Society for American Archaeology, Nashville.

2002   *Maya Wetlands: Ecology and Pre-hispanic Utilization of Wetlands in Northwestern Belize*. Doctoral dissertation, University of Arizona, Tucson. University Microfilms, Ann Arbor.

Baker, Robert
1996   Status Report on the Settlement Survey. *Archaeological Research at Blue Creek, Belize: Progress Report of the Fourth (1995) Field Season*, edited by Thomas H. Guderjan, W. David Driver, and Helen R. Haines, pp. 109–117. Maya Research Program, St. Mary's University, San Antonio.

Beach, Timothy, Sheryl Luzzadder-Beach,
Nicholas P. Dunning, and Vernon L. Scarborough
2003   Depression Soils in the Lowland Tropics of Northwestern Belize: Anthropogenic and Natural Origins. *The Lowland Maya Area: Three Millennia at the Human-Wildland Interface*, edited by Arturo Gómez-Pompa, Michael F. Allen, Scott L. Fedick, and Juan J. Jiménez-Osornio. Haworth Press, Binghamton.

Beach, Timothy, Jon Hageman, Jon Lohse,
Claudia Paxton, and Nicholas Dunning
1999   Ancient Maya Terracing in the Three Rivers Region, Northwestern Belize. Paper presented at the 64th Annual Meeting of the Society for American Archaeology, Chicago.

Beach, Timothy, Sheryl Luzzader-Beach, Nicholas
Dunning, Jon B. Hageman, and Jon C. Lohse
2002   Upland Agriculture in the Maya Lowlands: Ancient Maya Soil Conservation in Northwestern Belize. *Geographical Review* 92(3): 372–397.

Becker, Marshall J.
1971   *The Identification of a Second Plaza Plan at Tikal, Guatemala and its Implications for Ancient Maya Social Complexity*. Doctoral dissertation, University of Pennsylvania, Philadelphia. University Microfilms, Ann Arbor.

1979   Priests, Peasants, and Ceremonial Centers: The Intellectual History of a Model. *Maya Archaeology and Ethnohistory*, edited by Norman Hammond and Gordon R. Willey, pp. 3–20. University of Texas Press, Austin and London.

Berry, Kimberley, and Patricia McAnany
2000   Feeding and Clothing K'axob: Evidence for Wetland Cultivation at a Maya Settlement. Paper presented at the 65th Annual Meeting of the Society for American Archaeology, Philadelphia.

Bloom, Paul R., Mary D. Pohl, and Julie Stein
1985   Analysis of Sedimentation and Agriculture along the Río Hondo, Northern Belize. In "Prehistoric

Bloom, Paul R., Mary D. Pohl, and Julie Stein (*continued*)
Lowland Maya Environment and Subsistence Economy," edited by Mary Pohl, pp. 21–31. *Papers of the Peabody Museum of Archaeology and Ethnology* 77. Harvard University Press, Cambridge.

Bray, Warwick
1983   Landscape with Figures: Settlement Patterns, Locational Models, and Politics in Mesoamerica. *Prehistoric Settlement Patterns: Essays in Honor of Gordon R. Willey*, edited by Evon Z. Vogt and Richard M. Leventhal, pp. 167–193. University of New Mexico Press and Peabody Museum of Archaeology and Ethnology, Harvard University, Cambridge.

Brokaw, Nicholas, and Betsy Mallory
1993   *Vegetation of the Rio Bravo Conservation and Management Area, Belize*. Manomet Bird Observatory and Programme for Belize, Manomet, Massachusetts, and Belize City.

Carmean, Kelli
1991   Architectural Labor Investment and Social Stratification at Sayil, Yucatan, Mexico. *Latin American Antiquity* 2(2): 151–165.

Chase, Arlen F., and Diane Z. Chase
1998   Scale and Intensity in Classic Period Maya Agriculture: Terracing and Settlement at the "Garden City" of Caracol, Belize. *Culture & Agriculture* 20(2/3): 60–77.

Chisholm, Michael
1979   *Rural Settlement and Land Use: An Essay in Location*. 3rd edition. Hutchinson and Co., London.

Clagett, Heather L.
1997   Household Archaeology at Chan Cahal: A Step Beyond Functionalism. *The Blue Creek Project: Working Papers from the 1996 Season*, edited by W. David Driver, Heather L. Clagett, and Helen R. Haines, pp. 61–70. Maya Research Program, St. Mary's University, San Antonio.

Comas, Juan
1960   *Manual of Physical Anthropology*. Charles C. Thomas Press, Springfield, Illinois.

Culbert, T. Patrick, Laura J. Levi, and Luís Cruz
1990   Lowland Maya Wetland Agriculture: The Rio Azul Agronomy Program. *Vision and Revision in Maya Studies*, edited by Flora S. Clancy and Peter D. Harrison, pp. 115–124. University of New Mexico Press, Albuquerque.

Culbert, T. Patrick, Laura Levi,
Brian McKee, and Julie Kunen
1995   Investigaciones Arqueológicas en el Bajo la Justa entre Yaxha y Nakum. *IX Simposio de Investigaciones Arqueológicas en Guatemala*, edited by Juan Pedro Laporte and Héctor L. Escobedo, pp. 51–57. Mueso Nacional de Antropología y Etnología, Guatemala. City.

Culbert, T. Patrick, Vilma Fialko, Brian McKee,
Liwy Grazioso, and Julie Kunen
1996   Investigación Arqueológica en el Bajo la Justa: La Temporada de 1996. *X Simposio de Investigaciones Arqueológicas en Guatemala*, edited by Juan Pedro Laporte and Héctor L. Escobedo, pp. 367–371. Museo Nacional de Antropología y Etnología, Guatemala City.

Donkin, R. A.
1979   Agricultural Terracing in the Aboriginal New World. *Viking Fund Publications in Anthropology* 56. Published for the Wenner-Gren Foundation for Anthropological Research by the University of Arizona Press, Tucson.

Drennan, Robert D.
1988   Household Location and Compact versus Dispersed Settlement in Prehispanic Mesoamerica. *Household and Community in the Mesoamerican Past*, edited by Richard R. Wilk and Wendy Ashmore, pp. 273–293. University of New Mexico Press, Albuquerque.

Dunning, Nicholas P.
1996   An Examination of Regional Variability in the Prehistoric Agricultural Landscape. *The Managed Mosaic: Ancient Maya Agriculture and Resource Use*, edited by Scott L. Fedick, pp. 53–68. University of Utah Press, Salt Lake City.

Dunning, Nicholas P., and Timothy Beach
1994   Soil Erosion, Slope Management, and Ancient Terracing in the Maya Lowlands. *Latin American Antiquity* 5(1): 51–69.

2000   Stability and Instability in Prehispanic Maya Landscapes. *Imperfect Balance: Landscape Transformations in the Pre-Columbian Americas*, edited by David L. Lentz, pp. 179–202. Columbia University Press, New York.

Dunning, Nicholas P., Timothy Beach, and David Rue
1997   The Paleoecology and Ancient Settlement of the Petexbatun Region. *Ancient Mesoamerica* 8: 255–266.

Dunning, Nicholas P., Timothy Beach, Pat Farrell,
and Sheryl Luzzader-Beach
1998   Prehispanic Agrosystems and Adaptive Regions in the Maya Lowlands. *Culture and Agriculture* 20(2/3): 87–101.

Dunning, Nicholas P., John G. Jones, Timothy Beach,
and Sheryl Luzzadder-Beach
2003   Physiography, Habitats, and Landscapes of the

Three Rivers Region. *Heterarchy, Political Economy, and the Ancient Maya: The Three Rivers Region of the East-Central Yucatán Peninsula*, edited by Vernon L. Scarborough, Fred Valdez, Jr., and Nicholas P. Dunning, pp. 14–24. University of Arizona Press, Tucson.

Dunning, Nicholas P., Sheryl Luzzader-Beach, Timothy Beach, John G. Jones, Vernon E. Scarborough, and T. Patrick Culbert
2002 Arising from the Bajos: The Evolution of a Neotropical Landscape and the Rise of Maya Civilization. *Annals of the Association of American Geographers* 92(2): 267–283.

Dunning, Nicholas P., Vernon L. Scarborough, Fred Valdez, Jr., Sheryl Luzzader-Beach, Timothy Beach, and John G. Jones
1999 Temple Mountains, Sacred Lakes, and Fertile Fields: Ancient Maya Landscapes in Northwestern Belize. *Antiquity* 73(281): 650–660.

Eguchi, Teruyo
2000 Biface Lithic Tools from the Bajo Settlements of La Milpa, Belize. MS, Undergraduate thesis, University of Wisconsin.

Everson, Gloria
2003 Landscape and Settlement at La Milpa. MS, doctoral dissertation in preparation, Tulane University, New Orleans.

Fedick, Scott L.
1994 Ancient Maya Agricultural Terracing in the Upper Belize River Area: Computer-aided Modeling and the Results of Initial Field Investigations. *Ancient Mesoamerica* 5: 107–127.
1995 Land Evaluation and Ancient Maya Land Use in the Upper Belize River Area, Belize, Central America. *Latin American Antiquity* 6(1): 16–34.
1996a Introduction: New Perspectives on Ancient Maya Agriculture and Resource Use. *The Managed Mosaic: Ancient Maya Agriculture and Resource Use*, edited by Scott L. Fedick, pp. 1–14. University of Utah Press, Salt Lake City.
1996b [Editor] *The Managed Mosaic: Ancient Maya Agriculture and Resource Use*. University of Utah Press, Salt Lake City.

Fedick, Scott L., and Anabel Ford
1990 The Prehistoric Agricultural Landscape of the Central Maya Lowlands: An Examination of Local Variability in a Regional Context. *World Archaeology* 22(1): 18–33.

Fedick, Scott L., and Kevin Hovey
1995 Ancient Maya Settlement and Use of Wetlands at Naranjal and the Surrounding Yalahau Region. *The View From Yalahau: 1993 Archaeological Investigation in Northern Quintana Roo, Mexico*, edited by Scott L. Fedick and Karl A. Taube, pp. 89–100. Latin American Studies Program, University of California, Riverside.

Fedick, Scott L., Bethany A. Morrison, Bente Juhl Andersen, Sylviane Boucher, Jorge Ceja Acosta, and Jennifer P. Mathews
2000 Wetland Manipulation in the Yalahau Region of the Northern Maya Lowlands. *Journal of Field Archaeology* 27(2): 131–152.

Fialko, Vilma
2000 Recursos Hidraúlicos en Tikal y sus Periférias. *XIII Simposio de Investigaciones Arqueológicas en Guatemala*, edited by Juan Pedro Laporte, Héctor L. Escobedo, Ana C. Suasnavar, and Barbara Arroyo, pp. 685–695. Museo Nacional de Arqueología y Etnología, Guatemala City.

Fialko, Vilma, and T. Patrick Culbert
1997 Implications of the Tikal and Yaxha Bajo Communities for Understanding the End of the Classic Period in Peten, Guatemala. Manuscript in possession of the authors.

Flannery, Kent V., Editor
1982 *Maya Subsistence: Studies in Memory of Dennis E. Puleston*. Academic Press, New York.

Folan, William J., and Silverio Gallegos Osuna
1998 Uso del Suelo en el Estado de Campeche, Mexico y Alrededores. *Los Investigadores de la Cultura Maya* 5(2): 459–478. Universidad Autónoma de Campeche, Campeche, Mexico.
1999 Unas Observaciones sobre el Uso del Suelo del Sitio Arqueológico de Calakmul, Campeche. In *Los Camellones y Chinampas Tropicales*, edited by Juan José Jiménez-Osornio and Véronique M. Rorive, pp. 55–67. Universidad Autónoma de Yucatán, Merida, Mexico.

Folan, William J., Laraine A. Fletcher, and Ellen R. Kintz
1979 Fruit, Fiber, Bark, and Resin: Social Organization of a Maya Urban Center. *Science* 204 (4394): 697–701.

Fry, Robert E.
1969 *Ceramics and Settlement in the Periphery of Tikal, Guatemala*. Doctoral dissertation, University of Arizona, Tucson. University Microfilms, Ann Arbor.
1980 [Editor] Models and Methods in Regional Exchange. *Society for American Archaeology Papers* 1. Society for American Archaeology, Washington.

Genovés, Santiago
1964 Introdución al estudio de la proporción entre los

Genovés, Santiago (*continued*)
  huesos largos y la reconstrución de la estatura en restos mesoamericanos. *Anales de Antropología* 1: 47–62. Instituto de Investigaciones Históricas, Universidad Nacional Autónoma de México, México.

Gliessman, Stephen R., B. L. Turner II,
Francisco J. Rosado May, and M. F. Amador
  1983   Ancient Raised-Field Agriculture in the Maya Lowlands of Southeastern Mexico. In "Drained Field Agriculture in Central and South America," edited by Janice P. Darch, pp. 91–110. *BAR International Series* 189. Oxford, BAR.

Grazioso Sierra, Liwy, T. Patrick Culbert,
Vilma Fialko, Thomas Sever, John Murphy,
and Carmen Ramos
  2001   Arqueología en el Bajo la Justa, Peten, Guatemala. *XIV Simposio de Investigaciones Arqueológicas en Guatemala*, edited by Juan Pedro Laporte, Ana C. Suasnavar, and Barbara Arroyo, pp. 205–209. Museo Nacional de Arqueología y Etnología, Guatemala City.

Grube, Nikolai
  1994   A Preliminary Report on the Monuments and Inscriptions of La Milpa, Orange Walk, Belize. *Baessler-Archiv, Neue Folge,* Band 42: 217–238.

Grube, Nikolai, and Norman Hammond
  1998   Rediscovery of La Milpa Stela 4. *Mexicon* 20: 129–132.

Guderjan, Thomas H.
  1989   An Archaeological Reconnaissance in Northwestern Belize. *Mexicon* 11(4): 65–68.
  1991   [Editor] *Maya Settlements in Northwestern Belize. The 1988 and 1990 Seasons of the Río Bravo Archaeological Project*. Maya Research Program and Labyrinthos, San Antonio, Texas and Culver City, California.

Guderjan, Thomas H., and W. David Driver, Editors
  1995   *Archaeological Research at Blue Creek, Belize. Progress Report of the Third (1994) Field Season*. Maya Research Program and Department of Sociology, St. Mary's University, San Antonio.

Guderjan, Thomas H., and Robert J. Lichtenstein, Editors
  2001   *The Blue Creek Project: Working Papers from the 1998 and 1999 Seasons*. Maya Research Program, Texas Christian University, Fort Worth.

Guderjan, Thomas H., W. David Driver,
and Helen R. Haines
  1996   *Archaeological Research at Blue Creek, Belize. Progress Report of the Fourth (1995) Field Sea-*

son. Maya Research Program, St. Mary's University, San Antonio.

Guderjan, Thomas H., Helen R. Haines, Mike Lindeman,
Dale Pastrana, Ellen Ruble, and Pamela Weiss, Editors
  1994   *Excavations at the Blue Creek Ruin, Northwestern Belize. 1993 Interim Report*. Maya Research Program, St. Mary's University, San Antonio.

Guderjan, Thomas H., Helen Haines, Michael Lindeman,
Shirley Mock, Ellen Ruble, Froyla Salam,
and Lea Worchester
  1993   *Excavations at the Blue Creek Ruin, Northwestern Belize. 1992 Interim Report*. Maya Research Program, St. Mary's University, San Antonio.

Gunn, Joel D., John E. Foss, William J. Folan,
and Maria del Rosario Domínguez Carrasco
  2000   Environments of Elevated Cities in the Interior Yucatan Peninsula. Paper presented at the 65th Annual Meeting of the Society for American Archaeology, Philadelphia.

Gunn, Joel D., John E. Foss, William J. Folan,
Maria del Rosario Domínquez Carrasco,
and Betty B. Faust
  2002   Bajo Sediments and the Hydraulic System of Calakmul, Campeche, Mexico. *Ancient Mesoamerica* 13(2): 297–315.

Hageman, Jon B.
  1999a Ideology and Intersite Settlement Among the Late Classic Maya. Paper presented at the 64th Annual Meeting of the Society for American Archaeology, Chicago.
  1999b Were the Late Classic Maya Characterized by Lineages? Paper presented at the Tercera Mesa Redonda de Palenque, Chiapas, Mexico.

Hageman, Jon B., and Jon C. Lohse
  2003   Heterarchy, Corporate Groups, and Late Classic Resource Management in Northwestern Belize. *Heterarchy, Political Economy, and the Ancient Maya: The Three Rivers Region of the East-Central Yucatán Peninsula*, edited by Vernon L. Scarborough, Fred Valdez, Jr., and Nicholas P. Dunning, pp. 109–121. University of Arizona Press, Tucson.

Hammond, Norman
  1991   The Discovery of La Milpa. *Mexicon* 13(3): 46–51.
  2001   A New Maya Stela from La Milpa, Belize. *Antiquity* 75(288): 267–268.

Hammond, Norman, and Gair Tourtellot III
  1993   Survey and Excavation at La Milpa, Belize, 1992. *Mexicon* 15: 71–75.
  1999   Shifting Axes: Spatial Expressions of Power at

La Milpa. Paper presented at the 64th Annual Meeting of the Society for American Archaeology, Chicago.

Hammond, Norman, Gair Tourtellot III,
Sara Donaghey, and Amanda Clarke
1996 Survey and Excavation at La Milpa, Belize, 1996. *Mexicon* 18(5): 86–90.
1998 No Slow Dusk: Maya Urban Development and Decline at La Milpa, Belize. *Antiquity* 72(278): 831–837.

Hanratty, C. Colleen
2000 Excavations at the Structure 37 Plazuela. Manuscript on file, Maya Research Program, Texas Christian University, Fort Worth.

Hansen, Richard D., Steven Bosarth, Roger Byrne,
John Jacob, and Thomas Schreiner
2000 Climatic and Environmental Variability in the Rise of Maya Civilization: A Perspective from Northern Peten. Paper presented at the 65th Annual Meeting of the Society for American Archaeology, Philadelphia.

Hansen, Richard D., Steven Bozarth,
John Jacob, David Wahl, and
Thomas Schreiner
2002 Climatic and Environmental Variability in the Rise of Maya Civilization: A Preliminary Perspective from Northern Peten. *Ancient Mesoamerica* 13(2): 273–295.

Harris, David R., and Gordon C. Hillman
1989 *Foraging and Farming: The Evolution of Plant Exploitation*. Unwin Hyman, London.

Harrison, Peter D.
1977 The Rise of the Bajos and the Fall of the Maya. *Social Process in Maya Prehistory: Studies in Honor of Sir Eric Thompson*, edited by Norman Hammond, pp. 469–508. Academic Press, London.
1989 Functional Influences on Settlement Pattern in the Communities of Pulltrouser Swamp, Northern Belize. In "Households and Communities," edited by Scott MacEachern, David J. W. Archer and Richard D. Galvin, pp. 460–465. *Proceedings of the 21st Annual Chacmool Conference*. Archaeological Association of the University of Calgary, Calgary.

Harrison, Peter D., and B. L. Turner II, Editors
1978 *Pre-Hispanic Maya Agriculture*. University of New Mexico Press, Albuquerque.

Haviland, William A.
1981 Dower Houses and Minor Centers at Tikal, Guatemala: An Investigation into the Identification of Valid Units in Settlement Hierarchies. *Lowland Maya Settlement Patterns*, edited by

Wendy Ashmore, pp. 89–117. University of New Mexico Press, Albuquerque.
1985 Excavations in Small Residential Groups of Tikal: Groups 4F–1 and 4F–2. *Tikal Report* 19, *University Museum Monographs* 58. University Museum, University of Pennsylvania, Philadelphia.
1988 Musical Hammocks at Tikal: Problems with Reconstructing Household Composition. *Household and Community in the Mesoamerican Past*, edited by Richard R. Wilk and Wendy Ashmore, pp. 121–134. University of New Mexico Press, Albuquerque.

Healy, Paul L., John D. H. Lambert,
J. T. Arnason, and Richard J. Hebda
1983 Caracol, Belize: Evidence of Ancient Maya Agricultural Terraces. *Journal of Field Archaeology* 10(4): 397–410.

Houk, Brett A.
1996 *The Archaeology of Site Planning: An Example from the Maya Site of Dos Hombres, Belize*. Doctoral dissertation, University of Texas, Austin. University Microfilms, Ann Arbor.

Hughbanks, Paul J.
1998 Settlement and land Use at Guijarral, Northwest Belize. *Culture & Agriculture* 20(2/3): 107–120.

Hughbanks, Paul, and Julie Kunen
1997 1997 Season Report of the Ancient Maya Land and Water Management Project. Manuscript in possession of Fred Valdez, Jr., Programme for Belize Archaeological Project.

Irish, Joel D., and Christy G. Turner, II
1987 More Lingual Surface Attrition of the Maxillary Anterior Teeth in American Indians: Prehistoric Panamanians. *American Journal of Physical Anthropology* 73: 209–213.

Jacob, John S.
1995 Ancient Maya Wetland Agricultural Fields in Cobweb Swamp, Belize: Construction, Chronology, and Function. *Journal of Field Archaeology* 22(2): 175–190.

Jones, John G.
1999 Analysis of Fossil Pollen from Aguada Juan Pistola and Laguna Juan Piojo, Belize. MS on file at the Palynology Laboratory, Department of Anthropology, Texas A & M University.

Kepecs, Susan, and Sylviane Boucher
1996 The Pre-Hispanic Cultivation of Rejolladas and Stone-Lands: New Evidence from Northeastern Yucatan. *The Managed Mosaic: Ancient Maya Agriculture and Resource Use*, edited by Scott L. Fedick, pp. 69–91. University of Utah Press, Salt Lake City.

Killion, Thomas W.

1990   Cultivation Intensity and Residential Site Structure: An Ethnoarchaeological Examination of Peasant Agriculture in the Sierra de Los Tuxtlas, Veracruz, Mexico. *Latin American Antiquity* 1(3): 191–215.

1992   Residential Ethnoarchaeology and Ancient Site Structure: Contemporary Farming and Prehistoric Settlement Agriculture at Matacapan, Veracruz, Mexico. *Gardens of Prehistory: The Archaeology of Settlement Agriculture in Greater Mesoamerica*, edited by Thomas W. Killion, pp. 119–149. University of Alabama Press, Tuscaloosa and London.

King, Eleanor M., and Leslie C. Shaw

1998   The Ma'ax Na Project: Regional Archaeology at Upland Sites in Northwestern Belize. Paper presented at the 4° Congreso Internacional de Mayistas, Antigua, Guatemala.

2003   A Heterarchical Approach to Site Variability: The Maax Na Archaeology Project. *Heterarchy, Political Economy, and the Ancient Maya: The Three Rivers Region of the East-Central Yucatán Peninsula*, edited by Vernon L. Scarborough, Fred Valdez, Jr. and Nicholas P. Dunning, pp. 64–76. University of Arizona Press, Tucson.

King, Eleanor, Leslie Shaw, and Bruce Moses

1999   Agricultural Production as Occupational Specialization: A Case from the Site of Bolsa Verde in Northwestern Belize. Paper presented at the 64th Annual Meeting of the Society for American Archaeology, Chicago.

King, R. B., I. C. Baillie, T. M. B. Abell, J. R. Dunsmore, D. A. Gray, J. H. Pratt, H. R. Versey, A. C. S. Wright, and S. A. Zinman

1992   *Land Resource Assessment of Northern Belize, Bulletin* 43. National Resources Institute, Kent, U.K.

Kosakowsky, Laura J., and Kerry L. Sagebiel

1999   The Ceramic Sequence of La Milpa, Belize. *Mexicon* 21: 131–136.

Kunen, Julie L.

2001   *Study of an Ancient Maya Bajo Landscape in Northwestern Belize.* Doctoral dissertation, University of Arizona, Tucson. University Microfilms, Ann Arbor.

2003   Ancient Maya Agricultural Installations and the Development of Intensive Agriculture in Northwest Belize. *Journal of Field Archaeology* 28(3–4), forthcoming.

Kunen, Julie L., and Paul J. Hughbanks

2003   Bajo Communities as Resource Specialists: A Heterarchical Approach to Maya Socioeconomic Organization. *Heterarchy, Political Economy, and the Ancient Maya: The Three Rivers Region of the East-Central Yucatán Peninsula*, edited by Vernon L. Scarborough, Fred Valdez, Jr., and Nicholas P. Dunning, pp. 92–108. University of Arizona Press, Tucson.

Kunen, Julie L., Mary Jo Galindo, and Erin Chase

2002   Pits and Bones: Identifying Maya Ritual Behavior in the Archaeological Record. *Ancient Mesoamerica* 13(2): 197–211.

Kunen, Julie L., T. Patrick Culbert, Vilma Fialko, Brian R. McKee, and Liwy Grazioso

2000   Bajo Communities: A Case Study from the Central Peten. *Culture and Agriculture* 22(3): 15–31.

Lambert, J. D. H., and J. T. Arnason

1983   Ancient Maya Land Use and Potential Agricultural Productivity at Lamanai, Belize. In "Drained Field Agriculture in Central and South America," edited by Janice P. Darch, pp. 111–222. *BAR International Series* 189. BAR, Oxford.

Lanza, Felipe

1996   Informe trabajos clasificación de bosques Yaxha-Nakum. MS in possession of author.

Levi, Laura J.

1993   *Prehispanic Residence and Community at San Estevan, Belize.* Doctoral dissertation, University of Arizona, Tucson. University Microfilms, Ann Arbor.

1994   Center and Community at San Estevan. Paper presented at the 59th Annual Meeting of the Society for American Archaeology, Anaheim.

1996   Sustainable Production and Residential Variation: A Historical Perspective on Pre-Hispanic Domestic Economies in the Maya Lowlands. *The Managed Mosaic: Ancient Maya Agriculture and Resource Use*, edited by Scott L. Fedick, pp. 92–106. University of Utah Press, Salt Lake City.

Lewis, Brandon S.

1995   *The Role of Specialized Production in the Development of Sociopolitical Complexity: A Test Case from the Late Classic Maya.* Doctoral dissertation, University of California, Los Angeles. University Microfilms, Ann Arbor.

Lichtenstein, Robert J.

2000   Settlement Zone Communities of the Greater Blue Creek Area. *Occasional Paper* 2, Maya Research Program, Texas Christian University, Fort Worth.

Lohse, Jon C.

2001   *The Social Organization of a Late Classic*

Maya Community: Dos Hombres, Northwestern Belize. Doctoral dissertation, University of Texas, Austin. University Microfilms, Ann Arbor.

Lucero, Lisa J.
1999 Classic Lowland Maya Political Organization: A Review. *Journal of World Prehistory* 13(2): 221–263.

Lundell, Cyrus L.
1933 The Agriculture of the Maya. *Southwest Review* 19: 65–77.
1937 The Vegetation of Peten. *Carnegie Institution Publication* 478. Carnegie Institution, Washington.

Marcus, Joyce
1983 Lowland Maya Archaeology at the Crossroads. *American Antiquity* 48(3): 454–488.
1995 Where is Lowland Maya Archaeology Headed? *Journal of Archaeological Research* 3(1): 3–53.

McAnany, Patricia A.
1989 Economic Foundations of Prehistoric Maya Society: Paradigms and Concepts. In "Prehistoric Maya Economies of Belize," edited by Patricia A. McAnany and Barry L. Isaac, pp. 347–372. *Research in Economic Anthropology Supplement* 4. JAI Press, Greenwich.
1992 Agricultural Tasks and Tools: Patterns of Stone Tool Discard Near Prehistoric Maya Residences Bordering Pulltrouser Swamp, Belize. *Gardens of Prehistory: The Archaeology of Settlement Agriculture in Greater Mesoamerica*, edited by Thomas W. Killion, pp. 184–213. University of Alabama Press, Tuscaloosa.
1993 The Economics of Social Power and Wealth among Eighth-Century Maya Households. *Lowland Maya Civilization in the Eighth Century A.D.*, edited by Jeremy A. Sabloff and John S. Henderson, pp. 65–89. Dumbarton Oaks, Washington.
1995 *Living with the Ancestors: Kinship and Kingship in Ancient Maya Society.* University of Texas Press, Austin.
1998 *Where the Water Meets the Land: 1997 Excavations in Maya Residences and Wetland Fields, K'axob, Belize.* Boston University, Department of Archaeology and International Programs, Boston.

McIntyre, Roberta, Jonathan Lincoln, and Stanley Walling
1996 Geophysical Testing of Prehispanic Maya Settlement in Northwestern Belize. Paper presented at the 61st Annual Meeting of the Society for American Archaeology, New Orleans.

Neff, L. Theodore, Cynthia Robin, Kevin Schwarz, and Mary K. Morrison
1995 The Xunantunich Settlement Survey. *Report of the Xunantunich Archaeological Project 1995 Field Season*, edited by Richard Leventhal, pp. 139–163. University of California, Los Angeles.

Netting, Robert McC.
1977 Maya Subsistence: Mythologies, Analogies, Possibilities. *The Origins of Maya Civilization*, edited by Richard E. W. Adams, pp. 299–333. University of New Mexico Press, Albuquerque.

Paxton O'Neal, Claudia
1999 Archaeological Investigations of the Barba Group Terraces. MS, Master's Thesis, University of Cincinnati.

Pohl, Mary DeLand, Editor
1985 Prehistoric Lowland Maya Environment and Subsistence Economy. *Papers of the Peabody Museum of Archaeology and Ethnology* 77. Harvard University Press, Cambridge.
1990 *Ancient Maya Wetland Agriculture: Excavations on Albion Island, Northern Belize.* Westview Press, Boulder.

Pohl, Mary DeLand, and Paul Bloom
1996 Prehistoric Maya Farming in the Wetlands of Northern Belize: More Data from Albion Island and Beyond. *The Managed Mosaic: Ancient Maya Agriculture and Resource Use*, edited by Scott L. Fedick, pp. 145–164. University of Utah Press, Salt Lake City.

Pohl, Mary DeLand, and Charles H. Miksicek
1995 Cultivation Techniques and Crops. In "Prehistoric Lowland Maya Environment and Subsistence Economy," edited by Mary DeLand Pohl, pp. 9–20. *Papers of the Peabody Museum of Archaeology and Ethnology* 77. Harvard University Press, Cambridge.

Pope, Kevin O., and Bruce H. Dahlin
1989 Ancient Maya Wetland Agriculture: New Insights from Ecological and Remote Sensing Research. *Journal of Field Archaeology* 16(1): 87–106.
1993 Radar Detection and Ecology of Ancient Maya Canal Systems - Reply to Adams et al. *Journal of Field Archaeology* 20(3): 379–383.

Pope, Kevin O., Mary D. Pohl, and John S. Jacob
1996 Formation of Ancient Maya Wetland Fields: Natural and Anthropogenic Processes. *The Managed Mosaic: Ancient Maya Agriculture and Resource Use*, edited by Scott L. Fedick, pp. 165–176. University of Utah Press, Salt Lake City.

Pope, Kevin O., Mary DeLand Pohl,
John S. Jacob, John Jones,
and Eliska Rejmankova
2000   Ecosystem Dynamics: The Palaeoecological Imperative in Archaeological Research. Paper presented at the 65th Annual Meeting of the Society for American Anthropology, Philadelphia.

Popson, Colleen
2000   An Evaluation of Evidence for Formative Economic Behavior: Artifact Assemblage Diversity at Chal Cahal, Blue Creek, Belize. MS, Master's thesis, State University of New York, Albany.

Popson, Colleen, and Heather L. Clagett
1999   Excavations at Chan Cahal. *The Blue Creek Project: Working Papers from the 1997 Season*, edited by W. David Driver, Helen R. Haines, and Thomas H. Guderjan. Maya Research Program, St. Mary's University, San Antonio.

Potter, Daniel R., and Eleanor M. King
1995   A Heterarchical Approach to Lowland Maya Socioeconomics. In "Heterarchy and the Analysis of Complex Societies," edited by Robert M. Ehrenreich, Carole L. Crumley and Janet E. Levy, pp. 17–32. *Archaeological Papers of the American Anthropological Association* 6. American Anthropological Association, Arlington.

Puleston, Dennis E.
1977   The Art and Archaeology of Hydraulic Agriculture in the Maya Lowlands. *Social Process in Maya Prehistory: Studies in Memory of Sir Eric Thompson*, edited by Norman Hammond, pp. 449–467. Academic Press, London.

Pyburn, K. Ann, Boyd Dixon, Patricia Cook,
and Anna McNair
1998   The Albion Island Settlement Pattern Project: Domination and Resistance in Early Classic Northern Belize. *Journal of Field Archaeology* 25(1): 37–62.

Rands, Robert L., and Ron Bishop
1980   Resource Procurement Zones and Patterns of Ceramic Exchange in the Palenque Region, Mexico. In "Models and Methods in Regional Exchange," edited by Robert E. Fry, pp. 19–46. *Society for American Archaeology Papers* 1. Society for American Archaeology, Washington.

Rice, Don S.
1993   Eighth-Century Physical Geography, Environment, and Natural Resources in the Maya Lowlands. *Lowland Maya Civilization in the Eighth Century A.D.*, edited by Jeremy A. Sabloff and John S. Henderson, pp. 11–63. Dumbarton Oaks, Washington.

Rice, Prudence M.
1987   Economic Change in the Lowland Maya Late Classic Period. *Specialization, Exchange, and Complex Societies*, edited by Elizabeth M. Brumfiel and Timothy K. Earle, pp. 76–85. Cambridge University Press, Cambridge.

Ringle, William R., and E. Wyllys Andrews V
1988   Formative Residence at Komchen, Yucatan, Mexico. *Household and Community in the Mesoamerican Past*, edited by Richard R. Wilk and Wendy Ashmore, pp. 171–197. University of New Mexico Press, Albuquerque.

Robichaux, Hubert Ray
1995   *Ancient Maya Community Patterns in Northwestern Belize: Peripheral Zone Survey at La Milpa and Dos Hombres*. Doctoral dissertation, University of Texas, Austin. University Microfilms, Ann Arbor.

Romero Molina, Javier
1970   Dental Mutilation, Trephination and Cranial Deformation. *Handbook of Middle American Indians: Physical Anthropology*, edited by T. Dale Stewart. pp. 50–67. University of Texas Press, Austin.

Rose, John J.
2000   *A Study of Late Classic Maya Population Growth at La Milpa, Belize*. Doctoral dissertation, University of Pittsburgh, Pittsburgh. University Microfilms, Ann Arbor.

Sabloff, Jeremy, and Gair Tourtellot III
1991   The Ancient Maya City of Sayil: The Mapping of a Puuc Region Center. *Middle American Research Institute Publication* 60. Tulane University, New Orleans.

Sagebiel, Kerry L.
1999   The La Milpa Ceramic Sequence: Evidence of Renewal and Growth in the Early Late Classic Period. Paper presented at the 64th Annual Meeting of the Society for American Archaeology, Chicago.

2003   Shifting Allegiances: Ceramic Change at La Milpa, Belize, A Typological, Chronological, and Formal Analysis. MS, doctoral dissertation in preparation, University of Arizona, Tucson.

Sanders, William T.
1981   Classic Maya Settlement Patterns and Ethnographic Analogy. *Lowland Maya Settlement Patterns*, edited by Wendy Ashmore, pp. 351–369. University of New Mexico Press, Albuquerque.

Saul, Frank P.
1972   The Human Skeletal Remains of Altar de Sacrificios: An Osteobiographic Analysis. *Papers of*

the Peabody Museum of Archaeology and Ethnology 63(2). Harvard University, Cambridge.
1977   The Paleopathology of Anemia in Mexico and Guatemala. In "Porotic Hyperostosis: An Enquiry," edited by Eve Cockburn, pp. 10–15, 18, cover. *Paleopathology Association Monograph* 2. Detroit.

Saul, Frank P., and Julie M. Saul
1989   Osteobiography: A Maya Example. *Reconstruction of Life from the Skeleton*, edited by Mehmet Y. Iscan and Kenneth A. R. Kennedy, pp. 287–302. Alan R. Liss, New York.
1991   The Preclassic population of Cuello. *Cuello: An Early Maya Community in Belize*, edited by Norman Hammond, pp. 134–158. Cambridge University Press, Cambridge.
2000   The People of Rio Azul. *Rio Azul Reports 5, The 1987 Season*, edited by R. E. W. Adams, pp. 240–254. Mesoamerican Archaeological Research Laboratory, University of Texas, San Antonio.
2001   Cosmetic Alterations of the Face and Body. *The Archaeology of Ancient Mexico and Central America: An Encyclopedia*, edited by Susan Toby Evans and David L. Webster, pp. 291–295. Garland Publishing, New York.

Saul, Julie M., and Frank P. Saul
1997   The Preclassic Skeletons from Cuello. *Bones of the Maya: Recent Studies of Ancient Skeletons*, edited by Stephen L. Whittington and David M. Reed, pp. 28–50. Smithsonian Press, Washington.

Scarborough, Vernon L.
1983   A Preclassic Maya Water System. *American Antiquity* 48(4): 720–744.
1991   The Settlement System in a Late Preclassic Maya Community. *Archaeology at Cerros, Belize, Central America*, Vol. 3. Southern Methodist University Press, Dallas.
1999   The Engineered Environment and Political Economy of the Three Rivers Region. Paper presented at the 64th Annual Meeting of the Society for American Archaeology, Chicago.

Scarborough, Vernon L., and Nicholas P. Dunning
1995   An Accretive Model of Land and Water Use for the Ancient Maya of Northwestern Belize. MS, National Science Foundation Grant proposal.

Scarborough, Vernon L., Robert P. Connolly, and Steven P. Ross
1994   The Pre-Hispanic Maya Reservoir System at Kinal, Peten, Guatemala. *Ancient Mesoamerica* 5(1): 97–106.

Scarborough, Vernon L., Fred Valdez, Jr., and Nicholas P. Dunning
2003   Introduction. *Heterarchy, Political Economy, and the Ancient Maya: The Three Rivers Region of the East-Central Yucatán Peninsula*, edited by Vernon L. Scarborough, Fred Valdez, Jr., and Nicholas P. Dunning, pp. xiii–xx. University of Arizona Press, Tucson.

Scarborough, Vernon L., Matthew E. Becher, Jeffrey L. Baker, Garry Harris, and J. D. Hensz
1992   Water Management Studies at La Milpa, Belize. MS, report submitted to the National Geographic Society.

Shafer, Harry J., and Thomas R. Hester
1983   Ancient Maya Chert Workshops in Northern Belize, Central America. *American Antiquity* 48(3): 519–543.

Shaw, Leslie C., and Eleanor M. King
1997   Research in High Places: The Hilltop Center of Ma'ax Na, Belize. Paper presented at the 62nd Annual Meeting of the Society for American Archaeology, Nashville.

Shaw, Leslie C., Eleanor M. King, and Bruce Moses
1999   Constructed Landscape as Ideology: Archaeology and Mapping at Ma'ax Na in the Three Rivers Region of Belize. Paper presented at the 64th Annual Meeting of the Society for American Archaeology, Chicago.

Siemens, Alfred H.
1982   Prehispanic Agricultural Use of the Wetlands of Northern Belize. *Maya Subsistence: Studies in Memory of Dennis E. Puleston*, edited by Kent V. Flannery, pp. 205–225. Academic Press, New York.

Siemens, Alfred H., and Dennis E. Puleston
1972   Ridged Fields and Associated Features in Southern Campeche: New Perspectives on the Lowland Maya. *American Antiquity* 37(2): 228–239.

Stone, Glenn Davis
1996   *Settlement Ecology: The Social and Spatial Organization of Kofyar Agriculture*. University of Arizona Press, Tucson.

Tourtellot III, Gair
1988   Developmental Cycles of Households and Houses at Seibal. *Household and Community in the Mesoamerican Past*, edited by Richard R. Wilk and Wendy Ashmore, pp. 97–120. University of New Mexico Press, Albuquerque.

Tourtellot III, Gair, and Norman Hammond
1996   The Agriculturally Challenged at La Milpa, Belize. Paper presented at the 61st Annual Meet-

Tourtellot III, Gair, and Norman Hammond (*continued*)
ing of the Society for American Archaeology, New Orleans.
2000   The City Plan of La Milpa, Belize. Paper presented at the 65th Annual Meeting of the Society for American Archaeology, Philadelphia.

Tourtellot III, Gair, and Jeremy Sabloff
1989   Approaches to Household and Community Structure at Sayil, Yucatan. In "Households and Communities," edited by Scott MacEachern, David J. W. Archer, and Richard D. Galvin, pp. 363–369. *Proceedings of the 21st Chacmool Conference*. Archaeological Association of the University of Calgary, Calgary.

Tourtellot III, Gair, Amanda Clarke, and Norman Hammond
1993   Mapping La Milpa: A Maya City in Northwestern Belize. *Antiquity* 67(254): 96–108.

Tourtellot III, Gair, Jason Gonzáles, and Francisco Estrada Belli
1999   Land and People at La Milpa, Belize. Paper presented at the 64th Annual Meeting of the Society for American Archaeology, Chicago.

Tourtellot III, Gair, Norman Hammond, and Shannon Plank
1997   The City on the Hill: Investigations at La Milpa, Northwestern Belize. Paper presented at the 62nd Annual Meeting, Society for American Archaeology, Nashville.

Tourtellot, Gair III, John J. Rose, and Norman Hammond
1996   Maya Settlement Survey at La Milpa, Belize, 1994. *Mexicon* 18(1): 8–11.

Tourtellot III, Gair, John J. Rose, Nikolai Grube, Sara Donaghey, and Norman Hammond
1994   More Light on La Milpa: Maya Settlement Archaeology in Northwestern Belize. *Mexicon* 16(6): 119–124.

Tourtellot III, Gair, Marc Wolf, Scott Smith, Kristen Gardella, and Norman Hammond
2002   Exploring Heaven on Earth: Testing the Cosmological Model at La Milpa, Belize. *Antiquity* 76(293): 633–634.

Trachman, Rissa M.
2001   An Archaeology of Everyday Life: Domestic Labor Organization at the Maya Site of Dos Hombres, Belize. MS, National Science Foundation Dissertation Improvement Grant Proposal.

Treacy, John M., and William M. Denevan
1994   The Creation of Cultivable Land Through Terracing. *The Archaeology of Garden and Field*, edited by Naomi F. Miller and Kathryn L. Gleason, pp. 91–110. University of Pennsylvania Press, Philadelphia.

Turner II, B. L.
1979   Prehispanic Terracing in the Central Maya Lowlands: Problems of Agricultural Intensification. *Maya Archaeology and Ethnohistory*, edited by Norman Hammond and Gordon R. Willey, pp. 103–115. University of Texas Press, Austin and London.
1983   *Once Beneath the Forest: Prehistoric Terracing in the Río Bec Region of the Maya Lowlands.* Westview Press, Boulder.
1993   Rethinking the "New Orthodoxy:" Interpreting Ancient Maya Agriculture and Environment. In "Culture, Form, and Place: Essays in Cultural and Historical Geography," edited by K. W. Mathewson. *Geoscience and Man* 32: 57–88.

Turner II, B. L., and Peter D. Harrison, Editors
1983   *Pulltrouser Swamp: Ancient Maya Habitat, Agriculture, and Settlement in Northern Belize.* University of Texas Press, Austin.

Turner II, B. L., and William T. Sanders
1992   Summary and Critique. *Gardens of Prehistory: The Archaeology of Settlement Agriculture in Greater Mesoamerica*, edited by Thomas W. Killion, pp. 263–284. University of Alabama Press, Tuscaloosa.

Turner II, Christy G., and Lilia M. Cheuiche Machado
1983   A New Dental Wear Pattern and Evidence for High Carbohydrate Consumption in a Brazilian Archaic Skeletal Population. *American Journal of Physical Anthropology* 61: 125–130.

Walling, Stanley L.
1995   Bajo and Floodplain Sites along the Río Bravo: 1994 Survey and Excavations. *Programme for Belize Archaeological Project: 1994 Interim Report*, edited by Richard E. W. Adams and Fred Valdez, Jr., pp. 63–67. Center for Archaeology and Tropical Research, University of Texas, San Antonio.

Walling, Stanley L., Sharon Misdea, and Roberta McIntyre
1995   Ancient Terracing and Settlement in the Río Bravo Drainage, Belize. Paper presented at the 60th Annual Meeting of the Society for American Archaeology, Minneapolis.

Weiss-Krejci, Estella
2000   Investigating Depressions: La Milpa Archaeological Project, Report 2000. MS, Department of Archaeology, Boston University.

Weiss-Krejci, Estella, and Thomas Sabbas
2002   The Potential Role of Small Depressions as Water Storage Features in the Central Maya Lowlands. *Latin American Antiquity* 13(3): 343–357.

Wolf, Eric R.
  1966   *Peasants*. Prentice-Hall, Englewood Cliffs.
Wright, A. C. S., D. H. Romney, R. H. Arbuckle,
and V. E. Vial
  1959   Land in British Honduras: Report of the British
          Honduras Land Use Survey Team. *Colonial Re-
          search Publications* 24. Her Majesty's Station-
          ery Office, London.

Index

Abandonment
    of Far West Bajo, 35, 55, 56, 89, 101
    of La Milpa, 10
Acropolis, at La Milpa, 10, 11
Adams, Richard E. W., 11
Agricultural features
    artifacts in, 51–53
    construction of, vii–viii, 36, 37–55
    in Maya lowlands, 3–5, 6, 36–55
    See also Agriculture; Berms; Canals; Check dams; Fieldhouses; Platforms, in agricultural zones; Raised fields; Rockpiles; Terraces
Agricultural intensification
    accretionary development of, 49, 51, 54–55
    bajo soils transported for, 34, 55, 108. *See also* Soils, as bajo resource
    dating of, vii, 5, 49, 54–55
    landscape modifications for, 7–8, 35, 96–99, 105, 108. *See also* Berms; Canals; Rockpiles; Terraces
Agricultural zones
    in Far West Bajo, 36–55, 93–95, 96, 106
    rockpiles in, 32, 38
    Zone 1, 38–41
    Zone 2, 31, 41–45
    Zone 3, 34, 45–47, 80, 106, 107
    Zone 4, 47–49, 107
Agriculture
    ditched fields, 5, 13–14
    recessional (floodwater), 5, 107
    slash-and-burn, 35, 108
    swidden, 6
    See also "Pot irrigation"
Aguadas, 12, 13, 33, 59
Albion Island, Belize, 31–32
Altar de Sacrificios, Guatemala, 152
Ancient Maya Land and Water Management Project, viii, 9, 12–13, 118
Aquatic plants, 5. *See also* Vegetation
Architectural complexity, measures of, 90–93

Architectural features. *See* Ball court; Benches; Buttresses; Courtyards; Doorways; Floors; Patios; Plaster; Platforms; Plazas; Principal architectural groups; Roofing; Temples (pyramidal structures); Walkways
Architecture, typologies of, 57–59

Bajo, definition of, 1, 3
Bajo communities
    as specialized settlements, 8
    spatial organization of, 1, 96–105
    See also Agricultural zones; Residential zones
Bajo de Morocoy, Mexico, 4
Bajo de Santa Fe, Guatemala, 5
Bajo el Laberinto, Mexico, 32
Bajo hill, location of, 25–26
Bajo Hill site
    archaeological research at, 26, 56, 57, 59–69, 88–95
    burials at, 62, 64, 114–116, 147–148, 151
    founders of, 61, 88
Bajo la Justa, Guatemala, 4–5, 9
Bajo la Pita, Guatemala, 5
Bajo Pedernal, Guatemala, 4
Ball court, at La Milpa, 10
Beads
    of bone, 112
    of stone, 72, 113, 114
Belize River Valley, 14
Benches, 56, 64, 72, 91, 92, 102, 106, 110, 115
Berms
    at La Milpa, 13, 93–94
    in Far West Bajo, vii, 1, 4, 6, 25, 27, 35, 36–55, 59, 65, 69, 78, 79–80, 83, 85, 93–94, 96, 99, 105, 107, 109
    in Quintana Roo, 4
Blue Creek, Belize, x, 14
Blue Creek project, 13–14
Bolsa Verde site, Belize, 11
Booth's River, 14
Box gardens, 42, 43, 55. *See also* Garden-infield-outfield model

Bravo Hills region, 14–17
Burials, 62, 64, 71, 73, 76, 79, 102, 107, 108, 110, 114–116, 147–154
Burning, evidence of, 44, 45, 73, 85
Buttresses, 56, 74, 91, 110

Caches, 56, 61, 69, 71, 72–73, 75, 82, 102, 110, 111, 112, 113, 114, 151
Calakmul, Mexico, x, 3, 4, 6, 32
Canals, 3, 4, 5, 8, 55, 97
Candelaria River, Campeche, 3
Caracol, Belize, 51
Carbon isotope analysis, 34
Causeways. *See* Walkways
Ceramic vessels, 106, 107, 111–112, 114, 115
Ceramics
    curtain rod holder, 78–79, 110
    Early Classic, 41, 44, 45, 49–51, 61, 62, 64, 68, 72, 76–78, 82, 83, 87–89, 92–94, 100, 101, 118–126
    early Late Classic, 30, 31, 40, 41, 47, 49, 50, 51, 61, 63, 76, 87, 89, 92, 93, 118–126
    Early–Late Classic transition, 65, 67, 72, 74, 75, 118
    in agricultural zones, 40–55
    in Far West Bajo, 118–126
    in rockpiles, 30–31
    Late Classic, 49, 61, 82, 83, 86, 94, 101, 118–126
    Late Preclassic, 41, 44, 47, 49, 50, 51, 61, 66, 67, 72, 74, 83, 84, 86, 88, 92, 94, 100, 118–126
    Late/Terminal Classic, 31, 41, 44, 49–51, 61–69, 72–80, 83, 84, 86, 87, 89–90, 92, 93, 100, 101, 118–126
    Protoclassic, 49, 50, 83
Cerros, Belize, 3
Check dams, 8, 13
Chert
    as bajo resource, 4, 8, 32–34, 96, 99, 107, 108
    imported, 112

Abstract

The Far West Bajo is a seasonal wetland near the edge of the major Maya archaeological site of La Milpa in Belize. Information presented here demonstrates that from approximately 400 B.C. to A.D. 600, the activities of bajo inhabitants negatively impacted the environment, degrading the terrestrial and water resources on which their society depended. In response, the Maya developed new and more intensive strategies of resource exploitation, which allowed them to maintain and even gain greater prosperity. In some respects, the human impact on the landscape was one of severe degradation, as forests were cleared, slopes eroded, and the abundance of water adversely affected. But these processes also created new opportunities for agricultural exploitation and led the Maya of the Far West Bajo to develop innovative responses to these conditions that allowed them to persevere for several centuries more until their society's ultimate collapse.

The organization of three bajo communities was closely linked to their use and management of critical agricultural resources. The differences in access to these spatially variable natural resources resulted in a distinctive pattern of settlement across the landscape. The ancient farmers of the bajo identified and made use of three related environments, settling and tending gardens in the uplands, building terraces for intensive farming on the low slopes at the margins of the bajo, and obtaining water and other raw materials such as chert from the bajo itself. Access to these diverse resources was not equal, however, as pioneers settled in prime locations and claimed the best quality and most diverse resources for themselves. Descendants of these first settlers maintained this advantage and were successful in parlaying it into elevated socioeconomic status and positions as community leaders.

Understanding the landscape of the bajo requires tracing the intertwined histories of residential occupation and agricultural production, then placing these histories within a reconstruction of the paleoenvironment of the bajo throughout centuries of use. The reconstruction is based on syntheses of numerous strands of ecological data provided by specialists in geomorphology, hydrology, soil science, and palynology who

Resumen

El Bajo Extremo Occidental es un humedal estacional localizado en los alrededores del sitio arqueológico maya La Milpa, en Belize. La información presentada aquí demuestra que, desde aproximadamente 400 b.C. a 600 d.C., las actividades de los habitantes del bajo afectaron el medioambiente negativamente, degradando los recursos terrestres y acuáticos de los que dependió su sociedad. En respuesta, los mayas desarrollaron nuevas y más intensivas estrategias de explotación de recursos, las cuales les permitieron mantener e inclusive ganar mayor prosperidad. En algunos aspectos, el impacto humano sobre el paisaje fue uno de degradación severa, debido a que los bosques fueron cortados, las orillas erosionadas, y la abundancia de agua afectada adversamente. Sin embargo, estos procesos también crearon nuevas oportunidades para la producción agrícola que llevaron a los mayas del Bajo Extremo Occidental a desarrollar respuestas innovativas a estas condiciones, las que a su vez les permitieron perseverar por muchos siglos más hasta el colapso final de su sociedad.

La organización de tres comunidades del bajo estuvo estrechamente unida al uso y manejo de recursos agrícolas críticos. Las diferencias en acceso a estos recursos naturales espacialmente variables produjeron un distintivo patrón de asentamiento a través del paisaje. Los antiguos agricultores mayas del bajo identificaron y utilizaron tres medioambientes interrelacionados, viviendo y cultivando huertas en las zonas altas, construyendo terrazas para agricultura intensiva en las orillas alrededor del bajo, y obteniendo agua y materia prima tal como pedernal en el bajo mismo. Acceso a estos recursos diversos no fue equitativo, debido a que los pioneros se asentaron en lugares ideales y reclamaron los recursos de mejor calidad y mayor diversidad para sí mismos. Los descendientes de estos colonos mantuvieron esta ventaja y lograron utilizarla para alcanzar un elevado estatus socioeconómico y posición de liderazgo de su comunidad.

Para comprender el paisaje del bajo es necesario trazar las historias entrelazadas de la ocupación residencial y la producción agrícola, y luego poner estas historias dentro de una reconstrucción del paleoambiente del bajo durante los siglos de uso. Esta recons-

collaborated on this research. It is the thorough integration of all three lines of evidence, the settlement system, the agricultural system, and the ancient environment, that breaks new ground in landscape studies and in the study of Maya subsistence.

trucción está basada en la síntesis de numerosos datos ecológicos producidos por especialistas en geomorfología, hidrología, ciencia de suelos, y palinología, quienes colaboraron en esta investigación. Mediante la integración de tres líneas de evidencia, patrón de asentamiento, sistema agrícola, y paleoambiente, se ha podido aportar nuevas perspectivas al estudio del paisaje y la subsistencia maya.

ANTHROPOLOGICAL PAPERS OF THE UNIVERSITY OF ARIZONA

Anthropological Papers listed as O.P., D are available as Docutech reproductions (high quality xerox) printed on demand. They are tape or spiral bound and nonreturnable.